A — MINDFUL CAREER

Choose a Career, Find a Job, and Manage
Your Success in the 21st Century

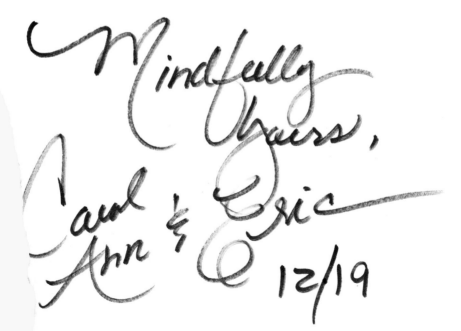

Mindfully Yours,

Carol Ann & Eric

12/19

Praise for *A Mindful Career*

CHIP CONLEY
Hospitality Entrepreneur, *New York Times* bestselling author of *Wisdom@Work*, Founder of The Modern Elder Academy

"The world is at a tipping point in the collective consciousness of how we work. The old structures and paradigms are being replaced by progressive companies and individuals with new thinking and practices. *A Mindful Career* introduces the concept of mindfulness at work to the conversation, demonstrating why it's needed and how it can be implemented. The results can be dramatic: individuals choosing careers that satisfy the soul and have a purpose, and employers creating company cultures that make the workplace a joy to be at. In a mindful working world perhaps someday people will say T.G.I.M—Thank God It's Monday!"

BRUCE CRYER
CEO/Founder, Renaissance Human, Stanford Adjunct Faculty, HeartMath CEO

"A beautiful, practical, inspiring book that draws you in for career-building ideas, and keeps you turning the pages with its personal development insights and inspiration. So much wisdom and actionable ideas are packed in these pages! Carol Ann and Eric Wentworth have produced a marvelous book that should be required reading for anyone in business, whether or not you need more fulfilling, more mission-aligned work. And especially if you do!"

TED PRODROMOU
LinkedIn Expert, Speaker, Coach, author of *The Ultimate Guide to LinkedIn for Business*

"*A Mindful Career* is the complete guide to managing your career and staying one step ahead of the ever-changing job market."

RANDY WILLIAMS
CEO/Founder, Keiretsu Forum,
world's largest angel investor organization

"*A Mindful Career* combines the Eastern philosophy of conscious mindfulness with Western methods to create a new dynamic that can help you find a career you love—and then succeed in the workplace."

PATRICK SCHWERDTFEGER
Speaker, author of *AI Anarchy, Inc.: Profiting in a Decentralized World with Artificial Intelligence and Blockchain*

"Labor markets are being disrupted at an unprecedented rate, and we're just getting started. Amidst rising chaos, job seekers and working professionals need a comprehensive and tactical roadmap for career development. Carol Ann and Eric Wentworth have compiled such a roadmap, all within the pretext of aligning career goals with individual purpose. What's the most efficient way to leverage your unique skill in today's high-tech market? This book provides refreshing guidance."

GURUGANESHA
Co-Founder, Conscious Selling,
sales training for Salesforce, Google, LinkedIn, Dropbox, and more

"Drawing from the ancient truths and the purest of common sense, *A Mindful Career* is a 21st century leading-edge guide for those seeking a career that deeply satisfies on multiple levels . . . financially, emotionally, and spiritually."

PETER ENGLER
Owner, Engler Career Group,
author of *Your Crystal Clear Career Path*

"*A Mindful Career* is an important new career guide that clearly identifies a powerful method—mindfulness techniques—to thoughtfully define your ideal career path and formulate an action plan to achieve your professional goals."

MIKE O'NEIL

CEO, Integrated Alliances, Forbes Top 50 Social Media Influencer, LinkedIn Trainer, author of *Rock the World with LinkedIn!*

"Deciding and choosing your career path based on your values is something you will always enjoy as it's part of the great journey in life. In this book you will learn how to chart your career to deliver benefits and rewards for your entire life."

BRUCE JANIGIAN

International attorney, Navy Captain,
Law Professor, U.S. Supreme Court Bar

"Fabulous and then some! The Wentworths produce marvelous books that I make required reading for my family."

JOE NOVAK

Founder, Empire Builders

"Careers and the workplace are often dysfunctional, despite the enormous amount of attention devoted to education, training, hiring the right people, and developing positive company cultures. *A Mindful Career* identifies the missing link that can change everything—mindfulness—and shows how it can positively affect both your career and the workplace environment."

DARREN JACKLIN

Real estate investor, Board of Directors, eXp World Holdings
DarrenJacklin.com

"*A Mindful Career* is packed full of content with so much practical information on how to be more mindful in your career and personal life. Well done!"

*"Your work is to discover your work and then
with all your heart to give yourself to it."* —Buddha

A
MINDFUL
CAREER

Choose a Career, Find a Job, and Manage
Your Success in the 21st Century

Carol Ann Wentworth
CEO, WENTWORTH EXECUTIVE RECRUITING

Eric C. Wentworth
AUTHOR OF A PLAN FOR LIFE

Charles Stephen Publishing
100 Leland Way
Tiburon, CA 94920
415-516-9343

amindfulcareer.com

First Print Edition

Library of Congress Cataloging-in-Publication Data
Wentworth, Carol Ann
Wentworth, Eric C.
A Mindful Career: The 21st Century Guide to Job Search
and Career Management

Includes index.
978-0-9911983-1-3 paperback
978-0-9911983-2-0 ebook

Library of Congress Catalog Number: 2019915982

1. Career Success—Guidance and resources. 2. Job Search. 3. Jobs. 4. Recruiting. 5. Motivation. 6. Education. I. Title

Cover and project management by Ruth Schwartz, thewonderlady.com

Interior layout by Lorna Johnson, lornajohnson.com

Dedicated to our dear friend and mentor Dick Bolles,
author of the all-time bestselling career guide,
What Color is Your Parachute?

With gratitude for being an inspiration
in our lives and millions of others.

My late husband Richard N. Bolles dramatically changed the lives of many people, including me. He was my soulmate. Everyone whose life was touched by this remarkable man will be forever changed—and grateful.

His book, *What Color Is Your Parachute?* has sold more than 10 million copies around the world, was a *New York Times* bestseller, and was named by *Time* magazine as one of the 100 most influential non-fiction English language books written since 1923. His book was also named by the Library of Congress Center for the Book as "One of the 25 books that have shaped readers' lives." A few of the other books in the list are the *Bible, War and Peace, Walden, To Kill a Mockingbird,* and *How to Win Friends and Influence People.*

There are not many people who can measure their loving admirers in the tens of thousands. But over the years, Dick acquired a legion of avid followers who had their lives changed by his teachings.

Dick worked hard, loved everyone, was endlessly curious about life, and deeply spiritual. A Harvard graduate, he chose to live a life of purpose and became a pastor at Grace Cathedral in San Francisco. It was while helping a few job seekers that Dick developed the original edition of *What Color Is Your Parachute?,* which he initially gave away at no cost.

Carol Ann and Eric Wentworth moved to San Francisco to work with Dick in 2005. They participated in the exclusive five-day career coaching workshop that Dick and I conducted in our home each year. We've become close friends over the years, and I am very pleased they have dedicated their book to my husband.

—Marci Bolles

"What did I come to earth to do?

Who did I come here to be?

What am I willing to give up
in order to become who I need to be?

How am I standing in my own way?

What do I want to do with my wild and wonderful life?

Your answers will be different from anyone else,
but they will take you to the right place."

—Elizabeth Gilbert, author of *Eat, Pray, Love*

CONTENTS

Putting Mindfulness to Work In Your Life

> *"Happiness comes when your work and words are of benefit to yourself and others."*
>
> Buddha

Busy, distracted, stressed-out modern Americans are not living mindfully.

Recent research says that the average person is "on autopilot" 47% of the time. We've all experienced this in our lives, driving for miles to a destination and not seeing anything along the way because we were so absorbed in our thoughts. A large portion of the population is disengaged, drifting through their days so mindlessly that they can't recall at the end of the day exactly what they did. The more we are on autopilot, the more vulnerable we are to anxiety, stress, and depression. All these conditions are on the rise in America.

This mindlessness shows up in the workplace too. According to a recent Gallup survey, 51% of employees in the U.S. are "unengaged" and 17% are actually "actively disengaged" in their work. The percent of disengaged workers closely mirrors the number of people who are dissatisfied with their career.

Learning to be mindful in your career and at work is the key to success and satisfaction. But what exactly is mindfulness? And how does it work?

1

Mark Coleman, author of *Make Peace with Your Mind* (markcoleman. org), describes mindfulness as "clear awareness. It is the power of attention. It is the ability to be present, self-aware, and cognizant of others and one's environment." Mindfulness is giving "close and caring attention to our immediate experience" and "freeing ourselves from the habits of mind that hinder our ease, responsiveness, and wellbeing." It's the ability to focus in the moment.

According to the Greater Good Science Center at the University of California Berkeley, "mindfulness is maintaining a moment-to-moment awareness—of thoughts, feelings, bodily sensations, and environment, through a gentle, nurturing lens."

In its rawest form, mindfulness simply means being honestly conscious—paying attention to our true thoughts and feelings without judging them in a non-reactive state of mind. This, in turn, will help you reach clarity of thought and feeling. And this will help steer you through the complexities of our often emotional and biased life to a deeper understanding of yourself and others.

> *"Mindfulness is the aware, balanced acceptance of the present experience. It isn't more complicated than that."*
>
> —Sylvia Boorstein, author
> of *Solid Ground: Buddhist Wisdom for Difficult Times*

Mindfulness requires time and attention, or nonconceptual awareness, where a person does not get stuck thinking about ideas they have had in the past and observes everything as if they are seeing it for the first time, which contributes to turning off the mental autopilot that is driving thoughts and actions.

There are several aids to help you achieve greater mindfulness. Time spent in a natural setting can help quiet the mind, reduce the distracting buzz that lies just beneath the surface for modern Americans, and reconnects you with a "nature bath" to cleanse your soul. Take a walk in an unspoiled forest or along the seashore. Unplug your mind for a day or two. And see how much better and grounded you feel afterward.

Meditation is an age-old and proven path to increased mindfulness.

Clearing the mind is like clearing the clutter from your home—a "feng shui" for your brain and soul. It's why 1 in 6 Americans now meditates regularly.

Adding music and art to your life will support greater mindfulness by tapping into a higher level of human consciousness and creativity.

Kindness enhances mindfulness. Kindness connects us with others through a uniquely human expression of love.

The side-effects of mindfulness are less stress and anxiety, better sleep, inner peace, more love, and improved health.

Being mindful changes your relationship with other people. It's honest, authentic, and true. Mindfulness can help you rise above our often negative, judgmental human nature. We are better human beings when we live mindfully.

Living mindfully enables us to live more consciously.

"We are what we think.
All that we are arises with our thoughts.
With our thoughts, we make the world."

—Buddha

According to the *Harvard Business Review* (July 18, 2018, Ellen Keithline Byrne and Tojo Thatchenkery), "research suggests that people who practice mindfulness have more cognitive flexibility, are able to see beyond what they've already done, and are better at solving problems requiring insight." This facilitates what creativity experts refer to as the incubation and insight stages of the creative process. Creativity, emotional intelligence, and the ability to work collaboratively with others are mindfulness "skills" that are important to success in the 21st century workplace. The "soft" skills that are so much in demand now by employers are largely a result of being mindful.

Many companies are incorporating mindfulness training into their business processes. Zappos incorporates mindfulness into their stated corporate values. Google offers mindfulness programs to increase the emotional intelligence and well-being of their employees. Big firms like Salesforce, LinkedIn, Dropbox, and Google have adopted mindfulness and applied it to their business through Conscious Selling teachings (ConsciousSelling.com). They have found that mindfulness training increases both employee satisfaction and their bottom-line by improving relationships within the company as well as with customers.

Achieving greater awareness of yourself by discovering who you really are through introspection and reflection, and by reaching a deeper level of clarity in thought, your path in life will become apparent and your path *through* life more satisfying and productive.

The practical application of mindfulness to your career can lead you to a richer working experience and greater success in something that is a core element of who you are and what your purpose is in life.

Although there are hundreds of examples of practical advice throughout this book, we will show you how in every aspect of your career you can be more successful by being more mindful.

"The more you see yourself as what you'd like to become
and act as if what you want is already there,
the more you'll activate those dominant forces that will
collaborate to transform your dream into your reality."
—Dr. Wayne Dyer, author of *The Power of Intention*

We want this book to do two important things: help you become a more mindful person—especially as it relates to your career—and give you the practical advice, knowledge, and tools to manage your career effectively.

A successful career is one of the cornerstones of a successful life. Learning to manage it *mindfully* is critical to creating a fulfilling career.

In this book, among many things, you will learn about:

✓ The principles of Mindful Career Management

✓ How mindfulness can improve your life

✓ Tips for the recent grad to choose your career mindfully

✓ How to search for a job effectively

✓ How to use social media to manage your job search and career

✓ The top interviewing skills and techniques

- ✓ How to write a resumé that gets read
- ✓ Salary negotiation tips for win/win solutions
- ✓ How to work with a recruiter and the two types of recruiters
- ✓ The most effective way to explain gaps in your work history
- ✓ Surviving being laid off
- ✓ The best job search websites
- ✓ How to maximize your LinkedIn presence for career success
- ✓ How to answer "impossible" interview questions
- ✓ What skills you need to succeed in the future
- ✓ Effective network building
- ✓ Setting yourself up for success during the first 90 days on the job
- ✓ How to be indispensable at work
- ✓ Personal development for career success
- ✓ How to stay relevant when you are over 50
- ✓ A library of recommended career books to read

Mindfulness—combined with the practical tools you need to succeed in your career—are a powerful combination to help you achieve productivity, creativity, happiness, and purpose in the work you choose to do. For many people, mindfulness at work is the missing ingredient for a successful career.

> *"There is no passion in playing small, in settling for a life that is less than the one you are capable of living."*
>
> —Nelson Mandela, human rights activist,
> former President of South Africa

Namaste.

Chapter 1

Your Most Important Decision

> *"Never forget that doing what you love*
> *is the cornerstone of having success in your life."*
> —Dr. Wayne Dyer, author of *Manifest Your Destiny*
> and *Change Your Thoughts—Change Your Life*

Your choice of a career—and how you manage it—is arguably the most important decision you'll make in life. Yet, it is a choice most people make with little thought or planning. Their life's work is "chosen" for them by circumstances or sheer lack of any conscious consideration.

As children, few people say they want to grow up to be a waitress or accountant or plumber. While these are honorable jobs, at that age we all still have bigger dreams and aspirations. But as adults, millions of people give up those dreams and "settle" for a job that pays the bills (hopefully). It's why more than half of all Americans are unhappy in what they do. It's also why roughly half of all Americans live paycheck to paycheck—with 46% in such dire financial condition they would be unable to pay for a $400 unexpected expense.

For most people, careers are not a mindful choice. Most "careers" are just jobs—people trading time and labor for a paycheck. A true career is more than a job. A career doesn't only put food on the table and pay the rent, a career becomes part of who you are as a person.

A career is work that often doesn't seem like work because you love doing it every day. A career ignites your passions and utilizes the skills you have developed. If you're fortunate enough to create a career for yourself rooted in something you love to do, it will be a lifetime source of personal satisfaction.

> *"There are three relationships you can have with work. A job, a career, or a calling."*
> —Chip Conley, Founder of Joie de Vivre hotels, Airbnb Advisor, author of *Wisdom @ Work: The Making of a Modern Elder*

People who only want a job are necessary to society. Those who view their work life as simply doing a job, separate from any passion or innate talent, fulfill critical functions in our society. There's nothing intrinsically wrong with simply wanting to work in return for a fair compensation.

Many people derive a sense of satisfaction in doing a job well and knowing it is necessary. The lady who has delivered our mail for nearly three decades absolutely loves her job (and we love her!). Delivering the mail isn't the kind of job you would characterize as a "career" but it's still a source of satisfaction and generates a dependable, livable income. And walking 20,000 steps every day has kept her in great health!

If you (for whatever reason) only want a job and not a career, then know you will likely be limited in the amount of money you'll be able to earn. You will also likely have to find emotional satisfaction in other areas of your life. Perhaps a passion for travel or helping young people at risk or collecting stamps—an interest that ignites your passion separate from your work.

It will be important for you to adopt a mindset of finding satisfaction in doing your job well, if not in the work itself. You can also find meaning and purpose in many jobs by connecting it to how it contributes to a company or society. The janitor at a hospital provides an important function in maintaining its cleanliness so the patients are safe. The cashier who checks out your purchases at the supermarket provides a needed service. We would all be much worse off if there were no trash collectors. But you should also be aware that in the 21st century there will be fewer "jobs" as many of these become automated, outsourced, or discontinued.

This book concentrates primarily on providing the guidance needed to develop a successful career based on a passion or calling. However, job seekers will also find much of value as well. A "good" job is always preferable to one chosen simply because it is available work and provides some income. A good job often means working for a company that treats you with respect and working alongside people you enjoy being around eight hours a day or more. A good job is one where you can find satisfaction and pride in providing a valued service.

In this book, you will find the collected advice, guidance, and resources from the world's top career experts, curated by Carol Ann Wentworth, one of the nation's most respected executive recruiters and small business owner, and Eric Wentworth, an entrepreneur, marketing executive, startup expert, and business owner. Both studied career planning with Dick Bolles, author of the bestselling career book *What Color is Your Parachute?* And both are co-founders of The Career ReBoot Camp, an innovative 2-day event to help job seekers get up-to-speed quickly so they are competitive in the 21st-century workplace. Besides recruiting, Carol Ann also provides one-on-one career counseling.

Our goal is to provide you with career guidance within the context of mindfulness. It hasn't been done before and we feel it is desperately needed in the 21st century. Whether you decide to create a more meaningful career for yourself or simply want to find a good job, *A Mindful Career* will help guide you in making well-informed decisions.

> *"Find out what it is in life you don't do well—*
> *and then don't do that thing!"*
>
> —Dos Equis beer commercial,
> career advice from "The World's Most Interesting Man."

NOTE:

You will find some redundancy in our book. This is done purposefully because it's easy to disregard some advice or forget it when it is offered in a body of work that includes hundreds of important items. Some things are essential to career success and we present them several times (usually with a new insight) so you will have the best chance of retaining it.

Chapter 2

Planning Your Career Mindfully

A FEW WORDS ABOUT PLANNING

In recent years, it's become trendy to disparage planning. The new trendy thing is to abandon all planning and just let life happen. It's too hard to plan, they say, plans don't often work out, and who knows what opportunity or interest may come your way.

There is a kernel of truth to feeling this way. Life is serendipitous. Unexpected roadblocks and opportunities will certainly happen during your life. And you should be prepared to deal with each one objectively and mindfully. But it doesn't negate the value of planning. In fact, it makes planning even more necessary.

Perhaps the most perceptive statement about planning came from the late President Dwight Eisenhower, a former 5-star general who also orchestrated the successful invasion of Europe during World War II. He said, "In preparing for battle I have always found that plans are useless, but planning is indispensable."

"Plans are useless, but planning is indispensable."

—President Dwight Eisenhower

Plans will inevitably change. But the direction and goals you plan will set you on a course of success, even if you arrive at a different destination.

Here's an example of what Eisenhower meant by planning being essential, but plans are useless. Let's say you are driving to New York from San Francisco. There are two ways you can do this. One is to point your car toward the rising sun and drive east. The other is to use a map or GPS.

Both methods will get you to New York eventually. But you can see it will likely take a lot longer just by driving aimlessly east. You may get lost. Or go the wrong way. Or the weather may be cloudy, and you start going south instead of east because you can't see the sun.

With a map, you'll arrive at your destination quickly and without stress. You will probably have time to stop to see the sights and enjoy the ride more. You can even take a detour to see an interesting site but still get back on course to arrive at your destination.

Or you can just hop on a plane and be there in four hours. There are always ways to improve your life plan by changing the way you get to your destination.

If your journey in life offers a new opportunity better fitting your long-term plans, or you find you have new priorities, you can always revise your plan. Just be sure you don't make changes based on expediency but on what you truly want in life—your goals. Expediency may take the form of accepting a job just for the money, even though you hate it. Or moving to a city you don't like just for a better job. Or allowing others to influence your path even when you know it isn't right for you.

Planning is important to stay focused on your goals, even if your plans change.

Here's what some of the greatest minds think about the importance of planning.

"A goal without a plan . . . is just a wish."

—Antoine de Saint-Exupéry, French author of *The Little Prince*

"A man who does not plan long ahead will find trouble at his door."

—Confucius

"If you don't know where you're going, you'll end up someplace else."

—Yogi Berra, Hall of Fame baseball player

"Give me six hours to chop down a tree and I will spend the first four sharpening the ax."

—President Abraham Lincoln

"Someone is sitting in the shade today because someone planted a tree a long time ago."

—Warren Buffett, American businessman, CEO of Berkshire Hathaway

"The reason most people never reach their goals is they don't define them. Winners can tell you where they are going, what they plan to do along the way, and who they will be sharing the adventure with them."

—Denis Waitley, author of *The Psychology of Winning*

"Plan your work and work your plan."

—Napoleon Hill, author of *Think and Grow Rich*

"Without goals and plans to reach them, you are like a ship that has set sail with no destination."

—Fitzhugh Dodson, clinical psychologist, author of *How to Parent*

> *"To accomplish great things, we must not only act but also dream; not only plan but also believe."*
>
> —Anatole France, French poet

Convinced?

Mindful Career Rules: Good luck and good "manifestations" are the results of sound, mindful planning. Failing to plan is planning to fail.

Chapter 3

A Well-Chosen Career
Is the Best Investment In Your Future

"The best prize that life offers is the chance to work hard at work worth doing."

—President Theodore Roosevelt

Mike Hogan wrote in *Barron's*, "Our career choices are among the most important investment decisions we'll ever make—because that paycheck underwrites so many other bets, like housing, education, and retirement." No matter what you decide to do in life, the financial prospects of your career will affect everything else you do. You need to factor this in and plan your life accordingly.

The key is to find work you love *and* provides the income needed to sustain your lifestyle. If the work you love doesn't pay well, accept that you may have to adjust your lifestyle to continue doing it. Chances are if you are doing what you love it will eventually reward you well. But, remember, there are no guarantees.

"It all begins and ends in your mind.
What you give power to has power over you."

—Leon Brown

FINDING THE PATH
TO MINDFUL CAREER SATISFACTION

While it's important to plan your career, the true path to finding work that enriches your soul while providing enough riches to support your lifestyle is learning to be mindful of yourself and the world around you.

Being mindful is learning to tap into your inner self to discover the truth about what makes you unique. It means breaking through all the rules and regulations governing our modern world—what you have been taught by parents and teachers, what society "thinks" you should do with your life—and authentically thinking for yourself.

It will likely require you to challenge the established social norms— the traditional methods of acquiring knowledge, the way we have been taught to work, religion, family structures, and inbred biases. We are all governed, and even controlled, by these accepted norms, so most people aren't truly "free" but operating according to an accepted framework that humans have devised to maintain social order. With the rapid changes taking place in all things during the 21st century, these control mechanisms are often no longer valid or workable for many people.

Evolved people and companies are recognizing the need to provide more emotionally satisfying working conditions. It's reflected in the introduction of remote work, flex time, paid sabbaticals to do charitable or community work, family leave, educational assistance, mindfulness training, and such tangible amenities as company lunchrooms and cafes, massages, and meditation rooms. This is already a reality at firms such as Google and Apple.

The trend toward more psychically rewarding work will continue too. The Baby Boomer generation introduced these changes and the Millennials and Gen Z will accelerate them as they create careers with purpose and meaning.

CHOOSE A 21ST CENTURY CAREER

You don't want to choose a "telegraph operator" career in the 21st century —something easily automated, outsourced, eliminated altogether, or changed radically. In truth, no one can predict the future, especially jobs and careers. Taxi drivers probably thought they were immune to the changes of the 21st century . . . until Uber and Lyft completely disrupted their industry. Hotels likely thought they were relatively protected from 21st century change . . . until Airbnb upended their business model. Borders Books was doing well—until it wasn't, a casualty of Amazon, Audible, and ebooks. Almost every industry is vulnerable to some degree of disruptive change.

Keep in mind that disruptive, destructive chaos also creates many new businesses and opportunities. Before the beginning of this century—less than two decades ago—giant employers such as Amazon, Google, LinkedIn, Costco, Facebook, Uber, Airbnb, Tesla and hundreds of others either didn't exist or were just getting established.

Before choosing a career path, think long and hard about where that career path is headed. Talk with people who are already doing what you want to do. What do they think the future of their profession looks like? It may be radically different than your preconceptions. In 2014, 9 in 10 physicians would advise their own children NOT to follow their career path. Not what you expected, is it?

Our friend Adam recently launched his career as a physician after many years of expensive education. In addition to the sizeable expenditure to establish his practice, he also must pay off more than $500,000 in student loan debt. This debt, and the rapidly evolving nature of healthcare, makes his future uncertain.

Try to imagine how your chosen profession will evolve over time (not easy to do). In 2000, authors had come to accept the framework and limitations of the traditional publishing business. A decade later, everything had changed. Today more books are self-published than are published by the big traditional publishers (who are scrambling to adapt). Now even big-name authors are establishing their own publishing companies and self-publishing their work and side-stepping the agents and publishers who take a cut of their profits.

Mindful Career Rules: Choose a career that meets the demands of the 21st century and has a low risk of being disrupted.

Chapter 4

The American Career

> *"Most men would feel insulted if it was proposed to employ them in throwing rocks over a wall, and then throwing them back again, merely so that they might earn wages. But many are no more worthily employed now."*
>
> —Henry David Thoreau,
> 19th century American essayist and philosopher

Here's how it works for most people in America when it comes to "planning" their career.

If you're fortunate you will have a strong interest or talent from the time you are a child. It's either inherent in your personality or was the result of someone or something making an indelible impression on you that resonated in some primal way. Child prodigies like Beethoven simply knew what their passion in life was almost from birth. These passions are callings. There is no other choice for a career.

Others, like Pablo Picasso, were exposed to artists and their work as children and "discovered" they too had a passion for it. And some will discover a passion when they are older, usually by trying several things or, in some cases, stumbling on a passion by accident. Dan, a Colorado River guide, was set to become a lawyer when he took a rafting trip and discovered his love for the adventure of that career.

My former teacher, the late Roger Ebert, realized from the time he was a small child his intense love for movies. He also liked to write. Combining these two "loves" led him to a successful Pulitzer Prize-winning career as a film critic.

But for the great majority of people, their career path is murky. Most will pursue a career they drift into without any direction and not a lot of thought about how well they are personally suited for it. Others will do what their parents and teachers have steered them into. And many will simply work, trading their time and effort for cash.

Your career is too important to be left to fate. It impacts too many of the things in your life that are most meaningful. Take the time and make the effort to get it right.

EVERYONE HAS TALENT—FIND YOURS

> *"What is it that you like doing? If you don't like it,*
> *get out of it, because you'll be lousy at it."*
>
> —Lee Iacocca, American automobile executive

In *"Do What You Love, The Money Will Follow,"* author Marsha Sinetar says this about people who know what they love to do in life, "It is as if they instinctively know what they must do with their time and energy and then determine only to do that." This mindful focus is what creates great careers.

Helen and Scott Nearing, in their book *"Living the Good Life,"* write "the objective of economic effort is not money, but livelihood." Some of the most satisfied people are those who are engaged every day in a passion . . . whether it is carpentry or computer coding or as a river rafting guide . . . and earn enough to live well.

> *"Pleasure in the job puts perfection in the work."*
>
> —Aristotle, Greek philosopher

If the money never comes to any great degree, the person who is doing what they love is rewarded by the sheer joy of doing something every day that provides happiness and soulful compensation. In the end, this will far outweigh financial remuneration.

MATCH YOUR PASSION TO YOUR PURPOSE

We don't want to categorically state that you must engage a personal passion as your career in order to be happy. While it reliably provides the most life-long career satisfaction, often it's enough to be passionate about what you do to earn a living.

It is important, no matter how you approach your career passions, that you also combine it with a purpose if possible. This is the highest form of mindfulness in directing your career path. It's also the path to greater productivity, according to science.

Morten T. Hansen, professor at UC Berkeley and author of *Great at Work: How Top Performers Do Less, Work Better, and Achieve More*, says "People who matched passion with purpose ranked 18 percentage points higher in the performance ranking compared with those who had neither passion or purpose." Performance correlates with success and success correlates with career satisfaction. Clearly, if you are an employer, you'll want the people who work for you to bring both a passion for what they do and a clearly defined purpose for their work.

> *"A man is a success in life if he gets up in the morning and goes to bed at night and in between does what he wants to do."*
>
> —Bob Dylan, singer and composer

If possible, your career path should begin by doing what you love. Otherwise, there's always the danger your "temporary" job could become permanent. Millions are "stuck" in jobs they hate simply because they took the job initially to make some money and life events conspired to keep them shackled to it.

Here are a few comments about doing what you love from the 2005 Commencement address at Stanford University by the late Steve Jobs, CEO of Apple Computer:

"You've got to find what you love. And that is as true for your work as it is for your lovers. Your work is going to fill a large part of your life, and the only way to be truly satisfied is to do what you believe is great work. And the most effective way to do great work is to love what you do. If you haven't found it yet, keep looking. Don't settle. As with all matters of the heart, you'll know when you find it. And, like any great relationship, it just gets better and better as the years roll on. So, keep looking until you find it. Don't settle."

"Your time is limited, so don't waste it living someone else's life. Don't be trapped by dogma —which is living with the results of other people's thinking. Don't let the noise of others' opinions drown out your own inner voice. And most important—have the courage to follow your heart and intuition. They somehow already know what you truly want to become. Everything else is secondary."

THE ROAD LESS TRAVELED

> *"The secret of success is making your vocation your vacation."*
>
> —Mark Twain, American author and humorist

Life isn't good for people who are unable to shape their own destiny. There's always an inner dissatisfaction lying just below the surface of consciousness, reminding them of their failure to create the life they really want to live. As a result, true happiness is elusive.

Embracing life is far too frightening for most people. It means risk. It means being willing to accept failure from time to time. It's hard work. And it requires the personal strength to face who we are and what we believe—and then play our hand in life with the cards we were dealt with. It's just too much for most people.

> *"There is no scarcity of opportunity to make a living at what you love. There's only a scarcity of resolve to make it happen."*
>
> —Dr. Wayne Dyer,
> author of *Don't Die with Your Music Still in You*

Many people say they "don't know" what they want to do. They "have no idea" what they're good at. This is sheer intellectual laziness. They simply haven't made the effort to examine their life or engage in self-reflection. They have already adopted a fixed attitude toward life, seldom being curious or adventurous or involved. Our society makes it easy to become observers rather than participants in life. They probably have some passions, some interests, but these are buried so deeply they never emerge into the light of day. As a result, many people just drift into a career, taking what comes along or what requires the least amount of effort.

It's important to be curious about life, to engage in adventures, to learn, discover, and create. The more a person seeks, the more they will find—and eventually discover their "passion" in life. It's also why life-long learning and "adventuring" are so important. As we grow, we evolve and our tastes change. Without continual involvement in life, we may not recognize a new "passion" when it comes along.

> *"Your work is to discover your work and then, with all your heart, to give yourself to it."*
>
> —Buddha

In a recent article about what people who were about to die said were their biggest regrets in life, an insurance executive said, "I always thought God had a greater plan for me, something that would give my life meaning, something special. But I never discovered what that was. I never figured out who I wanted to be when I grew up. Now I realize it was because I didn't really look for it." As the old man neared death, he said, "Tell my children—tell everyone—to resist going with the flow. Make a difference. Don't let them off the hook. Tell them to do the work necessary to discover their purpose in life, and then follow it without looking back."

Before the old man died, the company he had devoted his entire life to had replaced him with a younger man within days. A man's life in return for filling a cog in a wheel. Is this what life should be about? This is the reason why mindfulness of purpose and living is so crucial.

CAREERS VS JOBS

Life is simply too short and too full of possibilities to spend at least 25% of it doing something that has no meaning to you. Think back to when you were a child. Did you dream of having the career you now have? Are you working as an accountant? Short-order cook? Insurance claims adjuster? House painter? There's nothing wrong with these jobs. They are honorable professions. And necessary. But are they the jobs of dreams? Most likely no. These are jobs people have settled for because they didn't pursue their dreams.

The differences between careers and a job are significant:

1. A career is based upon a personal passion or work you feel is meaningful.

2. A career constantly evolves from ongoing learning and mastery.

3. A job is simply trading time/effort for money.

4. People with careers work because they want to work.
   People with jobs work because they have to work.

5. "TGIF . . . Thank God It's Friday" reflects the attitude of someone with a job . . . not a career.

One of the biggest fears most people have is living a meaningless life. A well-chosen career can give substance to your life. So, do whatever you can to make your life meaningful with a worthwhile career.

> *"One of the huge mistakes people make is that they try to force an interest on themselves. You don't choose your passions, your passions choose you."*
>
> —Jeff Bezos, Founder, Amazon.com

Find something to do with the potential to generate an obsession within you. Try several things out for size. Get past the awkward early learning stages. Mastery can ignite passion.

You never know where an interest will lead to if you follow it with passion. Anthony Bourdain loved travel, food, and writing. These interests led to a highly successful career as a chef, author of several bestselling books about the restaurant business *(Kitchen Confidential: Adventures in the Culinary Underbelly, A Cook's Tour),* as well as a popular TV show "No Reservations" that took him to restaurants around the world.

> *"Since you may fail when you don't follow your passion and you may fail when you do, then you may as well follow your passion."*
>
> —Jim Carrey, actor

Our friend Mary Beth Bond has always had a passion for travel. Mary Beth's "passion path" has taken her to more than 100 countries around the world, a career as a *National Geographic Magazine* author of twelve books, including *Gutsy Women: Advice, Inspiration, Stories,* a radio program about travel, a popular website (gutsytraveler.com), and more adventures than most people could have in five lifetimes. She followed her passion—a path that began slowly, was rocky at times, but eventually paid off in a uniquely rewarding career and life.

One of the joys of following a passion path is this—the more you learn about something, the more you will enjoy it and the more skilled you will be at it.

HOW TO DISCOVER
WHAT YOU MAY BE GOOD AT DOING

> *"The things that you love control your life."*
>
> —Richard Bolles, author of *What Color is Your Parachute?*

If you really don't have a career passion, one way to discover what you may be good at is to take a skills and personality assessment. I recommend the procedure the late Richard Bolles outlines in his book *What Color is Your Parachute?* It is both comprehensive and enlightening. *Time Magazine* called this book "one of the 100 best and most influential (non-fiction) books written in English since 1923."

Bolles recommends a thorough self-examination to determine who you really are and what your true interests are in life. He provides several useful exercises that can reveal what it is you really want in life—not what you *think* you want. This is critically important to your life-long success and happiness.

TOOLS TO HELP YOU KNOW MORE ABOUT YOU

Other useful tools to evaluate your personality and skills include the C. Jung and Myers-Briggs personality tests. The Myers-Briggs personality assessment tools have been around for decades. Thousands of organizations use the assessments to help them evaluate job candidates or facilitate more understanding within the workplace.

HumanMetrics has a brief version you can take to get started (HumanMetrics.com). Other job aptitude tests can be found at Mind Tools (MindTools.com). One of our clients uses the DISC personality assessment with every potential new hire to help determine how best to integrate the new employee into their company culture (discprofile.com).

A fun self-discovery assessment questionnaire (based upon the Myers-Briggs assertion that everyone is one of sixteen personalities, more or less) is 16Personalities (16personalities.com). Using established personality parameters, the company has developed its proprietary algorithm based on the latest psychometric research and more than 15 million test analyses. The free version provides a snapshot of your personality traits.

The paid version creates a 140-page eBook with some history of personality assessment theory and an analysis of your motivation and self-esteem, personal growth, romantic relationships, friendships, parenthood aptitude, academic path, career, and professional development. If you want to learn about other personality types, you can order all sixteen profiles.

The Career and Professional Development section is illuminating and can help you discover what your path in life could be, as well as how to succeed in it. We like that it covers all the key areas of your life since they are all intertwined and interdependent.

Another tool is the Birkman Method. The Birkman is a personality assessment tool that reveals your relationship to others, how you communicate, your response to incentives, your ability to handle change, and your stress triggers, among other things. When you have a deeper self-awareness, you are better able to understand what drives and inspires you.

Another new personality assessment tool is from Plum, a Canadian company conducting pre-employment evaluations. Their primary product is for employers, but they also offer a free personal assessment tool to help demonstrate your career strengths to a potential employer. In about 20 minutes you'll be able to find out what your strongest behavioral traits are and the types of working environments you are best suited for.

The Plum talent assessment is powered by "expert augmented AI" and provides insights to determine Adaptation, Persuasion, Leadership, Teamwork, Decision-Making, Communication, Innovation, Cultural Awareness, Task Management, Conflict Resolution, and Vision/Execution Abilities. If you like, you can then post the information on social media to showcase what makes you unique and valuable. Go to Plum.io to learn more.

There are other tools to help uncover what it is you have an aptitude to do well. But this doesn't mean if you have an exceptional aptitude for something that you should do it. Knowing you would make a great rodeo cowboy doesn't mean you should head west and start roping bulls. You still need to have a love for it—and it must be in the reasonable realm of possibility (although if you look at the career paths of many astronauts you will believe anything is possible).

Career assessment tools aren't perfect but can help open your mind to possibilities. Just be careful not to let them define you. In any case, if you don't have any strong interests or a driving passion to pursue in life, do the work necessary to discover what your purpose in life is. You'll thank yourself forever.

> *"Go confidently in the direction of your dreams!*
> *Live the life you've imagined."*
>
> —Henry David Thoreau, American philosopher and author

Ernie Zielenski writes in *Career Success Without a Real Job: The Career Book for People Too Smart to Work in Corporations,* that most work is "characterized by stifling boredom, grinding tedium, poverty, sexual harassment, loneliness, deranged co-workers, petty jealousies, bullying bosses, seething resentment, illness, exploitation, stress, helplessness, hellish commutes, humiliation, depression, appalling ethics, physical fatigue, and mental exhaustion." Yikes!

We have been fortunate in our careers to have enjoyed interesting work at enlightened companies. However, like most people, we have experienced at least one of these conditions at one time or another. How many have you experienced? Enough said.

Mindful Career Rules: Do the deep introspection to understand who you really are and what you love in life. Don't be fearful of following a personal passion as your career. And if you aren't certain about what you authentically feel passionate about (or have several passions) try it out to see how it resonates with your soul.

Chapter 5

It's Not Your Father's Job Market

"We can never really be prepared for that which is wholly new. We have to adjust ourselves, and every radical adjustment is a crisis in self-esteem."

—Eric Hoffer, author of *The Ordeal of Change and more*

If you haven't kept up with the changes in the modern workplace, you'll find it especially difficult to navigate the new world of work.

1. **Employers know how to do more with less.** New systems, outsourcing, contract labor, robots, automation, and weeding out the "dead wood" has made American business more efficient. And while corporate profits and CEO salaries are soaring, most workers are making nearly the same real wages as in 1975. This is a critical dynamic to be mindful of when deciding on your career path.

2. **Most people don't know how to look for a job.**

   • **Their resumé is badly written,** reflects poorly upon their abilities, and is not searchable easily by applicant tracking system software. The number of resumés with inaccuracies and inconsistencies is remarkably high.

- **Job seekers seldom know how to interview well.** They are often unprepared, don't know what questions to ask, don't have ready answers to questions, and have no understanding of how to make a positive first impression. Few people practice before an interview, instead they just "wing it."

- **Few people network effectively.** Even though it is still the #1 path to finding a good job. Not enough people are on LinkedIn who should be—and many of those who are, don't know how to use it. Few know how to use Twitter to find a job (it's the #2 online source of jobs). And almost no one understands the importance of friends and family to advancing their career aspirations.

- **Recruiters are swamped** and can't spend much time with you unless you are a stellar candidate. The typical resumé receives six seconds of their attention. Few people understand that recruiters aren't in business to find them a job, but to find top candidates for their clients (companies and corporations).

- **The hiring process has become ridiculously complicated.** Companies are looking for perfect candidates. They make decisions more slowly, conduct multiple interviews with several people, require the job seeker to take questionable personality tests, check multiple references, do deep online searches bordering on invasion of privacy, and frequently administer drug tests. Software programs to screen candidates are ubiquitous at large corporations. In the 21st century, you are more likely to be evaluated for a job at a large company by an algorithm rather than a human.

The job market hasn't been this complicated or daunting in modern history, yet a surprisingly large number of people are clueless about how to navigate their career.

TOO MANY AMERICANS ARE DISSATISFIED WITH THEIR CAREER

Far too often people abdicate the responsibility for the direction their life takes by following the dictates of others. They live a linear trajectory—go to school, get a job, work hard, get married, get a dog, have children, buy a home, work harder, acquire the trappings of the "good life," then retire so they can finally start "living."

The irony is that by retirement, life has been wrung out of them. They've forgotten how to live (if they ever really knew how). Or they are simply so exhausted getting to this point there is no life left in them. It's why so many people retire and then die shortly thereafter.

The compromises people make along their career paths often trap them in jobs they hate, a career they don't know how they ever selected, ongoing frustration, and anger.

- A Yahoo Finance survey found 60% would choose an entirely new career if they could start all over again.

- 90% of employees in 2016 are open to new career opportunities—what we recruiters call "passive" candidates.

- *CBS News* reported in a 2017 Gallup study that 51% of Americans "aren't engaged with their current job." Another 16% are "actively disengaged." Gallup estimates this disengagement "costs U.S. companies $450 to $550 billion per year."

- A 2018 Korn Ferry survey found that the top reason people looked for a job that year was that they were bored with their current job. One-third said they were looking for a more challenging position.

In still another study, 7 out of 10 "very dissatisfied" people said they disliked their job so much they would change to *any* job that paid as much or more . . . sight unseen. Think about this for a moment. If you were no longer in love with your husband would you take another man sight unseen just to be away from him? Well, maybe some would! It doesn't have to be this way IF you have a mindful career plan and follow it all your life.

> *"Business is easy. It's doing business with the people in business that's hard."*
>
> —Eric Wentworth, author of *A Plan for Life: The 21st Century Guide to Success in Wealth, Health, Career, Education, Place, Love . . . and You!*

WHAT IS NEEDED IS MORE MINDFULNESS IN THE WORKPLACE

Much of this dissatisfaction in the workplace can be attributed to a lack of mindfulness and consciousness among employees as well as employers. Despite thousands of articles, hundreds of books, and countless training programs designed to make people more effective in their jobs and as managers, the human factor intercedes and the desired result is blocked by vanity, ego, jealousies, insecurities, greed, and a lack of awareness.

As a result, American workers are angry with their employers and themselves. They take their anger out on easy targets to blame: the government, minorities, their families, and their employers. Their "mindless" behavior is affecting everyone in a blanket of negativity. Sometimes this mindlessness manifests itself with self-destructive behavior, including drugs, alcohol, suicide, and workplace violence.

This stream of harmful negative emotion could be easily avoided by adopting a mindful life. Yet, many employers, as well as employees, continue to operate under outdated, negative practices such as annual performance ratings, promoting people based on their tenure at the company, and outright prejudice against women, minorities, and older workers.

In the 21st century, the largest group of workers are now Millennials, followed by Gen Z, and they have an entirely different set of expectations than Boomers and Gen Xers. They are seeking a career, not just a job. They want jobs that are emotionally fulfilling, serve a purpose, and can make a difference in the world. "Nearly 9 out of 10 (86%) of Millennials would consider taking a pay cut to work at a company whose mission and values align with their own," according to LinkedIn's *Workplace Culture Report*. By contrast, only 9% of Baby Boomers would do so. More than 4 in 5 (83%) of Millennials say they would leave a job for one with better family and lifestyle benefits, including the time to do charitable work.

The good news on the horizon is the change in the labor market since 2016. At historically low unemployment rates under 4% in 2019—half of what it was in 2009, workers are now more secure and have more opportunities than at any time since 2005. Wages are even beginning to rise in many industries.

Workers today are impatient to capitalize on their skills to gain increased compensation and benefits, more challenging work and responsibility, and more freedom in the way they work.

> According to *World of Work,* in a 2012 survey by international employment matchmaker Randstad, more than half of today's employed people are actively searching for a new job. How must this feel if you are the CEO of a company and realize half of your employees have one foot out the door? As recruiters, we think this is good news. There is always a large pool of potential candidates for open positions. For corporate America, it's not such good news.

THE END OF THE 9-TO-5 JOB

Studies conducted in 2018 in New Zealand on the effects of a four-day workweek showed a sizable increase in productivity and worker satisfaction. While ingrained traditions are hard to change, a shorter work week seems destined to happen because of its positive impact on productivity.

In fact, the workforce is already moving quickly in this direction. By 2030, it's been predicted the 9-to-5 job will be a footnote in history with flexible hours—and days—as the new norm. And this means that you will need to adapt to these changes in order to succeed.

Bentley University released a study in 2015 revealing 77% of Millennials believe flexible hours would make the workplace more productive. Research by Stanford University backs up this claim.

Mindful Career Rules: Many workers report being dissatisfied with their careers. But the options for creating a meaningful career are expanding, if you have the courage to take advantage of the opportunities to live life on your own terms.

Chapter 6

Nothing Works
The Way We Used to Work

"The most basic requirement of the American Dream is a job."

—*Time* magazine

The new world of work has changed dramatically.

- The average job length is down to just 4.6 years in 2018, according to the Bureau of Labor Statistics. For workers age 25 – 34 years old the average tenure is just 3.2 years.

- The typical person will hold 11.7 jobs (11.8 for men, 11.5 for women) during their career, according to the Bureau of Labor Statistics. 25% held more than 15 jobs during their career.

- New companies employing thousands die (Circuit City) or are formed (Amazon) with increasing frequency. It's predicted that nearly half of the current Fortune 500 companies will be replaced in the next decade, according to Innosight.

- 21st-century skills are in high demand (millions of jobs are unfilled) but 20th-century skills are becoming obsolete (with millions unable to find work).

- The fast-changing and fluid character of the 21st-century workplace will continue to become more chaotic and uncertain.

- It's estimated one in seven jobs available to a college freshman upon graduation has not yet been invented. In 2000, the position of Social Media Marketing Manager or Uber driver did not exist. Solar panel installers and app developers were all but non-existent. Drone pilots weren't even a thing just ten years ago. The demand for battery storage developers has increased exponentially in the past decade.

The length of time workers can "make it" in their career has shortened drastically too.

> **According to payscale.com, earnings "top out" for men around age 45 and for women about age 38.**

In many careers, your "golden" years are between 30 and 45. In a youth-obsessed society, 50 is now considered "over the hill" for many jobs. Rampant ageism is a societal prejudice difficult to overcome. Eric worked in advertising for 35 years. Many of the very best people he worked with in the advertising business are now selling real estate or have given up trying to find work because of their age, not because they suddenly aren't talented anymore.

Many young people are unable to get their career started until they are in their mid to late 20s, so there isn't a large window of opportunity to build a successful life, at least "success" as it has been traditionally defined.

OUTSOURCING WILL CONTINUE TO INCREASE

> **"42% of American jobs . . . more than 50 million . . . are vulnerable to being sent overseas."**
> **—*Harvard Business Review* study (2012)**

Outsourcing talent, both in the U.S. and to other countries, barely existed in 1980. Now it is a fact of life at companies of all sizes as they reduce their operating overhead costs with "employees" who don't require expensive physical space, health benefits, worker's compensation, and other staffing costs. Outsourcing also provides the flexibility to quickly reduce or expand their workforce as conditions change.

It's reported that four in ten companies outsource jobs. In 2015 alone, more than 2.3 million jobs were outsourced to other countries. Since 2000, millions of jobs have been outsourced to China, although India is the current favorite outsourcing destination. But outsourcing is worldwide; countries currently seeing jobs transferred from America also include the Philippines, Bulgaria, Jordan, Lithuania, Egypt, and Indonesia, among others.

The global economy, the rise of skilled workers in many nations that were (or are) Third World countries with low wages, and ease of communication via the internet are the driving factors in a trend showing no sign of decreasing, despite the fact that 89% of economists surveyed said outsourcing hurts our economy.

The top professions at risk of being outsourced are:

✓ Computer programmers and software engineers.

✓ Accountants and auditors.

✓ Lawyers.

✓ Insurance sales agents.

✓ Real estate brokers/agents.

✓ Chemists.

✓ Physicists.

✓ Customer service.

In some markets, like San Francisco and San Jose, more than 1 in 6 jobs are outsourced.

WORK HAS CHANGED FOR MILLIONS IN THE 21ST CENTURY

As author and social observer Seth Godin (sethgodin.com) perceptively writes, "For 80 years, you got a job, you did what you were told, and you retired. People are raised on the idea that if they pay their taxes and do what they're told, there's some kind of safety net or pension plan waiting for them. But the days when people were able to get above-average pay for average work are over."

While employment has improved greatly since the peak of the Great Recession in 2008, the statistics don't reveal the extent of the disruption in the American workforce.

Americans are:

- ✓ **Working for less money.** The average national income (in constant dollars) has increased very little during the past 30 years (except for CEOs and the wealthy 1%). Many people are priced out of the markets where they work and must endure long commutes from more affordable areas.

- ✓ **Working at jobs they frequently don't like.** One in three are working at a job they didn't train for at school. According to the Wall Street Journal, in 2018 43% of college graduates "are underemployed."

- ✓ **Dropping out of the workforce altogether.** Fewer Americans are actively engaged in the workforce than at any other time since 1970.

Increased costs and the rising gap between the haves and have nots in America is straining our social fabric, with many people holding more than one job just to survive.

This is the "new norm" in the 21st-century workplace. Unfortunately, it doesn't look as if it will change much soon.

THE WORKPLACE IS AMERICA'S #1 CAUSE OF STRESS

Fully 1 in 4 people said workplace stress was the #1 stressor in their lives.

All this stress has physical consequences, such as neck pain (62%), eye pain (44%), and difficulty sleeping (34%). One million workers in America call in "sick" due to stress *every day*. 79% of men and 61% of women also reported stress on the job affects their personal relationships.

The major cause of stress isn't necessarily the longer hours and increased workload but other workers (53%) and management (53%). Stress costs American business hundreds of billions of dollars annually.

Americans are working longer hours for fewer benefits and stagnant pay than compared to just 20 years ago. Many feel they are trapped on an arduous treadmill they can't get off. Americans are stressed to the breaking point.

MINDFULNESS IN THE WORKPLACE

There is also good news happening in the workplace, some of it showing a more mindful approach by both companies and employees. Many companies now include meditation and yoga as a perk for their employees. Fashion designer Eileen Fisher has her staff meditate prior to every important meeting. Google has an internal course titled Search Inside Yourself. Neural Self-Hacking and Managing Your Energy is among several mindfulness classes the company offers. Then there are the company's regular series of Mindful Lunches.

When the Wisdom 2.0 Conference was held in 2016 in San Francisco, more than 1,700 people attended. Top executives from Ford, Cisco, LinkedIn, and Salesforce were featured.

Companies and individuals are finding mindful practices lead to greater cooperation, increased productivity, more creativity, and an improvement in emotional intelligence. Salesforce and LinkedIn conduct dozens of "Conscious Selling" programs every year in an effort to restructure the selling process to create "win/win" relationships.

Mindful Career Rules: The American workplace has become challenging. Learn how to navigate the new world of work. Learn to be mindful at work.

Chapter 7

The New World of Work

"Today's world of work is completely different from anything that's gone before."

—*The Economist*

Everything has changed in the 21st century.

Back in the "good old days" of the last century, finding a job usually wasn't very hard. Good paying jobs were plentiful for most of the period after World War II. Grads could take their time deciding what to do in life, unburdened by suffocating student loans. People often worked at jobs for ten years or more. Most companies still provided some job security and valuable benefits.

As recently as 1980 nearly 2 in 3 workers had defined-benefit pensions. Today, the figure is below 5%, according to an article in *Money* magazine. Not long ago almost everyone thought retiring at 65 to enjoy the rest of their days in comfort and leisure was the norm. According to *Bloomberg*, by 2024, 36% of 65 to 69-year-olds will still be working. Many Americans, hit hard by the Great Recession, say they will never be able to retire. Many others say they enjoy their careers and will only retire "when I'm dead." The 21st century couldn't be more different than the 20th century.

THE GREATEST UPHEAVAL IN WORK
SINCE THE INDUSTRIAL REVOLUTION

We've entered a period of change not seen since the Industrial Revolution when much of the world transitioned from a rural, agrarian society to an urban, industrial society. The Industrial Revolution created unprecedented disruption in the lives of millions of people—as well as widespread poverty. It also created massive amounts of wealth for those who adapted and took advantage of the creative chaos.

The revolution we are now experiencing will have similar effects. Already there are tens of millions of people who have been reduced to poverty by the transition from a manufacturing-based society to a working world dominated by service industries and technology. Conversely, there have been scores of billionaires created by these same changes. And it's all happening at lightning speed.

> In a little more than two decades after founding Amazon, in 2018 Jeff Bezos became the richest person in the world —and the wealthiest person to have ever lived.

The next 20 years will be a state of continued creative chaos throughout the world as technology, global interdependence, increased social interaction, massive information access, and disrupted industries make life uncertain and unpredictable. This is yet another reason to take a mindful approach when choosing a career path.

UNEMPLOYMENT WILL STAY LOW,
BUT THERE IS A SKILLS GAP

Even with unemployment currently below 4% (September 2019), good jobs are scarce—unless you have the specialized skills required for 21st-century jobs. Right now (2019), there are more than 7.3 million open jobs, according to the Bureau of Labor Statistics. But far too many Americans lack the 21st-century skills required to do those jobs. There are also more Americans of working age who have dropped out of the labor market than ever before . . . more than a half-million.

"Student loan debt is crushing the lives of millions of Americans."

—Senator Bernie Sanders

STUDENT LOAN DEBT WILL HIT $2 TRILLION BY 2022

Student loan debt hit $1.6 *trillion* in 2019, according to the Federal Reserve, and will be a drag upon the lives of many for years, even decades. Nearly 50 million Americans are indebted because they chose to get a college education. The average amount owed is $33,310 (2018), according to the U.S. Department of Education. Student loan debt may have been an abstraction of the future in college but will become a harsh reality when young people try to establish their lives, get married, buy a home or have children, and find there isn't enough money to do it. And since nearly 11% are delinquent on their payments, America now has a generation of people whose creditworthiness is harmed for decades, if not forever.

MORE TEMP, PART-TIME, AND CONTRACT WORK

"American work, American business, and the American Dream became temporary."

—Louis Hyman, author of *Temp: How American Work, American Business, and the American Dream Became Temporary*

The rapid move by companies toward hiring temp, part-time, and contract workers to reduce costs and remain flexible is changing the face of American business and the lives of workers. Since companies often don't provide job security or attractive benefits packages, more people are opting to work freelance to gain some control over their life. According to a study released in 2017, *The Intuit 2020 Report*, in less than ten years 4 in 10 working Americans will be temp or part-time workers, solopreneurs, contract workers, sole practitioners, consultants, freelancers or working "gigs."

A HUGE DEMOGRAPHIC SHIFT

*"By 2020, Millennials will surpass Baby Boomers
as the largest U.S. adult generation."*

—Pew Research Center, 2016

There is a huge shifting of demographics as Baby Boomers, the largest cohort in history, retires or dies. On the heels of this transition in the workforce is the Millennial and Gen Z generations, huge (and very different) cohorts of people. The different characteristics of each group will contribute to defining the future of work as much as The Greatest Generation and Baby Boomers left their mark.

Demographic data predicts a dearth of workers in the coming years. The birth rate is declining, and it looks as if restrictions on immigration may continue for years. More than half a million working-age adults have dropped out of the workforce for reasons as different as lack of modern skills to opioid addiction. As a result, there will likely be many labor shortages, especially since currently the skills of the workforce don't meet the market demands. Nearly two-thirds of employers say new hires lack the skills they need.

SCHOOLS DO A POOR JOB OF PREPARING STUDENTS FOR CAREERS

*"What if schools actually helped kids identify their
strengths by exploring their talents from a young age
and growing their skills over the 12 years instead of
letting them all follow the same routine like sheep and
leaving them confused in life after graduation."*

Tallie Dar in *Conscious Reminder*

Higher education, while more expensive than ever, is not doing the job of preparing graduates for the workforce of the 21st century. Only 11% of employers believe higher education "is very effective" in preparing grads to meet the skills needed today. In a survey of 501 American hiring managers, recruiters, and HR executives, 62% said students were unprepared to enter the workforce.

MANY PROFESSIONS WILL BE OUTDATED

> *"At least 40% of all businesses will die in the next 10 years ... if they don't figure out how to change their entire company to accommodate new technologies."*
> —John Chambers, Executive Chairman, Cisco Systems

Just as telegraph operators and horse-drawn buggy makers were replaced by technology, many professions will cease to be viable in the tech-driven 21st century. Your first career decision is to do something that meets the demands of the fast-evolving 21st century and can't be made obsolete in the new world of work.

Currently, the workplace has gotten exponentially more confusing as change occurs at an accelerated pace. So, you are mostly on your own as you try to navigate these turbulent times. For these reasons, it is vitally important to be a lifelong student and manager of your career. As Mark Twain put it, "I have never let my schooling interfere with my education."

The majority of college students graduate with little direction on creating a satisfying career, and almost no knowledge of the tools available to manage a career. A surprising number of people who have been in the workforce for many years also know little about how to do that either.

This book is just one resource of many you need to read to educate yourself on how to manage a career. It's up to you to educate yourself to stay relevant in the new world of work.

THE GOOD NEWS

The next few decades will bring more change—and opportunities—than any other time in human history. If you are just beginning your career (and you make the right choices) your life will likely be better than you ever dreamed. For those with the right education, skills, and creativity, the world is their oyster. But success in the new world of work depends more than ever on your ability to live mindfully.

You must be mindful of your own authentic self. You must be mindful of the world around you. You must be mindful of others. And you must be mindful (as much as possible) of what lies in the future. This won't be easy, because the 21st-century world will continually evolve, presenting new challenges to overcome, increased distractions, as well as opportunities that are difficult to see.

MANY YOUNG PEOPLE ARE CREATING THEIR OWN CAREER

Young people by the tens of thousands are eschewing the traditional career path in favor of utilizing the Internet-based tools now available (and which they are proficient at using) to forge their own path. Many see college as a giant financial scam that delivers little in return for decades of debt. They reject the traditional corporate structure, working with bosses, and climbing the ladder step by step to success (only to see these plans scuttled by mergers, acquisitions, and bankruptcies). They vividly remember what happened to their parents during the Great Recession and are determined that they will forge their own way.

Some create startups. While the number of startups that eventually succeed is small, the potential payoff for those that do can be great. Amazon, PayPal, LinkedIn, Oracle, Apple, Spanx, and hundreds of other big companies were all startups during the past 25 years. Their founders are all billionaires.

Other young entrepreneurs have become "influencers" online. Many travel around the world documenting their adventures with surprisingly professional video and photos, earning money by promoting the places they visit and the products they use. Many are earning high incomes, often in the millions of dollars, while doing what they love. Others are "digital nomads" who live in places as remote as Bali and Portugal. They have found online work—from writing to designing websites to creating an online business—that enables them to work from anywhere they want to work as long as it has an Internet connection.

None of these businesses could have existed as recently as 10 years ago. The internet and technology have changed everything. It's an exciting time to be young. The possibilities to create a sustainable, enjoyable, highly rewarding career are endless.

Mindful Career Rules: The career challenge of the 21st century is to find work matching the needs of the future—and *your* needs.

Chapter 8

The New Rules of Work

It's not your father's work world anymore.

In the 21st century, new rules of work are quickly being adopted by companies and employees.

WORK IS WHEREVER YOU WORK

With the costs and hassles of commuting increasing, and with the widespread availability of high-speed internet access, the need to work at a specific location becomes less necessary. Soon, you will be able to work virtually anywhere. SpaceX launched the first group of satellites in 2019 that will eventually help deliver high-speed broadband access to even the remotest parts of the planet.

Companies have been quick to see the advantages of having remote workers. In 2016, Forbes magazine published a list of the top 100 companies offering remote working as an option. Among these are Amazon, United Health, Xerox, Dell, IBM, Allergan, and Adobe. This is a big change from just 15 years ago. Companies are discovering that their remote workers are more productive and save on overhead costs. There are companies, like Automattic and Buffer, where 100% of the employees are working remotely, connected virtually from locations all over the world.

Remote work is on the rise because it, well, works. In one study, telecommuters completed 13.5% more calls than office workers. They performed 10% more work. They left the company at half the rate overall. And they also reported feeling more fulfilled on the job.

Since 2000, thousands of co-working spaces, like Rocket Space and Runway in San Francisco, have popped up. One large company, WeWork (wework.com), has made a huge impact worldwide in the shared office space concept with beautifully designed working spaces in more than two dozen countries. As of 2018, more than a quarter-million people work in one of their 450 offices located in 86 cities.

Bill and Michelle work from their home in Utah. Michelle sells her artwork on Etsy and her own website. Bill is a "troubleshooter" for IBM and is on-call to travel to spots all over the globe on a minute's notice. "We like spending more time together and really experiencing our kid's lives, unlike many of our friends who work traditional jobs," says Bill. He's lucky. His job, while intense at times, only requires about 25 hours a month.

Bill and Michelle made the mindful decision to give their lifestyle a try after a meditation retreat that awakened their desire for a more conscious life. Although they expected to earn less money, the reverse has been true. Both earn more than ever before. And they have achieved their dream of living more mindfully and consciously.

Ted, a freelance writer, works from his Airstream "home" on the road, as he travels around North America. "I can write anywhere," he said. "So, what is stopping me from seeing the country while doing so?" All he needs is his wi-fi hotspot or a local coffeehouse to connect to his clients.

Sofia, a 22-year old graphic designer, works from Bali, where a sizable number of American expatriates enjoy affordable living and wonderful amenities on American incomes. She designs websites. Her only complaint is the time difference. When it's 10 am in San Francisco, it's 1 am in Bali.

Remote work, in all its iterations, is a business trend that experts expect will continue to grow. Consider this as an option when creating and evaluating your life plan.

WORK IS 24/7

For much of the working world, the old 9 to 5 schedule is being replaced by a 24/7 reality. Employers often don't care where or when the work is done—as long as it's done on time. With easy internet access, tablets, and smartphones that means you may be "always on." While this provides you with some flexibility, it also erodes your private "away" time.

Over half of employed adults said they check work messages at least once a day over the weekend and more than four in ten while on vacation, according to a survey by the American Psychological Association (2013).

This new "always on" style of employment is also cutting into employees' weekends—even their sleep (a sizeable number of people now check messages at night, even waking themselves up in the middle of their sleep).

This 24/7 work world is not necessarily a good thing—just the opposite. Your productivity can be negatively affected when you don't have time to refresh yourself from your job. Learn to set limits. However, if you can incorporate your career into your lifestyle, you may enjoy the freedom of working when, where, and how you want.

Greg and Sue work from their suburban home as writers. They also keep a shared office for writers in the city to meet with clients and be around other writers. What they like about their lifestyle is the freedom to work out at their health club at 10 am, enjoy a relaxing lunch on their patio, and work until 2 am, if they want (Greg likes the solitude and lack of distraction late at night). Both like to get up early on weekends and put in a couple hours of writing time. If they want to go to the beach on a Tuesday, Greg and Sue arrange their working schedule to accommodate it. Neither would trade this flexibility and freedom for a higher paying office job.

Many people like the enforced regimen of the 9 to 5, Monday through Friday work life at a company office. It gives them "structure" within a framework that removes much of the uncertainty of daily work. If it suits your temperament, working 24/7 can be liberating and a path to greater career fulfillment.

THE DEMISE OF FULL-TIME JOBS WITH FULL BENEFITS

The current bare-bones working world can easily make you nostalgic for the "good old days" of the 1980s and 90s when jobs were typically 40 hours a week in length and came with benefits like healthcare, life insurance, investment plans, and a pension. The new rules of work in the 21st century include jobs with few or no benefits, part-time work, temp jobs, contract assignments, and "gigs." The new tax laws going into effect in 2018 with exemptions for pass-through income will only exacerbate the situation, with employees now having to decide if they should be independent contractors or pass on the deduction.

More than a third of the current workforce are freelancers. That's nearly 55 million workers. Some of these freelancers work because they enjoy the freedom and potential upside income potential. However, half report being seriously stressed and wish they were working at full-time jobs.

WORKING FOR MORE THAN JUST MONEY

In the last century and before, people mostly worked to earn money to pay their bills (and set a bit aside to take care of their future years). Now it's popular to want more out of a career . . . and rightfully so. This is especially true for the youngest generation of workers, the Millennials and Gen Z.

In the 21st century, many people want the work they do to have meaning, to contribute to the betterment of the world, to innovate change, and to provide soulful satisfaction. In a 2015 *Fortune* magazine article, human resource expert Adam Miller writes that the younger workforce wants three things from the workplace:

1. Flexible hours—the ability to fit work into their lifestyle.

2. Personal fulfillment—six in ten say a sense of purpose is the reason why they chose their current employer, according to a 2014 Deloitte Millennial Survey.

3. Personal growth—75% say learning new skills from inspired leaders is important.

Younger workers often see their parent's style of working as a failure. They want more from their career than just making more money or landing a bigger promotion. They want to work at something that has a purpose and makes a difference, if possible. And they want to integrate their work into their lifestyle.

The younger generation of workers isn't as loyal as their parents were to the company where they work. They've seen companies blithely lay off workers by the thousands, including long-time employees, or move their operations to a country with cheaper labor or better tax advantages. The bond of trust between employer and employee has been broken, perhaps forever.

As a result, the typical worker holds 6.2 jobs by age 26—far more than their parents, according to the Bureau of Labor Statistics (2018).

They also aren't afraid to delay their careers or try out several career paths. This is a more informed and enlightened generation and these decisions bode well for their future.

Younger people also have adapted their career aspirations to the technology they grew up with. Millennials and Gen Z are so comfortable with using technology that they almost seem "pre-wired" from birth. Many are using this knowledge to create apps, start new businesses, and becoming "influencers" to create careers that don't follow any traditional path.

It's not unusual for an "influencer" on social media with a million followers to earn well into the six figures annually. Some have even become millionaires. Kylie Jenner, a billionaire, earns more than $1 million per paid Instagram post. Kayla Itsines, a fitness blogger who has an enormous following for her Bikini Bod Guide, earns more than $15 million a year. There's even an eight-year-old boy who reviews toys on YouTube and earns well over $20 million a year, according to *Forbes* magazine.

Young people who embrace technology and a non-traditional career path often have exceedingly successful careers. There's no reason you can't too.

COGNITIVE AND SOFT SKILLS CAN OUTWEIGH A COLLEGE DEGREE

Many of the skills now required of workers are cognitive. Of course, those with highly desired specific skills that can't be outsourced or automated—like those who operate and service high-tech machinery, carpenters, writers, bricklayers—will be fairly safe in the changing economy. But everyone will be expected to operate on a higher plane intellectually.

Jeff Weiner, CEO of LinkedIn, goes as far as to say that in the new world of work what will separate the successful from others are "soft" skills. It's his belief that these skills are more important in the 21st century than many college degrees. Soft skills (which we will discuss in more detail later in the book) include communications ability, team building, and mindful leadership.

Here are twelve skills desired of the future workforce:

1. Sense-making. Higher-level thinking that machines don't do well

2. Social intelligence

3. Novel adaptive thinking

4. Cross-cultural competency

5. Computational thinking

6. New media literacy. Video and visual creation

7. Trans-disciplinary capabilities

8. Design mindset

9. Cognitive load management—the ability to filter and focus on what is important

10. Communications

11. Collaboration and team building

12. Leadership

These are not necessarily your parent's priorities. It's a decidedly more mindful view of work than any previous generation. We will discuss the importance of "soft" skills in more detail later in the book.

Chapter 9

The Internet
And the Changing Job Market

Like everything else in our life, the Internet has changed the world of work. If you aren't using the resources of the Internet to manage your career you are already at a disadvantage. But with this powerful career tool comes some potential hazards that can also derail your career.

Social media can affect your job prospects even before you are in the job market.

- One in ten college admissions professionals say they visit prospective students' online pages—and 38% reported they were negatively impacted by what they found (everything from inappropriate behavior and language to nude photos). Conversely, students who show a mature and sophisticated use of social media were viewed more positively.

- A 2017 study of randomly selected hiring authorities by the Society for Human Resource Management revealed that 85% now use social networking sites and Google search to help them screen job candidates (Facebook 66%, Twitter 53%, and LinkedIn 96%). A quarter said they made a hire after reviewing a social media profile.

Here are some of their other findings:

✓ 69% have rejected a candidate based upon what was found online.

The reasons?

✓ 13% of candidates lied about their qualifications.

✓ 11% posted lewd or inappropriate photos.

✓ 11% posted inappropriate comments.

✓ 11% said negative things about their previous employer.

✓ 10% posted content indicating they used illegal drugs.

On the positive side, 68% said they hired a candidate based upon what they found online. Here's why.

✓ 39% projected a positive attitude.

✓ 36% had a profile supporting their professional qualifications for a job.

✓ 36% showed creativity.

✓ 34% had good references.

In the SHRM survey, 61% reported they believed social media profiles reveal more information than is provided in a resumé and 50% use it to verify the information. At our firm, we review social media (and do background checks) before going forward with a job candidate.

Hiring authorities and recruiters look for "red flags" that could possibly spell trouble in the future.

A surprising number of college students, who are spending four or five years and tens of thousands of dollars for an education, blithely destroy their chance of getting a job by being stupid online. Those hilarious photos of you throwing up on your date when you got drunk at the college frat party may come back to haunt you someday. Worse, estimates are as many as one-third of 20-year-olds have posted a naked or revealing photo of themselves online, or "sexted" a revealing photo on their smartphone (or in this case, dumbphone).

That oh-so-cute naked photo of you having revenge sex that you emailed to your ex-boyfriend is lingering out there in cyberspace just waiting to go viral and mess with you. Those gorgeous photos of your genitals you sexted to your girlfriend ought to really impress the hiring managers. What company would hire someone who displays such poor judgment?

Since it's estimated that 70% of all resumés contain inaccurate information—and 43% include downright lies—designed to enhance a job prospect's work, personal or educational history, what appears online is often a reality check for employers. Most HR Directors say even one lie or distortion is enough to disqualify a candidate. So, resumés are cross-checked against other available data—including social media, criminal records, credit scores, and past employment dates. In many cases, discrepancies are found that could disqualify a candidate. Again, what company would want an employee who is dishonest?

Your life is an open book and the Internet is the library. If a company really wants to drill down to find out personal and professional information about you, well, it's easier than ever. Several companies and websites provide information that was only available to private investigators in the recent past. Whether or not you are on the internet, your personal privacy is, for all intents and purposes, gone.

HOW EMPLOYERS JUDGE YOU
IN THE NEW WORLD OF WORK

The new world of work isn't anything like your father's workplace. Employers now often judge potential employees on:

1. Google presence and ranking.

2. Online reputation.

3. Business social media presence.

4. Personal website.

5. Blog.

6. Facebook presence.

7. LinkedIn Profile, connections, recommendations.

8.   Twitter followers and Tweets.

9.   YouTube presence.

10. Instagram posts and followers.

By reviewing all these online sources, a recruiter can easily discover the "real" person behind the resumé.

Not only has the job market become more competitive, managing a career effectively today is significantly more complex. Before doing anything online be mindful of its impact on your life and career.

JOB SEARCH 3.0

The days of sending a typed cover letter and resumé to answer a job posted in the newspaper or a trade magazine are long gone. Job search is now conducted online.

Data compiled by the Pew Research Center in 2016 and Glassdoor (2016) illustrates the amazing change in where job seekers find their jobs today.

✓   79% of job seekers now use social media to get hired.
    (86% of those who are in the first decade of their careers).

✓   More than one in five have applied for a job through social media.

✓   More than nine in ten job seekers have a profile on a social
    media site.

Twenty years ago, few people could have conceived of the importance social media now plays in career management. The fact is if you're not online, you're probably in the unemployment line.

THAT WAS THEN, THIS IS NOW

Career management expert Josh Waldman, author of *Job Searching with Social Media for Dummies* and the popular blog Career Enlightenment (careerenlightenment.com) points out several key ways today's job search is different.

1.   **Google and LinkedIn have replaced the resumé.** Sure, you still need
     to have a resumé on steroids, but recruiters today are using Google
     and LinkedIn searches to find talent.

2. **Your resumé summary is key to getting noticed.** It's the open or closed door to your qualifications. The average time spent reviewing a resumé is said to be just six seconds (it's actually longer if you appear to have the right qualifications for the job). If you don't grab the attention of the recruiter or hiring manager in the space of a TV commercial, you've probably wasted your time applying. Make sure your summary includes the right keywords and appeals to the self-interest of the company. Customize your summary for each job description.

3. **"Social proof, testimonials, and recommendations seriously reduce the perceived risk of you as a candidate,"** says Waldman. Consider including a real testimonial statement or two in your resumé.

4. **Relationships outweigh resumés in importance.** Personal networking is still the top path to getting a job, and probably always will be. References are important to recruiters when evaluating a job candidate.

5. **Employers only care about what they want.** Keep the focus of your resumé and job search on what you can do for the employer.

6. **Keywords are king.** Study up on how to select and use keywords to find a job. Applicant tracking software and keyword searches on LinkedIn have changed how resumés (and profiles) need to be structured. It's important to develop several resumés—each with a different focus—customized for every job application, matching as closely as possible with the advertised position. Incorporate words from the job description as keywords in your custom resumé.

    Recruiters sometimes use Jobscan (jobscan.co) to compare resumés to the keywords in job descriptions. You can do the same to customize your resumé to fit the Job Description more closely. This is especially helpful for resumés that must pass the Applicant Tracking System gauntlet. The Jobscan Learning Center section also offers a range of pre-vetted formats you can use to build your resumé, as well as job search tips.

    You can also analyze your LinkedIn Profile against relevant job descriptions and industry data by using Jobscan's LinkedIn Optimization Tool.

7. **You are your brand** in 21st-century career management. Carefully decide what personal image you want to project to support your goals and is based on core truths about you and your capabilities, then apply it consistently in every area of your life—online and offline.

Career expert Dick Bolles adds these key points:

1. Sending out resumés blindly to companies has an atrocious success record—only 1 in 270 lands a job. Your new "resumé" is online.

2. There are more jobs available than you think. At any given time, there are millions of openings. Learning to use a wide range of online resources is key to successful career management and job search.

3. Small companies with 100 employees or less are the best ones for job-hunters to approach—especially for older workers, those with handicaps, or returning vets. Research companies online to discover the rising stars.

4. Recruiters scour job boards to find potential candidates. Be sure to have your updated resumé listed on the job boards that are pertinent to your industry and career goals.

Mindful Career Rules: The workplace is constantly evolving—rapidly. Be mindful of how these changes can affect your career path.

Chapter 10

21st Century Macrotrends Affecting Your Career Path

> *"If you change the way you look at things, the things you look at change."*
>
> —Dr. Wayne Dyer, author of *The Power of Intention*

More change has taken place since 2000 than at any other time in human history.

During the next 15 years, the rate of change will only increase. To survive it you will have to change too. You'll need to look at your life and career path knowing that the only thing you can be certain of is that you can't be certain of anything.

At times, you will feel as if the world has gone crazy and you're barely able to hold on for dear life. Hundreds of millions will be severely disrupted by the changes to come. But if you plan for it (and make the right choices) you can adapt to the changes and live a happy and successful life. The potential exists to live a life better than at any other time in history.

More than at any other time in history it's important to dust off your crystal ball and try to predict what the future will be like. Sure, you say, there's a good use of my time. Who can predict what the world will be like in ten or twenty years?

Well, you can—and you can't. In 1975, few of us had any idea just 40 years later we would be making movies on our phones (portable phones, at that) or wasting millions of hours on the internet playing Grand Theft Auto. Most of the best-paying jobs today didn't exist in 1975. But with a little foresight, (something in short supply back in the 70s) you could have predicted some emerging fields would grow into lucrative sources of jobs. Imagine if you had extrapolated the introduction of the personal computer to its inevitable ramifications upon society. Or the Internet in the mid-90s. You would have had a plethora of career choices. Or you could have possibly become a billionaire, like Bill Gates, Jeff Bezos, Elon Musk, and Steve Jobs.

We're (hopefully) smarter now and have more resources to help us see possibilities in the next twenty or thirty years. The science of trend analysis and demographic projections give clues to where the world is heading, at least in the next few decades.

MACROTRENDS AFFECTING YOUR FUTURE

> *"The new wave is coming. Some people who catch up with the wave will be rich, will be more successful. But for those who fall behind, the future will be painful."*
>
> —Jack Ma, Founder, Founder of Alibaba

Here are 30 macrotrends likely to shape the way our world evolves in the 21st century. Nearly all of them have the potential to affect your future career prospects. Any of these trends could also be your ticket to a fulfilling career suited to the realities of the 21st century.

1. **Artificial intelligence.** *Forbes* reported in early 2019 it's estimated that as many as 5 million jobs will be replaced by artificial intelligence by the end of 2020.

    Machines will soon be smarter than you are. Maybe they are already. When a machine can do your job better than you (e.g. accountants, science research, doctors) what will you do?

    While artificial intelligence may destroy many current jobs, it will also create many excellent jobs. As the New York Times reported in October 2017, "Tech's biggest companies are placing huge bets on artificial intelligence, banking on things ranging from face-scanning smartphones and conversational coffee-table gadgets to computerized health care and autonomous vehicles." Artificial intelligence specialists "can be paid from $300,000 to $500,000 a year or more in salary and company stock." Some are paid millions of dollars.

2. **Automation.** Nearly half of all jobs will be automated by 2025, according to *Harper's* magazine.

   Businessman and billionaire Mark Cuban said at SXSW 2019 "Research shows that by 2026 one million jobs in the U.S. are expected to disappear because of automation." McDonald's—which currently employs 210,000 workers worldwide—is testing out completely automated restaurants. At many companies, products get produced without ever having the need for human intervention. Soon, any repetitive work not absolutely requiring a human being will be done by an automated machine. Controlled by sophisticated computers, automation produces better work much faster than even the most capable humans. PR writers are being replaced by automated press releases. Tax preparation is fast becoming automated. One study predicts more than nine in ten cashiers will be out of work by 2030. The challenge in the coming years is to choose a career not easily automated.

3. **Robotics.** Automobiles are 90% built by robots (who do a much better job than humans ever have). Amazon uses robots in its warehouses to stock and fulfill millions of orders. They work 24-hours a day, never take "sick days" or quit suddenly. Robots do what they're told without complaining, and don't require benefit packages. The military is testing robotic soldiers, tanks, and planes. Robots have replaced baristas at dozens of new "coffee shops." Robotics will permeate 21st-century life, creating thousands of high-paying jobs (as well as eliminating thousands of repetitive jobs).

4. **Connectivity—The Internet of Everything.** Cisco Systems projects by 2020 more than 50 billion devices will be connected or functional through the Internet. Nearly anything you want to know about can

be found on the internet. What once took weeks or months to find now takes seconds.

The Internet is the driving force behind an increasingly connected world. From autonomous cars to fitness trackers to the refrigerator in your home, the Internet of Things (IoT) will continue to transform how we work and live—even how long we live. Virtually every human activity will be affected. The spinoffs from this hyper-connectedness have already created millions of jobs.

Just four years ago the *MIT Technology Review* wrote, "What if every vehicle, home appliance, heating system, and light switch were connected to the internet? Today, it's not a stretch of the imagination, it's a reality." Nothing has the potential to change our world more than the Internet of Things . . . or Everything.

"Modern cars already have hundreds of sensors and multiple computers connected over an internal network." Your car is essentially a rolling computer. Your home appliances and security can now be connected to the IoT. Home personal assistants, like Alexa, provide access to nearly anything you want to buy or know.

The first library without printed books has opened, enabling readers to download books to their smartphones or tablet devices with no need for librarians.

The Internet has likely produced as many new career opportunities as it has replaced. The role of Social Media Manager did not exist just 15 years ago. Remote work is possible primarily because of the Internet. Thousands of new online businesses (e.g. eBay, Slack, Medium, LinkedIn, Trello, Skype) are a result of Internet access. And thousands of jobs in support industries—from fiber optics to cloud computing—depend upon the Internet.

5. **Climate change.** Despite a few holdouts who think it's a "hoax," 98% of all the scientists in the world think climate change is real and happening because of human activity. Most experts agree that climate change is accelerating more rapidly than anticipated, with all the adverse effects it causes.

A rapidly warming planet affects everything from the hundreds of millions who live along the coasts impacted by rising ocean levels to the insurance companies paying out more for damages caused by extreme weather. Nothing short of nuclear war has more potential to destroy the earth than climate change. At the same time, thousands of new jobs are being created to address this problem. Big corporations, like Amazon, are investing hundreds of millions in renewable energy in everything from wind farms to solar energy. Enormous infrastructure building programs will also be required to protect cities, defense facilities, and businesses located along the coastline, creating tens of thousands of jobs.

Related global challenges—from species extinction to ocean pollution—will create hundreds of thousands of meaningful careers as the dire reality of the threat to human survival finally becomes apparent to everyone.

Careers addressing climate change have the potential to save our planet. If you desire a career with purpose, you can't find one better than addressing climate change.

6. **Renewable and alternative energy sources.** Some nations are already running almost entirely on renewable energy sources. The cost of solar power has dropped dramatically in recent years, making it more affordable than fossil fuel sources. Wind, water, geothermal and other types of renewable energy are all increasing. The increased power and decreasing cost of rechargeable batteries will make electric-powered vehicles and machines commonplace in the 21st century. Every major automobile company is rapidly converting its entire line of cars and trucks to electric power. Some states (and nations such as Germany) have mandated a total conversion to electric-powered vehicles within 20 years.

With billions of gallons of fuel being used every day in the world, fossil fuels will become extremely expensive as supplies diminish (there are 100,000 passenger planes in the air every day using an average of 28,000 gallons of fuel each and a cruise ship uses a gallon of fuel for every 130 feet it travels!). Renewable energy is a field with excellent career opportunities.

7. **Human Genome Project.** The decoding and mapping of human DNA
    will open thousands of applications, creating many new enriching
    careers. Already, thousands of jobs, hundreds of companies, and
    hundreds of billions of dollars have been generated by the HGP. A
    popular company created as a direct result of the HGP is 23andMe.
    At 23andMe anyone can get their ancestry unlocked and several
    genetic trait health reports for just $199 (23andme.com).

    Healthcare companies are using DNA to prevent, predict, and treat
    illnesses. Helix and LoseIt! (a nutrition and weight-loss app) teamed
    up to create a custom diet and exercise recommendations based
    on your DNA. Other healthcare startups are changing healthcare
    with DNA-based treatment and prevention programs. The field of
    pharmacogenomics—the study of how variations in an individual's
    genes affect their response to medications—will open another
    avenue to personalized medicine.

    In the rapidly growing field of forensic science, DNA is a game-
    changer. Crimes are routinely solved using DNA proof, "cold
    case" crimes are being solved (sometimes decades after the crime
    occurred), and many falsely-convicted people have been released
    from prison based on new DNA evidence. Jobs in forensic science
    are interesting, challenging, and meaningful.

    Genome sequencing is changing fast, analyzing a greater percentage
    of DNA, and dropping in price. In 2016, the Mayo Clinic treated
    more than 12,000 patients using genetic information. The prospects
    for an exciting and worthwhile career based on DNA usage is
    enormous.

8. **Driverless transportation.** Driverless vehicles will radically impact
    several industries: highway construction and maintenance, auto
    manufacturers and their suppliers, insurance companies, traffic
    control, land use, and the way people do business and spend their
    extra time. Most of the nation's 3.5 million truck drivers may need
    to find new employment, as will taxi, Uber and Lyft drivers, among
    others. In 2017, Elon Musk announced his plans to build a self-
    driving electric pickup truck and a semi-tractor trailer. Electric and
    driverless vehicles will change the way business operates in America.

9. **Big Data analysis and predictive analytics.** Our lives are increasingly being tracked and analyzed with Big Data. It is endemic in our society and will affect everything we do in the future. Companies will incorporate more data into their operations to stay competitive. The government's use of data is also growing exponentially. This trend will only increase, providing a wealth of opportunity. Already, towing companies use predictive analytics based on ongoing scanning of license plates to predict with remarkable accuracy where to find cars whose owners are delinquent on payments. And police departments use predictive analysis to predict where crimes will be committed before they happen, enabling them to allocate resources more efficiently.

    Data skimmed from the Internet is being used by criminals to scam Americans and by foreign governments to disrupt our democratic process. Large companies like Sony and Target have been hacked using retrieved and manipulated data. Big Data security will be important for any company using it—and will create thousands of high-paying jobs in cybersecurity.

10. **Wearable technology.** From fitness trackers to Apple smartwatches to police body cams, the trend toward wearable technology is just beginning. Soon we will be able to wear clothing with the technical capability to monitor our vital health signs, enabling doctors to monitor their patients' health remotely.

    Imagine earrings able to track your vital signs, shoes that can track your exercise, buttons with embedded GPS tracking, and solar-powered clothes capable of charging up your electronic devices. This isn't the future of wearables; all are available now. Wearable technologies will create many new companies and thousands of new jobs.

11. **The wealth gap between rich and poor.** The wealth gap between the top 1% of Americans and everyone else will continue to increase as a few individuals and families consolidate their control over wealth creation—and as millions of people lose jobs to automation, robotics, and other 21st century societal changes. According to Politifact, the Walton family "owns more wealth than the bottom

40% of the American population." Combined, Bill Gates, Jeff Bezos, and Warren Buffet have more wealth than 160 million Americans.

There are 540 billionaires in the U.S. with a combined wealth of $2.4 trillion, according to *Forbes* (2016). Meanwhile, the average income of Americans has remained much the same since 1975 (in constant dollars) while prices for most things have risen dramatically. The takeaway from this trend is to avoid being disrupted by change by anticipating the future . . . and learn how to manage and invest your money wisely. Choose your career wisely, your company carefully, and include the value of benefits (such as matching 401k contributions) in your compensation package. In the future you want to be a "have" and not a "have not."

12. **The transformation of the food system.** The transformation of our global food system will impact every person on the planet. Big agriculture and chemical companies continue to consolidate their control over-farming. At the same time, there is a dramatic rise in small farming and sustainable, organic food as health-conscious people avoid food grown using pesticides and genetically modified plants. Small farming will be a viable career path for many who like the idea of getting back to the land and providing a product they can be proud to produce. Startups addressing agriculture efficiency— from drone crop spraying to precise nutrient allocation to moisture monitoring to robotic harvesters—are promising to radically alter farming. Lab-created foods, like the popular Impossible Burger made from vegetables, will continue to erode the meat industry's market share. Additionally, research conducted by the Business and Sustainable Development Commission shows how meeting the challenge of food security "could unlock 14 major business opportunities (e.g. eliminating food waste, more nutritious food products, improved small farm production) worth almost $2.3 trillion annually by 2030."

13. **Increased global conflict.** After a few decades of relative peace in the world compared to the past 100 years, the rise of right-wing ideologies, the proliferation of nuclear weapons controlled by unstable governments, increased religious conflict, and more nationalism will

create a perfect storm environment for armed conflict around the world. Besides careers in the military and contracted security firms, there will be thousands of excellent jobs created in cyberwarfare.

Cyberwar is the next phase of warfare. Stuxnet, the world's first digital cyber weapon, was a "worm virus" used by the Americans and Israelis to disable the centrifuges at Iranian nuclear plants in a stealth cyberattack. The election of 2016 was hacked by the Russians to disrupt our democratic process, an attack just as potentially harmful as Pearl Harbor. A career in cyber warfare has (unfortunately) a bright future.

14. **Cybercrime.** The Pentagon, Equifax, National Security Agency, Sony Pictures, Home Depot, Target and hundreds of other supposedly secure companies have been hacked in recent years. The personal records of millions of their customers and employees are now laid bare for any tech-savvy criminal to steal. The chance that your personal data is out there in the dark web cyberspace somewhere, available to even petty criminals, is extremely high. More than one in seven Americans have already had their identity stolen. Financial institutions have lost hundreds of billions of dollars by hackers. And it's only getting worse. Careers fighting cybercrime—in cyberwarfare and cybersecurity—will be in high demand.

15. **The rise of women and minorities in the workplace and politics.** More women are obtaining college degrees than men now. This and rising demands for gender equality will eventually result in women taking a full seat at the table in most professions. In most areas of law and medicine, there are now just as many women entering these critical professions as men. The infamous "glass ceiling" is being shattered with a steadily rising number of female CEOs and entrepreneurs. The prospects for exciting careers for women have never been brighter.

At no other time has the outlook looked better for minority populations in America. The Census projects the U.S. population will become a minority "majority" by 2045. Despite the continuation of racism, minorities are finding more and better opportunities in careers, politics, and lifestyle. Younger people embrace diversity more than older Americans, so the trend toward inclusion will increase in the future. While there is still a long way to go, minorities will make a big impact on the workplace in the 21st century.

16. **3-D printing.** 3-D printing has already been used to build houses, automobiles, and prosthetic devices, among many other things. This technology has launched slowly but will eventually permeate the manufacturing of most items. Already it's possible to create a product entirely from a computer CAD design. Perhaps the industry that will embrace 3-D printing the most is the medical field, especially if it becomes possible to print bones and tissue items (a 3-D printed heart?). Nearly anything mankind can design or manufacture can also be 3-D printed, creating hundreds of thousands of rewarding jobs.

17. **The end of privacy.** Unless you're a cloistered nun, privacy is a thing of the past. And as big data continues to find and learn more about you whenever you go online, walk the streets observed by millions of surveillance cameras, and provide your personal records to the government, hospitals, and companies, there's little chance you will have any privacy left. The protection of privacy will become a big business in the future as people try to escape from the gaze of both legitimate surveillance and criminal elements.

18. **Communal and small space living.** As the planet becomes more crowded and livable incomes more difficult to achieve, people will band together in communal living arrangements. Communal living appeals to Millennials and retirees; people who are most likely to be both lonely (40% of Americans—43 million—suffer from loneliness) and on a budget. Intentional communities living at places such as Pure House, We Live, and Commonspace allows people to interact with others as well as enjoy their own private room. Milagro in Tucson, Arizona, is a cluster of 28 homes gathered around a central shared green space and community center. In the San Francisco Bay Area (where we live) housing prices are so high that several shared living spaces have sprung up recently so people can find an affordable place to live. It's a trend that is likely to continue. The Fellowship for Intentional Living estimates there are 1,539 shared communities spread across the United States (2018).

Smaller living spaces are already becoming popular as people decide that living in a "tiny home" or mobile home eases the burdens of rent or a mortgage. Look for more creative small living possibilities in the future—and many opportunities to take advantage of this trend.

19. **Socialism and the welfare state**. With robots and automation and outsourcing, there may not be enough jobs for everyone in the future. Already, some thinkers are proposing a universal minimum income to keep society from devolving into chaos. Despite our nation's "go it alone" individualism it's likely socialism will become the norm in the coming decades. Creating and administering social welfare programs can be an exciting and rewarding career path.

20. **Miniaturization.** The reason your cellphone has replaced cameras, books, newspapers, foreign language dictionaries, GPS devices, scanners, road maps, voice recorders, alarm clocks, watches, calculators, photo albums, wallets, flashlights, and many other things is miniaturization. Miniaturization will impact nearly everything, especially in healthcare and technology. And it will create thousands of jobs.

21. **Species extinction.** Global warming, pollution, and habitat destruction will hasten the extinction of many species. But efforts are underway to combat and prevent a complete collapse of all life on earth. The Svalbard Global Seed Vault in Norway is a secure vault protecting thousands of plants from extinction. The 1973 Endangered Species Act has protected 99% of species in the U.S. from extinction (prior to this legislation more than 500 species, subspecies, and varieties of our nation's plants and animals had become extinct). The hundreds of thousands of jobs being created to reverse species extinction will be among the most important ever created by humans.

22. **Drones.** Drones are here to stay and are already being used for everything from aerial photography to delivering medical supplies to remote areas to bringing a hot pizza to your door. Tethered drones, capable of staying aloft for weeks, will increasingly be used for security, media coverage, scientific analysis, farm management, the military, and exploration. Military drones are already embedded around the world among our armed forces. Thousands of jobs have

been created already utilizing drone technology and the future is looking up for this industry.

23. **Body part replacement.** 3-D printing, miniaturization, cloning, recent advances in biotechnology, and other emerging technologies have made it easier to replace human body parts when they are damaged or diseased. The career prospects in this field to do good work that also pays well is exciting.

24. **Virtual reality.** Virtual and augmented reality is expected to be a $162 billion industry as soon as 2020, according to IDC. In everything from gaming to virtual travel to medicine and news, VR and AR will change how we view the world, creating thousands of jobs.

25. **New forms of construction and architecture.** The intersection of technology with new materials and modes of construction promise to make this an outstanding career in the future as the world rebuilds its infrastructure and expands business and living spaces. Construction is moving from "blue-collar" to "new collar" jobs as the technical skills necessary to excel in this field grow. College graduates, who once shunned construction as a viable career path, are now embracing the industry for its robust potential growth and use of advanced technology.

26. **Everyone is in business for themselves.** There are 29 million small businesses in America, according to the SBA. They represent 99.7% of all businesses in the U.S. While risky (only three in ten survive ten years or more), it's still the best way to experience independence (no crazy bosses, unless *you're* crazy), freedom to do what you want and when you want (although you may work longer hours than salaried employees), and the surest road to great wealth (there are no billionaires who work for others).

It's also predicted that by 2020 freelancers may comprise half of all workers, up from 35% in 2016, according to a 2017 report in *Forbes* magazine. Today, there are 53 million freelance workers and millions more who work part-time or do contract work. It's a trend younger Americans have embraced and should only continue to expand in the years ahead. What's exciting is the large and growing number of resources supporting people who are working for themselves (see several at the end of this book).

Over the years, we've owned several businesses (and have also worked for companies), worked freelance and on contract jobs. The most money (and fun) we have had is when we directed our own destiny. As people realize how important it is to do mindful work, the number who will venture out on their own will continue to increase.

If you choose to work for a company, as most people still do, it is wise to think of yourself as a business of one, as LinkedIn founder Reid Hoffman suggests. Thinking of yourself as a business incorporates a wider range of skills you will need to develop and manage, skills that will help you succeed in the 21st-century workplace, like creating and marketing your personal "brand." Reid posits that we can no longer think of ourselves as hired "labor" but as entrepreneurs, with all the creativity and resourcefulness the self-employed use to succeed. As he writes in *The Startup of You: Adapt to the Future, Invest in Yourself, and Transform Your Future* we must all be "founders of our own lives."

27. **Lifelong education.** We like Albert Einstein's quotes about living a mindful life, including what he said about lifelong learning, "Learning is not a product of schooling but the lifelong attempt to acquire it." What is shocking is 40% of high school graduates and 13% of college grads report not having read a book in the previous year, according to a 2015 Pew Research study. According to research, people who read more books also generally make more money. Bill Gates reads a book a week. Warren Buffet often reads several books every week. They understand lifelong education is important to success.

It's important for your career to be constantly learning and evolving.

The opportunities for learning are greater than ever, with several online resources like Coursera, Khan University, Udemy, Udacity, CodeAcademy, edX, Skillshare, Stanford Online, MIT OpenCourseware, and many others offering a wide range of courses, often from major colleges and universities (some for credit).

If you want to impress a current or future employer, taking a course from Yale or UCLA that expands your knowledge in your career will do the trick. It demonstrates you are ambitious and invested in becoming more valuable to your employer.

> *"A formal education will make you a living,*
> *self-education will make you a fortune."*
>
> Jim Rohn

28. **A revolution in healthcare.** If you can stay healthy enough long enough there's a good chance the revolution in healthcare will find a cure for whatever ails you. Technology, the internet, human genome sequencing, biomedicine, robotics, and the other myriad developments converging in the 21st century will create exponential advancements in healthcare—and hundreds of thousands of excellent jobs.

    Healthcare also intersects with many other macrotrends, including software development, DNA testing, 3-D printing, life extension, travel . . . and more. So, it's possible to combine a passion in any of these areas with the expanding field of healthcare.

29. **Extended human lifespan and an aging population.** Humans born today will, barring wars and global warming's effects on the planet, live to 100 or longer. Anti-aging as a field of endeavor is a fascinating one but won't create a large number of jobs directly. Most new jobs will be created helping people live healthier and more physically fit lives or caring for those who aren't healthy.

    With more (and better) years of life, it's important to think further ahead. Despite age discrimination, there are opportunities for a remunerative and mindful career as you grow older. Most will be self-created. It's important to think ahead about how you will work in your later years. A good place to begin is by reading Chip Conley's book, *Wisdom@Work: The Making of a Modern Elder.* There will also be a substantial number of career opportunities in healthcare and gerontology, as an increasing percentage of the population will be over 65 in the future.

30. **Increased leisure activities.** Americans are finally embracing leisure time. Despite America's worldwide reputation for being lazy, we are just the opposite. Americans work longer hours than the famously industrious Japanese. And we get fewer vacation days than any other modern nation (and then don't use six of the days we earn on

average). 54% of Americans have unused vacation time at the end of the work year. One in four working Americans gets no paid time off at all, even for holidays. Unlike the French or Germans, who enjoy five or six weeks of leisure time every year, Americans get just 23 days of paid vacation and holiday time off.

This uniquely American lack of time to recreate and recover is beginning to change, if ever so slightly. People of all ages report wanting more time to travel and relax—and they are finally doing something about it. Travel and leisure activities are increasing among Americans. This provides a wealth of opportunities for employment in hospitality and travel fields. From fishing guides to hotel managers and massage therapists (and hundreds of more jobs) the potential to find exciting and rewarding work in leisure activities will only increase in years to come.

21ST CENTURY MACROTRENDS CAN HELP CREATE A MINDFUL LIFE OF PURPOSE

Many more people now want a career with meaning and purpose . . . a more mindful life. As you can see from this list of macrotrends, there are ample opportunities to achieve this goal, as well as earn a good income.

Keep in mind though that finding a life of meaning and purpose is primarily derived from yourself. A purpose-driven career is just icing on the cake. As author Penelope Trunk says, "A career is like a mate. The relationship is limited by what you bring to the table." Strive to achieve a mindful and conscious life first, then find a career path in alignment with your mindful life. If you do this and adjust to the disruption of the 21st century, you'll have the greatest opportunity to live a fulfilling and rewarding life in human history.

TECHNOLOGY IS KING

What this list of macrotrends demonstrates is the danger of choosing a career path that can be made obsolete by technological and social changes. But what it also shows is the need to become technically proficient to take advantage of these changes. Already, here in the San Francisco Bay Area, where Wentworth Executive Recruiting is located, we see the high demand for tech-savvy job candidates every day. Technology jobs, and positions requiring tech knowledge are paying superior salaries and benefits. And they are often difficult for us to fill because they are in such high demand.

Creative jobs, such as art direction or content creator now often require knowledge of several supporting software programs. Many "blue-collar" manufacturing jobs now include technology expertise as a requirement. Tech knowledge is pervasive in most industries. Even forest service personnel must understand how to use GPS-enabled equipment or internet-connected surveying software.

If you have tech skills, don't assume (as many young people do who grew up with technology and take it as second nature) that a potential employer knows you have them. Be sure to include specific information on your resumé about your technical knowledge. If you don't have technical skills, we strongly advise learning at least the basics or you will seriously limit your career options in the future.

"The secret of change is to focus all of your energy, not on fighting the old, but on building the new."

—Socrates, ancient Greek philosopher

NOTE:

Roughly half the jobs in the top income quartile (those earning $57,000+ annually) require at least some computer coding skills, according to a recent study by Burning Glass and Oracle of 26 million job postings.

Mindful Career Rules: The changes in the 21st century will provide many opportunities for the mindfully aware and technologically savvy.

Chapter 11

Plan Your Life, Then Your Career

"If you want something you've never had,
you must be willing to do something you've never done."

—President Thomas Jefferson

"Nothing is really work, unless you would rather be doing
something else."

—J.M. Barrie, Scottish author of *Peter Pan*

You've heard it dozens of times: do what you love and the money will come. It's mostly good advice—as long as doing what you love is also something others love to pay you for doing. Most people who have successful careers are obsessed with their work, whether it is writing novels or painting or building a chain of coffee shops. They love going to work—for these folks it's TGIM! (Thank God It's Monday), unlike the hordes of Americans you see every night on the freeways literally fleeing from their jobs.

Successful people have a passion for their work often beginning at an early age. The pop singers Justin Bieber and Britney Spears knew from the time they were children they wanted to become singers. Many actors started out in television commercials as kids. Most successful authors have been writing stories from the time they first learned to spell.

Others try out several different things before they settle on a career path. Dr. Ruth Westheimer, the famed TV sex therapist, once trained as a sniper in the Israeli military. Harrison Ford worked as a carpenter before becoming an actor. Former Secretary of State Madeline Albright worked at Jocelyn's department store selling bras. Ralph Lauren was a glove salesman. And Brad Pitt once dressed up as a chicken for El Pollo Loco restaurants. Some people need to "try on" a few career paths before discovering their passion, or take a job to simply earn some money.

YOUR FOUNDATION FOR CAREER SUCCESS: MIND, BODY, AND SOUL

A mindful, conscious career is about successfully combining mind, body, and soul into the framework of your life. When these are in alignment, your career path will become easier and your work more fulfilling.

Health and Fitness. Your health and fitness are critically important to achieving success in every other area of life. Besides the fact that people who are fit and vibrant are offered more jobs, if you want to perform at your best you'll need to be as healthy as possible.

The components of good health include fresh wholesome food, plenty of pure water, clean air, regular exercise, restful sleep, loving relationships, daily meditation, lack of stress, and a positive mindset.

> *"To keep the body in good health is a duty . . . otherwise, we shall not be able to keep our mind strong and clear."*
> —Buddha

Relationships. Your friends, relatives, and loved ones will provide the substance in your life. Life will feel empty without it. And your success depends upon their input and support. Nearly everything that happens to you in life—both good and bad—will be the result of another person's actions or reactions to what you do. Surround yourself with people who see your value and appreciate it. Invest time and effort into building and maintaining your personal and professional relationships.

Also, be sure to marry someone who supports your career aspirations. Facebook CEO Sheryl Sandberg considers this to be the #1 ingredient in a successful career. This is especially true for women. You don't want a husband who expects his career to always take precedence over yours. If you can't get this agreed upon upfront, consider staying single until you find someone who will. Remember, when you marry someone you marry their lifestyle as much as the person. And their lifestyle will eventually meld into your way of life, altering who you are as an individual.

> *"Give the ones you love wings to fly, roots to come back, and reasons to stay."*
>
> —Dalai Lama

Education. More than ever it's important to be knowledgeable. The value you provide to others largely determines the level of success you will achieve. And with a rapidly evolving world, it is imperative to always be learning. Remember the old adage—knowledge is power. Also, keep in mind that the average income rises with every additional year of education.

Today there are literally hundreds of online opportunities to gain more knowledge. For example, LinkedIn provides dozens of courses and videos to expand your career expertise. MOOC (massive open online course) is a link to colleges and other resources that provide online courses to facilitate lifelong learning.

> *"Education breeds confidence."*
>
> —Confucius

Place. Often overlooked as an important contributor to your success in life, your place—the country, state, city, neighborhood, and shared values of the people in the place you reside—will impact your career, your love life, and your health. To have the best chance of succeeding at your goals, it is important you live among the people and resources that can support your goals and where you feel is most in alignment with your soul.

> *"Surround yourself with people who can hear the sound of your soul."*
>
> —Jeff Hood

Wealth management. Money really can buy happiness. Without it, you can't make things happen and you can't afford many of the choices that bring you happiness. Your health will suffer because you won't be able to afford good healthcare, nutritious food, and a safe environment. Your ability to create the kind of life you envision will be seriously hampered. It's critical you learn to create wealth, grow it, use it wisely, and manage it well.

> *"If you would be wealthy, think of saving as well as getting."*
> —Benjamin Franklin, American inventor, statesman, and Founding Father

Spirituality. Despite mainstream religions having many fervent followers, religion in America is on the decline, especially among younger people. In recent years, religions have disappointed many people with well-publicized instances of corruption and abuse. Many others seem to be in it for the money, with pastors living in grand style at the expense of their church members. Terrorism and wars also often have a religious component. Disillusionment in religion is understandable.

At the same time, spirituality is on the rise. A core component of mindfulness is spirituality, often based on Buddhist beliefs. And a common path to spirituality is through mindful meditation and greater consciousness.

In your career, meditation can have several scientifically proven benefits:

1. **It enhances health,** reducing stress and improving sleep. Meditation bolsters mindful practices. It helps restore the body and mind after arduous physical and mental effort.

2. **It supports happiness** and well-being, improving mood and more focused, calm decision-making.

3. **It helps connect with and manage inner emotions,** tapping into innate intuition, and bringing the mind back to the present moment.

4. **It enhances creativity** by supporting a state of "flow" that calms the mind, improves focus, and creates new neural structures through a process called neuroplasticity.

Many people say that meditation has radically transformed and improved their life. It's worth giving it a try to see if it can help you too.

> *"Just as a candle cannot burn without fire,*
> *mankind cannot live without a spiritual life."*
>
> —Buddha

CREATE YOUR CAREER PERSONAL BOARD OF DIRECTORS

Ongoing education is greatly enhanced by the advice you receive from a band of mentors, people who believe in you and want to see you succeed. Few people are "self-made" successes. Arnold Schwartzenegger said, "It is not true that I am self-made. Like everyone, to get to where I am, I stood on the shoulders of giants." No one becomes a success without the support of other people. You can speed up the process up by actively seeking out mentors.

Sally Krawcheck relates in Chip Conley's book, *Wisdom @ Work: The Making of a Modern Elder,* "all the important decisions about your career are made when you're not in the room. People decide to hire you, fire you, promote you, fund you, send you on the overseas assignment, all when you're not there." To even the playing field she recommends creating a Personal Board of Directors to support your career evolution. Having a support team in place who you can call on to answer questions and provide guidance is an important, but seldom used, method of helping you make better decisions. Find mentors and experts who you can turn to when you have a question about your career—or life. Don't be shy; people are universally generous and happy to share their expertise and advice. To learn how to ask, read Jack Canfield's and Mark Victor Hansen's book *The Aladdin Factor.* It provides a wealth of information on the right way to ask for what you want.

For more information on how to create a solid foundation for a successful life, pick up a copy of *A Plan for Life: The 21st Century Guide to Success in Wealth, Health, Career, Education, Love, Place . . . and You!* (available at Amazon.com). You can also go to Best Life (bestlifeonline.com) for great advice on living your life well. Tim Ferriss is also a prolific source for cutting-edge information on living successfully.

Mindful Career Rules: Your career is only one component of a successful life. It's a successful balance of mind, body, and soul. Do the necessary work to create success in every area of your life: Wealth, Health, Career, Education, Love, Place . . . and You.

Chapter 12

Choose Your Lifestyle First

A dependable way to achieve career happiness and satisfaction is to decide first what kind of lifestyle you want to lead, then choose what it will take to support it, including where you decide to live. The key is to choose a place that supports your career aspirations as well as your mind, body, and soul.

1. **Choose where you want to live first.** Your decision to live in a place that is in sync with your soul—and supports your desired lifestyle—is crucial. Our friend Larry Mindel, founder of the Il Fornaio restaurant chain (and many other restaurants), advised our son to do this as he began his career. There's always the possibility that you will get "stuck" in a place you hate if you don't make this choice first. A job, marriage, friends, and a home will make it difficult in the future to move to where you want to live.

2. **Make sure where you live supports your career goals.** Obviously, if you are an actor you will want to live in New York or Los Angeles. While there are acting jobs elsewhere, these two markets have a supportive environment, connections, and quantity of work you'll need to succeed. Building a career as an actor in Fargo will be challenging.

    Fortunately, the expansion of the U.S. population, more local support services, and Internet access have made smaller markets a viable alternative for many professions. Working remotely, you can now be a successful stockbroker and live in places like Fargo. (We're not picking on them; it just seems *so* remote).

Give serious thought and do the research into where you want to live.

Consider:

1. What city or place will support your career goals?

2. Determine the places that you feel are in alignment with your personality.

3. What are the future career prospects in the places you are considering?

4. How important is it to be near your family and friends?

5. Visit for several days any place you might want to live for the rest of your life.

6. Do you like the weather?

7. Are you in sync with the intellectual level of the area?

8. Are there enough recreational and cultural activities?

9. Are you okay with the taxes and cost of living?

10. Do you know anyone?

Once you do this basic research, jot down the pros and cons of each place.

Be mindful of the reasons you are moving someplace new—and the eventual possible repercussions.

You will be surprised how much the place you live shapes the kind of person you become.

Where you live will impact not just your career but your overall happiness too, from the person you will likely marry to the type of friends you'll make. So, choose carefully.

BEST PLACES FOR YOUR CAREER

> *"When we think about crafting our lives, we tend to concentrate on two questions: 'What will I do for work?' and 'Whom will I marry?' But happiness is, in fact, a three-legged stool, with the where question forming the third leg."*
>
> —Bret and Kate McKay, authors, *The Art of Manliness: Classic Skills and Manners for the Modern Man*

THE IMPORTANCE OF PLACE

As we've pointed out in other parts of this book, your environment will have a major impact on your life. One place can provide many more opportunities than another. The friends you meet will be a result of where you choose to be. Your spouse will likely be someone you meet where you choose to live and work. Some states and cities provide more job opportunities than others.

Here are eight factors to consider when choosing where to live:

1. **Professional opportunities.** Richard Florida, the author of *Who's Your City,* says the importance of where you live has only increased in recent years, despite the ability to work remotely. That's because of what he calls "clustering." This is the aggregation of people, support services, and culture that professions create in specific locations. Silicon Valley is an example of this—entrepreneurs and technical types flock there because of the number of firms supporting the "tech" businesses, the angel investors and VCs who fund new ventures, and the networking among peers and mentors.

2. **Aesthetics.** Richard Florida's research has found that "The higher people rate the beauty of their community, its physical environment, and recreational offerings, the higher their overall level of community satisfaction." Our surroundings affect our mood, health, and sense of well-being.

3. **Recreational opportunities.** People generally like places more where there are many opportunities to enjoy their favorite pastimes.

4. **Climate.** Choose a place with the kind of climate you prefer. This can vary substantially from person to person. Minneapolis ranks among the "worst" climates in America yet has one of the highest happiness rankings. Some people flourish in warm, sunny climes and can become clinically depressed in cloudy, cold environments. Others enjoy the change of seasons. Just know that the weather will affect you nearly every day, so choose your place carefully.

5. **Geography.** There are "beach" people, "mountain" people—even "swamp" people. Research shows that personality types tend to cluster in certain areas. For the most part, the folks you meet in Alabama will be different from those you meet in California (at least politically). While diversity is preferred by many, most people tend to want to be around like-minded people.

6. **Cost of living.** Factor in all the costs—including housing, taxes, food, and transportation—to determine if you can afford to live where you want. In the big cities, where most professional opportunities are centered, the costs tend to be much higher than in smaller markets. This may be a career factor you will need to accept. Just know you will need to allow for it.

7. **Proximity to family and friends.** Friends and family are a major key to happiness and good health, both physical and mental. While you can (and will) make new friends wherever you go, if family is important to your happiness then you need to consider this in your choice of place.

8. **Potential mates.** Here's the thing, the place you choose to live and work at is where you will most likely find a person to marry. And some places have much better odds than others. The male/female ratio may not be in your favor or the pool of attractive potential mates may be too small in some places. Also, as mentioned, certain types of people tend to cluster in like-minded places.

"Economic opportunity is tied to location, more than ever before."

—Economic Innovation Group (2017)

THE BEST PLACES TO FIND A GOOD JOB

Factoring in the growth rate, unemployment percentage, starting salaries, and average wages, here are the top ten states for overall employment prospects, according to *U.S. News & World Report* (May 2019).

1. Utah
2. Colorado
3. Minnesota
4. Hawaii
5. Idaho
6. New Hampshire
7. North Dakota
8. Wisconsin
9. Massachusetts
10. Nebraska

The line between financial success and stagnation can often be drawn on a map," according to Kim Hart, writing in *Axios.* "New jobs are clustered in the economy's best-off places." Most of the distressed areas of America—clustered mostly in the South, Midwest, and rural areas—saw zero net gains in employment and new businesses since 2000. The best career prospects are in or near the major cities.

According to the job site Indeed, the top ten cities that have the best prospects for finding a good job (as of 2018) are:

1. San Jose
2. San Francisco
3. Boston
4. San Diego
5. Los Angeles
6. Minneapolis
7. Sacramento
8. Miami
9. Seattle
10. Washington, DC

And finally, here are the top 10 cities with the highest average salaries, according to *U.S. News & World Report* (2019):

1. San Jose
2. San Francisco
3. Washington, DC
4. Boston
5. Seattle
6. New York
7. Hartford
8. Anchorage
9. Denver
10. San Diego

"Best Places" lists change somewhat all the time and different criteria are used to determine them. So, do an online search for the most recent recommendations. Be sure to factor in your career area of interest and lifestyle preferences before making any decision about where to live.

DON'T OVERLOOK THE OVERLOOKED MARKETS

Unlike in the past, many smaller or "secondary" markets are now supporting excellent career opportunities. Small cities such as Boise, Idaho and Lincoln, Nebraska now have a wide range of opportunities combined with enviable (and affordable) living conditions. The Internet expanded communication methods, and fast shipping to virtually anywhere in the world has made the location of businesses less important than in the past when most needed to depend upon the resources of a large city. Since the choice of where you live impacts so many other areas of your life (and happiness), it's important to include this in the overall equation of career management. Source: *Business Insider, 2017*

The high cost-of-living in tech-centric markets such as the San Francisco/San Jose area, Seattle, Los Angeles, Boston, and New York has enabled smaller cities to develop their own "Silicon" valleys. Austin has boomed (and become more expensive) as an alternative market. Other cities such as Atlanta, Orlando, Miami, Chicago, Denver, Minneapolis, and Phoenix offer jobs in technology as well as other fields that pay well. The living costs in these markets are generally lower as well.

To find out how different the costs are from one city versus another, check out one of the cost-of-living calculators at cnn.money.com, sperlingsbestplaces.com, or bankrate.com.

Mindful Career Rules: Your Place—where you choose to live—will have a major impact on your career and life. Choose it wisely.

Chapter 13

Love What You Do

> *"Life is too short to afford living it miserably."*
> —Benjamin Disraeli, former British Prime Minister

Everyone doesn't dream of writing a novel, starting a business, joining the SEALS, or becoming an architect. They may not have a passion they want to make into a career. In fact, most people don't have a clear idea of what they want to do in life.

But it doesn't mean they can't find career satisfaction. Our mail carrier loves what she does and is proud of her 26 years with the Post Office. It's low stress. She gets a lot of exercise. The salary and retirement benefits are excellent. And she knows hundreds of people who love her. Not too shabby for a career.

Careers don't have to be out of the ordinary. They don't have to be exceptional at all. But you must find fulfillment and pleasure in the job you are doing.

BE PASSIONATE ABOUT DOING GREAT WORK

The hard truth about work is that most people will not work at something they have a passion for in life. They will work at a "job." But that's okay. If you haven't discovered your passion in life, then be passionate about doing great work—no matter what you're doing. If you are only half engaged in what you do, waiting for your passion to magically appear someday, you'll never find career satisfaction.

YOU DON'T HAVE TO BE GOOD AT SOMETHING TO BE GOOD AT SOMETHING

"Success is liking yourself, liking what you do,
and liking how you do it."

—Maya Angelou, American poet,
and author of *I Know Why the Caged Bird Sings*

Our friend Daniel runs a youth center for disadvantaged kids. He is passionate about what he does but it doesn't require a "talent" to do it. The work he does every day requires a range of skills from fund-raising to coaching. These are tasks well within the ability range of most intelligent people. The point is you don't have to be naturally good at something to be good at something.

Babson College President Leonard A. Schlesinger, Innovation Associates president Charles F. Kiefer, and *New York Times* contributor Paul B. Brown, authors of *Just Start: Take Action, Embrace Uncertainty, Create the Future* (JustStartTheBook.com), say if job fulfillment is not possible, for whatever reason, and it looks as if things won't change soon, accept the fact and find fulfillment elsewhere.

They point to the many famous people who held ordinary jobs while pursuing their dreams during their free time. Writer Wallace Stevens, the winner of a Pulitzer Prize and two National Book Awards, worked as an insurance lawyer his entire life. Albert Einstein worked in a patent office. Actor Harrison Ford was a carpenter. All eventually found a path to success and fulfillment.

Their advice:

1. Continue to do excellent work at your primary job.

2. Don't moonlight on company time.

3. Don't talk about your outside activities.

4. Schedule time in the evenings or on weekends to develop the skills you will need to succeed in what you are passionate about doing.

5. Develop your network and get out to meet people.

6. Develop a basic business plan to eventually make your side gig a full-time business.

For other people, outside hobbies, their family, church activities, raising great kids, or pursuing personal interests are what provide fulfillment in life apart from their career.

Mindful Career Rules: Not everyone has a driving passion for something they love to do. But you can still find career satisfaction and success by being passionate about doing your work capably.

Chapter 14

How People Look for a Job

It's useful to look quickly at how people search for a job. Job boards are most job seekers' default choice, perhaps because these are the oldest and most familiar method of finding available jobs. But research shows that other methods are gaining ground.

95%	Job sites
72%	Employer sites
66%	LinkedIn
63%	Word-of-mouth
52%	Recruiters
7%	Social media sites

While social media sites appear to be the least favorite way to find a job, their popularity is dramatically different among age groups, with Millennials and Gen Z naturally utilizing Facebook, Twitter, Instagram, and YouTube more frequently.

JOB BOARDS

The largest job boards—Monster, Indeed, Careerbuilder.com, and Simply Hired—are the "big ponds" of job opportunities.

The reason it's important to participate in the big job boards is that recruiters use companies like Zip Recruiter and Talent Hunt to scour the boards to find possible candidates.

Here's a handy list of the top job fifteen boards.

1. LinkedIn
2. Simply Hired
3. Indeed Job Search
4. Glassdoor Jobs
5. LinkUp
6. Craigslist Jobs
7. Google Jobs
8. US.Jobs
9. Monster
10. ZipRecruiter
11. Facebook Job Search
12. Job.com
13. USAjobs.gov
14. CareerBuilder
15. Snag

NICHE JOB BOARDS

Niche job boards are the smaller, industry-targeted or job-specific sites. They often include openings that seldom, if ever, show up elsewhere. Sometimes they even post the hiring manager, bypassing the HR Department entirely. Imagine getting your resumé into the hands of someone you might actually work for someday. Examples of niche job boards are Dice for tech and engineers, AngelList for tech and startups, Engineering.com for engineers, MediaBistro for public relations and advertising, SalesGravy or TalentZoo for sales professionals, and Idealist for jobs at non-profit organizations.

Nearly every industry has a niche job board. Some began as community sites or blogs that list job openings—mainly because the site administrator could make a few hundred bucks off the job posts and advertising. That doesn't diminish their importance. Au contraire. As Ford Myers, a noted career coach and author of *Get the Job You Want Even When No One's Hiring* points out, simply applying for a job through a niche site shows that you are part of the industry, an insider.

You can use niche job boards as part of your overall job sleuthing plan to find out who the key players are at a target company—then do an end-run around the HR Department to the real hiring authority.

Don't adopt the "spray and pray" technique for your job search, sending out hundreds of resumés to jobs you can't do because you're desperate to get a job, any job. This very seldom works. Even worse, encouraging this wasteful approach to job search are many amateur recruiters who also use the "spray and pray" approach to searching for job candidates, so it's understandable why job seekers might think this is a valid approach to finding a job.

A popular job search story you see regularly is about the person who sends out 982 resumés over six months but finally lands their dream job. This is not a mindful way to find a job. The people who do succeed in this way are like lottery winners—with about the same odds of success. What works is an intelligent, *targeted* job search plan.

Nearly everyone has received an invitation to apply for a job that makes no sense at all with their experience, skills, and education. That's because the invitation came from a job mill, often staffed in a foreign country. They operate on the same principle as robocalls, making thousands of calls and hoping to get .001% response from some clueless person. Don't respond to these solicitations. They rarely translate to a legitimate job interview and some are scams.

You may feel productive sending out dozens of resumés every day, but you're really just wasting time. Do the work you need to do to learn how to search for a job intelligently.

The best way to land your dream job is to prepare yourself for it with the right education and experience, learn how to search for a job properly, create a job search plan, and have a flexible, long-term career management strategy.

Mindful Career Rules: Be focused and targeted in your job search. Use job boards mindfully. Never adopt the "spray and pray" method of sending out hundreds of resumés.

Chapter 15

Take Your Time Choosing a Career

"Take time for all things, great haste makes great waste."
—Benjamin Franklin, American inventor,
statesman, and Founding Father

The current process for selecting a career path usually begins in high school, when a career counselor and well-meaning parents begin to steer their 16 or 17-year old adolescent into "thinking about what you want to do in life." The timing of this coerced decision-making could hardly be worse. Science has already proven the prefrontal cortex (responsible for making decisions) is not yet fully functional in teenagers. It's why they frequently make some pretty stupid choices in their lives.

Remember, these teens were just children a few short years ago. Teens are just discovering the opposite sex, learning algebra, getting their driving permit—and adults expect them to begin choosing their career path for life. It's amazing there aren't more unhappy lawyers, business executives, and electricians in the world, given the near-total lack of preparation we give these kids. Our advice to parents and high school students (except those lucky enough to know what they want to do already) is to take their time. Kids born after 2000 are likely to live to be at least 90 years old, healthier than any previous generation. If you begin your career at 20 or 25 or even 30 makes little difference—if it's the right career.

> **Studies of college seniors have found more than two
> in three have serious doubts about the major they selected.**

We would even go so far as to recommend a two or three-year break between high school and college or beginning a training program. Consider doing something different and mind-expanding . . . join the Peace Corps or the Coast Guard or travel. Discover new worlds beyond your home and neighborhood. These years will provide more time to mature, you'll save up some money, and discover new things that may become a passion.

 Asking an 18-year old person to choose a career during a time of unprecedented change, and at a time in their life when they often have little self-knowledge or understanding of what they like or don't like, doesn't make sense.

MONEY

There's also the issue of money. College education costs have risen faster than most other costs. Even a modest outlay will be in the tens of thousands of dollars. An Ivy League education can easily cost a quarter-million dollars. It is particularly dumb to go into debt (the average college debt now is $37,000) when job prospects are mixed, career preferences may change, and the pressure of paying back the debt begins immediately. It's a recipe for disaster.

 The high school—college—go into debt—meet a girl—get married—buy a dog—have children—buy a house—go into more debt—work like a maniac to make enough money to support the life you've drifted into—send the kids to college—load up more debt—and retire path doesn't meet 21st century standards. It's your life and you must choose to live it as best you can. Don't mindlessly follow the well-worn path of the masses.

Choose yourself.

Choose your own life.

Choose mindfully.

FINDING WHAT TO DO IN A CHANGED WORLD

The truth is most people, even those who pursue a passion, will work for someone other than themselves. Which means they must find a job.

Job-hunting is now a constant subtext in 21st-century career management. Nearly everyone will be "between jobs" at some time during their career. You must be prepared to go job-hunting for the rest of your life—to constantly be "in the game." Staying current with the tools, resources, and the personal support network required to maintain a healthy career is job number one. It's up to you to create and direct your career.

Massive layoffs and downsizing over the past quarter-century have broken forever the loyalty bond between employees and employers. Deep structural changes in the U.S. and the global economy have resulted in the permanent elimination of many jobs. The internet and digital technologies, as well as competition from foreign economies, has changed American business forever.

For example, 90% of music is downloaded digitally, which means CD sales are down drastically (and will soon disappear entirely). This means record stores are closing at record rates (some Gen Z young people don't even know what a "record store" is). Which means fewer record store employees are hired. That's how it works. The modern workplace is fluid and shapeshifting.

Technology, while creating many new jobs, will also eliminate millions of jobs. As more things become automated by technology, fewer people will be required. Keep this in mind when choosing a career path. Can your job be done by a machine someday?

Many of our manufacturing industries are dying, beaten into submission by high-quality goods produced by lower-paid workers overseas. America is becoming primarily a service economy. And service economies are highly vulnerable to the whims of the marketplace—and geopolitical activity.

Our automobile industry employs more than a half-million fewer people than just twenty years ago. American cars and trucks, once made entirely in the U.S., are now also made in Mexico and Canada. Parts for American cars come from dozens of countries. It's difficult to buy anything 100% Made in the USA any longer. In a global economy, the career environment is always evolving and changing.

> When ABC-TV News emptied out a typical American home
> of all the foreign-made products as part of their series
> *Made in America,* the entire home was left bare—
> except for the kitchen sink.

While some products can still be found that are made in America, most Americans aren't buying them.

The impact of this historic change in the economy upon jobs means we are fast becoming a nation of haves and have-nots. Future jobs will be concentrated at the low end and high end. Obviously, your goal is to be in the high end. That will require specialized skills and advanced education in careers suited for the 21st century—or a career based on a unique skill. More than ever before, career success will also rely on developing social and "soft" skills.

It also requires keeping an eye on the future. You don't want to enter a field that can easily be disrupted or may disappear altogether—unless you are doing whatever replaces it. The startups now replacing obsolete business models are hiring thousands of new team members.

GOOD NEWS FOR RECENT GRADS

The good news for anyone about to enter the job market is that it is the best it's been in years, except for those who are in obsolete professions, minimum wage work, and without education. The current unemployment rate is less than 4%, the lowest it has been in many years. And the labor shortage that exists is likely to continue for several years or more because of demographic reasons.

The top cities for the number of jobs available for new grads in 2019 are:

1. New York
2. San Francisco
3. Chicago
4. Washington, DC
5. Boston
6. Los Angeles
7. Dallas/Ft. Worth
8. Atlanta
9. Seattle
10. Austin

These ten cities account for nearly a million available entry-level jobs. Nationwide, there are more than seven million open jobs.

Employers in nearly all industries are looking for qualified, skilled people—from application software developers to registered nurses to truck drivers. There hasn't been a better time in recent memory to launch a career doing what you love to do—whether it's as a renewable energy product manager or physical therapist or social media marketing manager.

Glassdoor (glassdoor.com) recently listed several jobs with excellent starting salaries and plenty of openings:

1. Project Manager
2. Physician Assistant
3. Software Engineer
4. Marketing Manager
5. Nurse Practitioner
6. Business Analyst
7. Operations Manager
8. Occupational Therapist
9. Electrical Engineer
10. Product Manager

The lowest paying of these positions has a median base salary of more than $75,000 and the highest at more than $117,000.

You have more flexibility now than in the past to move into a career that isn't defined by your college major (one of the benefits of a strong workplace market). Here are the ten college majors that eventually led to the most different kinds of jobs:

1. Business Administration and Management
2. Marketing
3. Psychology
4. Economics
5. Finance
6. Political Science
7. Communications
8. Computer Science
9. Information Technology
10. Sociology

What this says is that now you have more room to move into something you may find you like to do more as you discover what is available. These college majors cast a wide net in moving to a job that is only sometimes directly related to what you learned in school.

Unless you are already on a path to a career doing what you love, you'll likely try on a few different roles in the years just after graduating college before deciding what resonates with your soul. Just be mindful of your choices and make them for the right reasons.

Mindful Career Rules: If you don't have a career "calling" or "passion," take your time deciding on a career path. Don't choose to work in "obsolete" jobs. Learn the new success skills important in the 21st century. There has never been a better time in recent memory to be mindful about choosing your best career path.

Chapter 16

Timely Advice for the Recent Graduate

"You may delay, but time will not."

—Benjamin Franklin

Olympic high divers say the approach is the most important part of completing a successful dive. So too the first years after college have a long-term impact on your career. A graduates' first job has an inordinate influence on their career path and lifetime earnings, according to Austan Goolskee, former Chairman of the Council of Economic Advisors. Don Peck, author of *Pinched: How the Great Recession Has Narrowed Our Futures and What We Can Do About It* writes that fully "2/3 of real-lifetime wage growth typically occurs in the first ten years of a career."

In this competitive job market getting your career off to a good start is especially important. Yet most college grads have little or no idea what they want to do—or how to go about finding what to do. It's almost as if it's a surprise to them. If you graduate and don't know what to do with your fresh college degree, then you are already behind the loop. This is one of the critical junctures in your life. You can drift and let yourself be carried along to wherever life happens to lead you, or you can take the first step along the road to career fulfillment.

Conversely, it's important for many college grads who don't know what they want to do in their career to try out a few things before deciding on a career path. If you haven't done this already through a college internship, now is the time to experiment before you get locked into a profession. You may even want to ask a business owner or executive if you can "shadow" them for a week or two to see what it's actually like working at a job before committing to it.

We also suggest taking some time after graduation to travel. Travel has a way of expanding your consciousness and creativity. It was through traveling to Europe that Eric was inspired to create a travel business that was successful for several years.

EVEN RECENT GRADS NEED EXPERIENCE

In the 21st century even recent college grads need experience. Employers don't want to take the time or spend the money to train employees, especially when they know most people in their 20s will find another job within three years. A 2013 Chronicle of Education Survey of Employers listed these qualifications as most desirable in college grads.

23%   Internship

21%   Employed during college

13%   College major

12%   Volunteer experience

10%   Extra-curricular activities

8%   Relevance of coursework

8%   GPA

5%   College reputation

These findings are the opposite of popular belief. Perhaps instead of spending big bucks on that Ivy League education and burying yourself in the library to make good grades, you should be working summers or volunteering for Habitat for Humanity.

ACTIONS SPEAK LOUDER THAN WORDS

The resumé of the typical new college grad is rather thin. After all, you are mostly potential at this point. But employers want more than just promising words on paper, they want to see accomplishments.

Grade inflation has dampened the value of a 4.0-grade point. And real-world executives know that your ability to take tests well doesn't necessarily translate to doing a job well. They're looking for those "soft" skills that indicate you can take initiative and get the job done. That's why Internship, Employment, Volunteer Experience, and Extra-Curricular Activities weigh in heavily on the new grad's resumé. It shows you have done something.

Most of all, they want to see leadership ability. If you are the class president, captain of the football team, or head of the community service club you have a leg up on your less-involved classmates. The surest route to a scholarship at a top-tier school is not always straight A's, but what you do outside of the classroom. This is the new reality for students in the 21st century. Likewise, employers want to see these activities to determine if you have the "right stuff" for them to take a chance on hiring you.

The bottom-line is colleges want graduates who will go out into the world and reflect well upon their school. And employers want graduates who will add value to their business.

ONLINE SUPPORT FOR THE RECENT GRAD

There are a number of excellent websites for the recent grad to get peer-reviewed advice on launching your career. One of the best is The Muse (themuse.com). A unique feature of The Muse is the ability to see photos of the working environment at companies reviewed by the site. It's often enlightening to see what the working conditions are like. If you like a company but don't care to work in a large open area with rows of tables with computers, as with most startups, you may want to pass on a particular job for that reason. After all, you spend more than a fourth of your life working. You may as well work in an office you love (assuming you have the luxury of that choice). Many of the companies include listings of available jobs. The Muse also features a large number of job-search and career management instructional videos.

Another site to check out is AfterCollege.com, ranked by Education-Portal.com as one of the Top 10 Job sites for recent grads. It's designed to assist new grads to find entry-level positions in a wide range of industries.

Glassdoor.com is another valuable resource for recent grads. The site lists available opportunities and it also provides insights/critiques from current and previous employees at many firms.

Bright.com enables applicants to build their resumé and then aligns your qualifications with positions that best suit your skills. It then creates a list of jobs that match. You'll also receive a "Bright" score—a number ranking assigned to each open position that rates the relevancy to jobs listed on the site. It even factors in the weight of your contacts, a validation that who you know is often as important as what you know. Bright.com's Friends with Opportunities (sorta like friends with career benefits) can hook you up (professionally speaking) with Facebook connections.

Other sites you may want to take a look at include iHipo.com, for job seekers who want international work experience, and CollegeRecruiter.com, a site with links to thousands of internships and entry-level jobs.

The recent grad is at a huge disadvantage in the job market. Finding a job is something most people only do a few times during their life—so most aren't good at it, no matter how far along they are in their career.

Think of it as buying a car or a house. You likely won't be good at this either because you don't do it often. But your best approach to something you don't do well is to research it like crazy—find out as much as you can about the job-search process and career management. Learn all you can about the "soft" factors—like enthusiasm, confidence, persistence, how to work well with others, and the best way to suck up to your boss without losing your integrity—-because these are just as important in being successful as your hard skills. Your first job can be critically important to your career, so approach it like a final exam you need to ace to graduate.

THE DISCONNECT BETWEEN EMPLOYERS AND EMPLOYEES

A study by the Career Advisory Board in 2014 found that there is a HUGE disconnect between how well job candidates felt they were presenting themselves for job opportunities and how the companies they interviewed with perceived them. Fully 59% of applicants thought they were doing an excellent job, but 14% of employers felt that candidates presented themselves poorly.

The study shows the importance of learning how to apply, interview, and follow-up on job openings. And it demonstrates the need to research the company as fully as possible. Learning to manage your career mindfully and consciously cannot be overstated—it's the most important first job of the recent graduate.

Mindfulness Career Rules: Experience, timing, and finding support are all important in launching and supporting your career objectives.

Chapter 17

No Degree, No Problem

A trend that is increasing in the 21st century is hiring people based on their skills, unique expertise, or relevant experience. Apple (founded by a college dropout), Google, IBM, and other top-tier companies have removed the bachelor's degree requirement from many of their positions. "Half of our employees last year (2018) were people that did not have a four-year degree," said Tim Cook, Apple CEO.

Thousands of young entrepreneurs have demonstrated that a degree isn't always a requirement to be successful. It's the *doing* that is important to success, not necessarily a degree. Far too many college students spend most of their time partying and socializing and graduate without usable career or life skills—or even a general education. They (or their parents) have paid a huge price just for obtaining a credential because it is still an entry ticket to many jobs.

In *The Hechinger Report*, Lawrence Lanahan writes, "In late 2017, a research project led by the Harvard Business School, a workforce organization called Grads for Life, and the consulting firm Accenture concluded in a report, *Dismissed by Degrees*, that employers 'appear to be closing off their access to the two-thirds of the U.S. workforce that does not have a four-year degree.'" More than 60% of business and HR leaders, as well as recruiters, admitted in a recent survey that they rejected resumés without a four-year degree, even if the applicant was qualified. The positive news is that about four in ten did not. It's also important to note that 63% of business and HR leaders in a recent survey admitted they have trouble filling middle-skills jobs—positions that frequently don't require a college degree.

If a college education isn't possible (or sometimes even desirable) there are still many excellent career paths that can be pursued by acquiring skills in high demand, at "middle tech" jobs, in the trades, or by starting your own business.

OCCUPATIONS THAT DO NOT REQUIRE A FOUR-YEAR COLLEGE DEGREE

Here are the percentages of professionals with only a high-school or Associate degree in major occupations:

26%	Mechanical Designer
25%	Electrical Technician
25%	Chef
19%	Manufacturing Technician
18%	Telecommunications Technician
17%	Computer Network Technician
17%	Information Technology Technician
14%	Food and Beverage Specialist
13%	Technical Support Specialist
13%	Public Safety Officer
11%	Customer Service Representative
11%	Network Operations Analyst
10%	Insurance Agent

Many other professions don't require a college degree. Only a third of beginning farmers have a four-year degree. Less than half (44%) of business owners have a degree. You can even become a commercial pilot without a degree (although the training and certifications required typically exceed that of any four-year college).

MILLION DOLLAR IDEAS TRUMP MBA'S

You certainly don't need a degree to find career satisfaction or get rich. What you need are great ideas—and the desire to succeed. Many million-dollar ideas are staring you in the face. Just find a need and fill it well. As motivational speaker Zig Ziglar frequently said, "You can get everything you want in life if you will just help enough other people get what they want."

And often people don't know what they want until someone creates it.

When David and Angie Porter developed the FURminator, they didn't have an MBA in business. He didn't have a college degree. But he saw a need (eliminating pet hair) and created a product to solve the problem. We are certain he didn't say to himself, as a child, "When I grow up, I want to invent a brush that removes dog hair." But when the idea came to him, he acted on it. Today the FURminator is a $45 million a year business. In 2011, the Porters sold their business for $140 million.

Don't let the lack of a college degree become a stumbling block to achieving your dreams. There are plenty of people who did quite well without one. Here are just a few:

Richard Branson	Billionaire owner of more than 100 businesses, including Virgin Atlantic
Coco Chanel	Founder of the House of Chanel, high-fashion clothes and fragrances
Mary Kay Ash	Founder of Mary Kay Cosmetics
Travis Kalanick	Billionaire founder of Uber
Michael Dell	Billionaire founder of Dell Computers
Barry Diller	Billionaire broadcasting executive
Walt Disney	Billionaire founder of Disneyland, movies, cartoons
Henry Ford	Founder of the second-largest auto company in America
Ty Warner	Billionaire creator of Beanie Babies
Frank Lloyd Wright	Iconic American architect

Jack Dorsey	Billionaire Twitter founder
Sheldon Adelson	Billionaire former court reporter who built a multi-billion-dollar casino empire
Ben Affleck	Oscar-winning actor, writer, producer, and director
Carl Bernstein	Famous journalist who uncovered the Nixon Watergate scandal
Sergey Brin	Billionaire co-founder of Google
John Paul DeJoria	Once lived in his car, now billionaire owner of Paul Mitchell, Patron brands
Thomas Edison	America's greatest inventor: phonograph, movies, the light bulb
Larry Ellison	Billionaire founder of Oracle
F. Scott Fitzgerald	Famous American author
Harrison Ford	Former carpenter turned hugely successful actor
Benjamin Franklin	Founding Father of the United States and prolific inventor
John Glenn	Astronaut and U.S. senator
Tom Hanks	Perhaps America's most successful modern actor
Quincy Jones	Musician and music producer
Thomas Kinkade	Multi-millionaire American artist
Stanley Kubrick	Creative American film director
Ralph Lauren	Multi-billionaire former sock salesman and founder of Ralph Lauren company
Rush Limbaugh	Bombastic right-wing radio personality with a net worth of $300 million
Steve Martin	Famous American comedian, musician, and author

Steve McQueen	Iconic masculine American actor
Drew Houston	Billionaire Dropbox co-founder and CEO
Jillian Michaels	Multi-millionaire fitness guru
David Oreck	Inventor of Oreck vacuum cleaners
Joel Osteen	Multi-millionaire preacher
Larry Page	Billionaire co-founder of Google
Sean Parker	Billionaire co-founder of Napster, Airtime, and Plaxo; First Facebook president
Brad Pitt	Famous American actor and "sexiest man alive." Net worth $300 million
Wolfgang Puck	Multi-millionaire chef, restaurateur, and businessman
Vidal Sassoon	Billionaire founder of Sassoon salons, hair care line
Dave Thomas	Founder of Wendy's hamburger chain
Harry Truman	Former President of the United States
John Mackey	Founder of Whole Foods markets
Mark Twain	Arguably America's greatest author and journalist
Jerry Yang	Billionaire founder of Yahoo!
Mark Zuckerberg	Mega-billionaire founder of Facebook
Steve Jobs	Billionaire co-founder of Apple Computer and Pixar Animation Studios

Convinced? This is only a small portion of the people who went on to great fame and/or fortune who did not earn a college degree.

OF THE 400 RICHEST AMERICANS, 63 DID NOT GRADUATE FROM COLLEGE

You probably noticed how many billionaires are among this list. What distinguishes these people from others is not the amount of education they attained, but the ideas they created or talent they developed.

Almost anyone with average intelligence and the means can be a college graduate. It is no formula for success—as many discovered in The Great Recession. The multitudes of college grads who can't find a good job, coupled with an outstanding $1.6 trillion student loan debt, will cause many to wonder whether college was a smart decision. A 2019 Payscale survey of 248,000 respondents found that two-thirds of employees had regrets about their advanced degrees, citing student loan debts as the primary reason. Some regretted their choice of majors, with three-quarters of Humanities, Social Sciences, Physical and Life Sciences, and Art majors regretting their education.

- More than 500,000 college grads were working as cashiers or waiters in 2013, as reported by *Fox Business News*. 46% are in jobs that require only a high school diploma (2018).

- 53.6% of college graduates under the age of 25 are unemployed or underemployed, according to the U.S. Department of Labor (2018).

  Source: *How to Build a Successful Life Without a Four-Year Degree,* Blake Boles

> *"He is well paid that is well satisfied."*
> —William Shakespeare

Our firm places people every month in excellent positions in the construction industry, where salaries often exceed $120,000. Although a college degree often is not required, you will still need to train and acquire skills because construction has become very sophisticated. Computer skills are especially valued. "New collar" jobs, as we call the skilled blue-collar positions, will require a much higher level of technical expertise in order to succeed in the 21st century.

Currently (2019), there are more than seven million unfilled jobs in America. The majority of these open positions do not require a college degree. As Mike Rowe of *Dirty Jobs* fame has said, "The massive $1.6 trillion student debt is a scandal." Americans have been led to believe that obtaining college degree credentials are all that you need to succeed and be happy in your work. This just isn't true.

Rowe relates the story of one woman who worked hard for a college degree and then spent the next 15 years paying off her student loans. Frustrated with how little her career was advancing, she entered an apprenticeship training program in the construction business. This led eventually to her launching her own licensed construction firm—and more money and job satisfaction than she experienced in her previous career.

Obtaining a college degree has reached mythological proportions in America. But it isn't always the route to career happiness.

"NEW" COLLAR JOBS

We've often thought that LinkedIn should create a division of their business called LinkedIn Blue devoted to "blue-collar" jobs. Because what has evolved over the past three decades is a new reality among blue-collar jobs. Today, many require a degree of sophistication and skill that matches or exceeds many positions held by white-collar workers.

Many blue-collar jobs now require significant education and training. As computerization and the internet become entwined with manufacturing processes and the administration of many jobs—from recycling trash to tool and die making—the requirements of these positions demands more from workers. And jobs now done by automation or robotics must be programmed, operated, and repaired. This requires humans who know how to do these things.

Our firm places many blue-collar positions. An experienced and skilled construction supervisor can easily make $150,000 or more. And in many markets, construction is booming as office space continues to increase and infrastructure projects are funded. Also, recent natural disasters caused hundreds of billions of dollars in destruction across America, all of which will need to be repaired or rebuilt during the next decade.

In fields such as hospitality, a restaurant or hotel manager can earn more than $100,000 a year. Landscapers who own their own business often earn in excess of $150,000. Top auto mechanics routinely earn more than $100,000. And technical service reps can easily top $100,000 after just a few years on the job.

Former "blue-collar" jobs that now require technical training—"New collar" jobs—are among those in highest demand now. And many don't require a full college education. "Skilled trades show among the highest potential among job categories," according to economic-modeling company Emsi.

Many other "blue-collar" jobs are held in high regard—and high demand—now. And these careers can provide a great deal of personal satisfaction too. For example, most woodworkers, farmers, and tailors love their jobs and revel in mastering their craft.

Our parents and grandparents believed that only a college education and an office job would be the ticket to success. That thinking still exists, but with a plethora of college grads seeking these kinds of jobs, now is a good time to think about a "blue-collar" career, where skilled workers are often in high demand.

Mindful Career Rules: While more education usually pays off, a college degree isn't the only way (and may not be the best way) to achieve career success. Don't overlook the "New Collar" jobs as a potential career path, combining career satisfaction, high growth potential, excellent compensation, and technical skills as a potential career path.

Chapter 18

Parting Is Such Sweet Sorrow

"If you refuse to change your job (if you don't like it), the only sensible thing you can do is practice loving it every day."

—Dr. Wayne Dyer

WHEN SHOULD YOU QUIT YOUR JOB?

Before quitting your job first ask yourself if YOU are the problem. Is it the company or are you not a good employee? Are you disengaged? Unmotivated? Do you have poor work habits? Are you undependable? Do you lack enthusiasm? Are you pessimistic? Do you only do what's asked of you and nothing more? Are your skills current? Do you have personality flaws that make others not want to work with you or give you additional responsibilities? Are you mindful at work?

If you decide to stay, then change your mindset and do your best to contribute, learn, and grow.

However, there are many reasons why changing jobs makes sense.

13 VALID REASONS TO QUIT YOUR JOB

1. Work stress is harming your health.

2. Your boss is a jerk, abuser or sociopath.

3. The company culture is toxic.

4. You get criticized publicly.

5. You are grossly underpaid.

6. There is no room for advancement.

7. The company is in a failing industry.

8. Your commute is more than an hour each way.

9. You are in a position that doesn't align with your talent and education.

10. You are repeatedly passed over for promotion.

11. You have been offered a much better job.

12. Your input is disregarded—or not even wanted.

13. You have discovered a passion that is in alignment with your personal values.

Perhaps you've decided to try out an entrepreneurial venture. Or you simply realized the career direction you are in is not what you feel is right for you. If you are being conscious and mindful about your life and career there are a myriad of valid reasons to quit your job and do something else.

HOW TO QUIT YOUR JOB

There's a right way and a wrong way. The worst "wrong" way is to air your grievances and storm out of the office without any notice and a loud "I'm outta here."

Take the physician's motto when treating patients, "First, do no harm." Don't burn your bridges with your current employer under any circumstances. There is no upside to doing this and much potential harm to you. Remember, be mindful.

Quit this way:

1. Give two-weeks' notice. It's the norm and it's the mindful thing to do.

2. Don't leave your company in a bind. If you are engaged in the final stages of a critical project, see it through (or offer to do so).

3. Notify your boss in person. Keep the meeting upbeat and short.

4. Submit a formal letter of resignation to the HR Department. This should be just a few lines stating that you are leaving. Do not air grievances or brag about the better job you have been offered.

5. Don't provide reasons for leaving. It's nobody's business but yours.

6. Thank the company for hiring you as an employee and show gratitude. Even at its worst you had a job and got paid.

7. Do not engage in angry emotional outbursts, detailing all the reasons why the company or your boss failed you.

Leaving this way will show professionalism and provide the best possible future references.

WHAT IF YOU LOST YOUR JOB? NOW, WHAT?

"Everything that has a beginning has an ending. Make peace with that and all will be well."

—Jack Kornfield, Buddhist monk, author of *Buddha's Little Instruction Book* and *No Time Like the Present*

Okay, you just got your pink slip. You're in shock, angry, fearful, and feeling disconnected. How do you respond and recover?

First, don't take it personally, as hard as that is to do. Tens of millions of Americans have experienced the same thing in recent years—and most were doing a good job just like you. Take a deep breath and schedule a meeting with your HR Department or the owner of the company. You want to negotiate the best severance deal possible. Realize that in many cases, perhaps yours, you may not be able to do anything other than pack a box full of belongings and exit the building. There may be no recourse. There may be no other option than taking what is offered and get on with the next chapter of your life. Before you leave, you should attempt to get a commitment from that employer to provide a positive recommendation in the future—assuming you didn't get let go for stealing widget secrets and selling them to the Chinese.

BE GRATEFUL

> *"Gratitude is the healthiest of all human emotions. The more you express gratitude for what you have, the more likely you will have even more to express gratitude for."*
>
> —Zig Ziglar, motivational speaker, author of *See You at the Top*

Grateful? You just lost your job. Why be grateful?

First, losing a job isn't the end of the world. You will get another job. Or start a business. You will survive this and you will be a better person for the experience. Really.

Don't look at losing your job as a failure. It is what it is. But if you do think of it as a failure, remember the wise words of Oprah Winfrey—"Failure is just another stepping stone to greatness." The list of people who failed or experienced setbacks in their career but then went on to something much better and more aligned with their talents is extensive.

Here's something that will change your life forever. Every day (no skipping) write down three things you are grateful for in your life. We guarantee doing just this one simple act will reset your mind to a better, more positive point that will shower you with unforeseen benefits.

Here are a few examples:

1. I'm GRATEFUL I have an education.

2. I'm GRATEFUL for my home.

3. I'm GRATEFUL I am in good health.

4. I'm GRATEFUL for my family.

5. I'm GRATEFUL I live in America.

Here's the thing, billions of people in our world cannot make these claims. You are fortunate to be you living where you do in a time like we live in. Be grateful for this. Trust us, this mindfulness will change your mindset—and your life.

MEDITATE

> *"15 minutes of meditation can have the same positive effects on your well-being as one vacation day."*
>
> —The Journal of *Positive Psychology*

As we mentioned earlier, few things are as transformative in life as meditation. Meditation is described as "the act of engaging in mental exercise to reach a heightened level of spiritual awareness and mindfulness." Jack Kornfield, Ph.D., meditation teacher, author, Buddhist elder, and founder of Spirit Rock Center, says, "Unconscious reactions and fear create problems. With a peaceful and kind heart, whatever happens can be met with wisdom." Losing a job can mess with your mind. On the Life Change Index Scale, losing a job ranks as one of the ten most stressful life events (#8). It's not the best time to make important decisions, without some support. Meditation can center your mind and enable you to think more clearly.

Meditation allows you to calm your body, eliminating annoying mind chatter so you can stay focused on the present, free from future worries. Yoga, a form of moving meditation, has similar benefits, with the added dimension of improved muscle tone, balance, and lymphatic circulation to keep your immune system strong.

A Harvard University study recently found that just 27 minutes per day of mindfulness meditation significantly increased the gray matter of the hippocampus, the area of the brain associated with introspection, decision-making, and compassion, and decreased gray matter in the amygdala, the brain's anxiety and stress center.

Both meditation and yoga flood the brain with feel-good neurotransmitters and hormones, such as serotonin, melatonin, DHEA and endorphins, and lowers the stress hormones cortisol and adrenaline, according to the National Institutes of Health. As a result, you'll sleep better, feel less anxiety, have more energy, and your mood will be improved. This is exactly what you need when you've lost your job.

More people are learning of the benefits mediation provides and its popularity is soaring. In 2012, just slightly more than 4% of Americans were meditating. By 2017 more than 14% reported incorporating meditation into their lives.

If you don't already meditate daily there is no better time to start than when you have just lost your job or suffered some other setback. This is not the time to be fearful, anxious, and impulsive. Meditation can help calm your mind so that you can think clearly. Meditation will help you get past this difficult time and emerge even better than before.

There are many resources (some listed at the end of this book) to learn how to meditate. Search online to find them. If you live in the San Francisco Bay Area you may want to make the trek to Spirit Rock Meditation Center in Marin County (spiritrock.org). This is where we go on Monday evenings to meditate with a group of like-minded people.

THE FIRST 60 DAYS AFTER LOSING A JOB ARE CRITICAL

What you do in the first 60 days after losing your job is critical.

While seven out of ten job seekers think they know exactly what to do to get their next job, according to a survey by Right Management, a global outplacement firm, that figure drops to just two in ten once they go through the outplacement process. Here are some suggested steps:

1. Utilize whatever outplacement services are available to you from your employer. These can range from classes, seminars and workshops to resumé evaluation, and networking events. If you are offered an outplacement consultant, spend time personally with her, don't just communicate online. The adjustment from job-holder to job seeker will be easier if you take proactive steps immediately.

2. If you have the means, go on a short vacation or long weekend trip. You need time to settle your thoughts, regroup, consider options, and relax. Remember, you will be working hard to find a new job. And after you land the new job there likely won't be a real vacation for at least a year, so get some R&R while you can. Making important decisions when you are still in shock, angry, and stressed usually results in a poor outcome. This is the time to be clear-headed and focused.

3. Create a job search plan. Just putting down on paper all the action steps you will take to land a new job will give you a boost in confidence and energy. There's a lot you can do to improve your job-hunting opportunities.

    ✓ **Call friends and former colleagues** to let them know you are actively looking for a job. A surprisingly large number of jobs are acquired through friends, relatives, and former co-workers.

    ✓ **Sign up for online job boards.** See if there are niche job sites in your industry.

    ✓ **Schedule at least two lunch dates a week**—one with a friend and another with someone who can help with your job search.

    ✓ **Begin due diligence on companies that could be potential employers.** Don't just take anything that comes along. Direct and control your search.

    ✓ **Brush up on job skills that are important to your career.** Now is the time to finally learn how to use PowerPoint or get that certificate in social media marketing.

    ✓ **Review job recruiters** and contact those you consider reputable. Recruiters can be extraordinarily helpful, so get on their radar screen.

    ✓ **Set aside an hour a day to exercise**—bike, swim, workout at the gym, play tennis, run. You'll feel more confident, look better, sleep better, and feel a sense of accomplishment at a time when you are most vulnerable to negative emotions.

    ✓ **Begin a healthy nutrition program.** You'll have more energy, lose a few pounds, and feel a sense of purpose.

✓ **Consider a change in direction.** Now might be a good time to make a move into another area of your field. If all the marketing jobs are filled, try your hand at sales. Or consider starting your own business. Many entrepreneurs became one because they lost a job. It's tough work and risky but business owners can make considerably more money than employees. Try a part-time job in the business first to see if the change would be right for you. Want to open a coffeehouse? Go work for Starbucks as a barista first.

✓ **Spruce up your social media presence.** If you don't have a LinkedIn, Twitter, Instagram or Facebook account, consider getting one. Learn how to fully utilize these to expand your network and create a dynamic online presence.

✓ **Start a blog.** Comment on the industry you work in. Do this one or two times a week. A blog can set you apart from other job candidates. It shows you're "current" and provides a forum to subtly promote your capabilities. For example, if you are an insurance claims adjuster you can post news, comment about developments in your field, and provide a forum for people to contribute suggestions to improve the claims adjusting practice.

✓ **Freshen up your look.** Have your hair styled professionally. Purchase a couple of killer outfits or suits. Get a professional manicure. Ladies, have an upscale salon do your makeup. When you know you are looking great your confidence level will rise a few notches at the interview.

✓ **Track the progress of your job search plan daily.** Keep all receipts and record all mileage—these are potentially tax-deductible.

✓ **Apply for unemployment benefits immediately.** You've paid into this fund all your life, now you deserve to get some of it back.

✓ **Carefully craft a resumé** that is searchable online by keywords, has an attractive layout, is "lean and mean" with every word and phrase working to show why you are the best choice for the job. Be sure it's error-free.

GET OUT OF THE HOUSE

> *"The wrong thing to do is sit at home in your pajamas and apply for jobs online. It's isolating and depressing."*
>
> —Ford Myers, author of
> *Get the Job You Want, Even When No One's Hiring*

Looking for a job is tough. When your ego is already scabbing up from all the rejection wounds it's easy to just hide behind the internet and your computer. Many newly unemployed people are ashamed to face friends, their identity so wrapped up in their job; they simply want to go into hibernation until that day when they can emerge with a newer and better job to show they're whole again.

If you haven't been nurturing your network of personal and professional contacts, now is the time to do some catch-up. Force yourself to get out of the house and meet up with people, especially those people who you can network with that might lead you to possible job leads. Attend social networking events. Go to industry conferences. Participate in seminars relevant to your career aspirations. Don't be shy about introducing yourself. You never know how a new personal connection can affect your career search. Our biggest career breaks came to us through attending events.

Depression is a constant stalker of the unemployed. Getting out into the world will buoy your spirit, even if it's just for a tennis game or coffee with a friend. So, unplug the TV, stop raiding the fridge, turn off the video games, and get out into the real world. Because that's where your next job awaits.

GO BACK TO SCHOOL

Don't forget your alma mater. Colleges and universities have made tremendous strides in supporting the career goals of their grads—past and present. Many have their own online social networking presence. Most large schools have local chapters in major cities and host events for their grads. If the CEO or HR Director is a fellow grad of your school, you likely will have an advantage over other applicants.

One easy way to find fellow alumni is on LinkedIn. It automatically alerts you of anyone who attended the same schools as you.

Finally, join associations or trade groups in your industry. It will give you contacts at companies you may want to work at and provide built-in networking opportunities.

THE HIDDEN JOB MARKET

"Experts estimate that between 80% – 85% of all job openings are unlisted."

—Fred Coon, CEO, Steward, Cooper & Coon

The percentage of unlisted job openings is debatable, but many job openings fly under the radar of most job seekers because they aren't publicized to the public. These include active job listings as well as positions that are more passive. As we write this, our clients have several openings they would consider filling if the right person came along, but they aren't in such dire need to hire for these positions that they are actively looking.

The changing job market has also changed the way companies source candidates for positions they wish to fill. Many have turned to social media, looking on platforms such as LinkedIn, Reddit, Twitter, Instagram, and Facebook. Others have their own in-house recruiters or have established relationships with top independent recruiters to help them find the talent they need.

Whatever the case, if you can tap into the unadvertised hidden job market you will be one giant step ahead of your competition—which could be hundreds of other highly qualified candidates.

Here are some tactics you can use to find unlisted jobs . . . and be noticed by employers who have positions they wish to fill.

1. Tap into your network of connections to see if they know of any positions that are open or about to be added to their or other companies in your industry. Tell them you are looking for the next challenge in your career. Describe the kind of position you can fill. And mention a few target companies you would like to work at.

2. Check the career pages on the websites of companies you might like to work at. Often, they list jobs on their site that aren't listed elsewhere.

3. Join industry-related groups: associations, Chambers of Commerce, trade groups, meet-ups, etc. and begin building contacts before you need them—dig your well before you're thirsty.

4. Establish yourself as a source of information or an "authority" about a key area.

5. Follow companies on LinkedIn, Twitter, and Facebook.

6. Build and maintain relationships with a few key recruiters. They often know about jobs with their clients before they are listed.

7. Maximize your LinkedIn presence. Top recruiters have access to members who have activated an anonymous alert indicating they are open to new opportunities in the Jobs section of LinkedIn.

8. Target the companies you would like to work at. Research them. Check Glassdoor.com to see how their employees rate the company. Attend conferences where the company has representation. Reach out to anyone who you know that works at the company (or once worked there).

9. Do an online search of the company and its competitors. Often you will find a job at a similar company's career section that meets your needs.

It's important to put together a holistic plan to find your next career opportunity. Take a break for a few days to gather your thoughts and assess your situation. Then go forward aggressively and confidently.

DO SOMETHING–ANYTHING

While you look for work, do what work you can, even if it's part-time or contract work. Or begin building a business from a hobby or interest in your spare time. There are many successful businesses that had their start this way.

The other benefit to working while you look for work is you can legitimately put something on your resumé to explain the gap in your work record. If you are an accountant and do some freelance work helping local businesses or friends, it keeps you in the game. In many cases we suggest giving your part-time work a name, as you would if you were in business. You can explain this away by saying you gave your own business a shot but decided you like working as part of a company team more.

Working during a period of full-time unemployment will keep you busy, focused, and distracted from thinking too much about being out of work. And it will keep the money flow coming in, even if only a trickle. It might even be successful enough for you to start your own full-time business.

YOU LIKELY AREN'T TRYING HARD ENOUGH

"Not Dead, Can't Quit."
—Richard Machowicz, Navy Seal

Active job seekers only spend an average of 3 hours, 16 minutes a day searching for a new job, according to the Bureau of Labor Statistics. The fact is that most people are not trying hard enough. Lack of sustained, focused, hard work to find a job is why so many unemployed people are still unemployed. Perhaps this lack of a good work ethic is even *why* they are unemployed.

Wealth expert Tom Corley, the co-author of *Rich Habits, Poor Habits*, found that one of the differentiating factors between people who create a great deal of wealth and those who create very little wealth is their willingness to work hard. If you're suffering from a case of the lazies, you'll probably never succeed in your career—or life.

"Nobody has ever been truly successful who didn't work ridiculously hard."
—Gary Vaynerchuk, entrepreneur, author, speaker

Track just how much time and effort you spend on searching for a job. If it isn't much, then you've got a problem.

The same is true when managing your career. While long hours don't necessarily equate to success on the job, being focused and controlling your time effectively leads to accomplishment—which leads to success. A good work ethic is a major "soft skill" that is valuable to employers and a sign of emotional intelligence.

As we write this book in 2019 America is experiencing near full employment, with an unemployment rate below 4%. But it's important not to get complacent. The job market can change quickly and dramatically. As recently as 2015 nearly 3 million Americans had been out of work for six months or more, according to the U.S. Bureau of Labor. And in 2010, the unemployment rate reached almost 10% (9.8%).

So, if you are only investing minimal effort in looking for a job and managing your career effectively you will likely not be successful at either one. Remember, finding the right job is now your job. Invest as much time in searching for a job as you would if you had a job.

Success comes to those who are focused, manage their time well, and work diligently to achieve their dreams.

Mindful Career Rules: The way you transition from your last job to your new job is important. Incorporate gratefulness and meditation into a job-search plan. By being mindful, you will make this time valuable to your future success.

Chapter 19

LinkedIn Is Your Link
to Professional Success

> *"If you want to be found, be where people are looking."*
> —Eric Wentworth, author of *A Plan for Life:*
> *The 21st Century Guide to Success in Wealth,*
> *Health, Career, Education, Love, Place . . . and You!*

LinkedIn should be the primary platform for your professional networking and career management. We encourage everyone, whether they are currently in the job market or not, to create a consistent engagement with LinkedIn. You never know when you will need LinkedIn and you don't want to be starting from scratch at a time when you have decided that a professional network can help with a new venture or to find a job.

We encounter people all the time who have been out of the workforce for years, perhaps raising a family, and now find they need to get a job. Without a network of contacts to tap into it is usually difficult.

College students who want to jumpstart their career should begin building their professional network and learning the career management tools available on LinkedIn while still in school.

People who have been in a job or business for years and haven't thought they need LinkedIn often unexpectedly find they must find a new position (due to a layoff or downsizing or business failure).

Without a rich network of professional contacts on LinkedIn, it will be more difficult to find a new job.

Most people, even some users, think LinkedIn is only for finding a job. It can certainly help you with that, but it's also a career management platform with many tools that can help increase your effectiveness in your profession. It's also a strong B2B lead-generation tool for businesses looking for new customers.

The power and reach of LinkedIn is impressive:

- LinkedIn has more than 630 million members (June 2019) with two new members joining every second. If LinkedIn was a country it would be the third largest in the world

- 90% of Fortune 100 companies use LinkedIn Talent Solutions to augment their HR capabilities.

- 44% of LinkedIn users earn $75,000 or more annually.

- LinkedIn has more than 15 million active job listings.

- 26 million companies participate on LinkedIn.

With LinkedIn, you can easily expand your reach to hundreds of thousands—even millions—of professional contacts. It's the ultimate networking tool.

Use LinkedIn to establish your personal brand, find employees, discover job opportunities, demonstrate your expertise, stay current with news and trends in your industry, advertise your products and services, share information, increase your knowledge by taking LinkedIn Learning courses, and make key connections that can enhance both your professional and personal life. Also, you can do all this on your smartphone if you prefer—60% of LinkedIn users access the site on them.

✓ LinkedIn, according to the Bullhorn Reach Social Recruiting Activity report, is the most important networking tool for career management.

✓ LinkedIn is the largest job posting site, with a new person hired through it every ten seconds.

✓ A 2016 survey by DMR found 94% of recruiters use LinkedIn to find qualified job candidates, compared to 66% for Facebook and 54% for Twitter. Nearly half (48%) of recruiters only use LinkedIn for social outreach.

✓ Fully 95% of LinkedIn users are open to receiving unsolicited InMail from other members.

Although Facebook and Twitter are trying to become both a personal and professional network, currently neither comes close to matching the career tools available on LinkedIn. LinkedIn gets 5.7 times more job views than Facebook and three times more than Twitter.

Under the direction of Jeff Weinstein, CEO, LinkedIn has evolved into a powerful tool that can have a major impact on the success of your career or business. The tens of millions who use LinkedIn frequently are among the most successful professionals in America. LinkedIn has become much more than simply a job-hunting platform.

The demographics of LinkedIn users show they are the cream of the crop—54% are either high or medium-income earners, usually in professional positions. More than 50% of internet users in the U.S. who have a college degree use LinkedIn.

As LinkedIn continues to expand, and as the technical requirements of formerly "blue collar" professions increase, it's likely that you will find more people in these jobs as well. Our firm uses LinkedIn Recruiter to augment our other search tools in order to find top candidates for management positions in the construction industry. For other industries in which we place talent—technology, biopharmaceuticals, cleantech, sales, marketing—LinkedIn is our primary search tool because nearly all of the professionals in these industries are members.

> *"People will review your LinkedIn Profile 83% of the time before they meet with you the first time."*
>
> —Hubspot, *State of Inbound* report

Surprisingly, LinkedIn as the ultimate career management tool has not reached most people. Even among LinkedIn users, fully three out of four use it infrequently, mostly to post a resume. Most people simply don't understand that much of your success in life is a result of having built and nurtured a robust professional and personal network. People lead busy lives and building a network isn't usually top-of-mind with them. And frankly, most people haven't developed a long-term career management strategy. They aren't prepared to take advantage of new opportunities or what is next in their career progression. This is not a mindful approach to arguably the most important ingredient in your personal and professional happiness—your career.

LINKEDIN AS A SEARCH ENGINE

Most people don't think of LinkedIn as a search engine—but it is. In fact, it is the largest business-oriented search engine in the world. The way you create your Profile and your activity on LinkedIn enables you or your company to be found easily. LinkedIn results often show up on Google searches. If Google respects the data on LinkedIn, you should too. The two search engines working together give you a powerful online presence.

If you learn to combine and connect a Facebook, Twitter, or Instagram account to LinkedIn it increases your exposure exponentially.

LINKEDIN IS CHANGING RAPIDLY

We feel the revisions to LinkedIn are mostly positive. Older users like us (we first started using LinkedIn in 2004) can adapt to the "new" LinkedIn easily. But it may be daunting for a new user. Our best advice is to jump in with both feet, use their Help and Tutorials, and don't get discouraged. It isn't brain surgery. If more than half a billion people can figure it out, so can you.

For a deep dive into how you can use LinkedIn to its fullest advantage, we recommend picking up a copy of *The Ultimate Guide to LinkedIn for Business* (third edition) by our friend Ted Prodromou. Unlike many LinkedIn guides, Ted walks you through each step with easy to understand directions. Whether you are searching for a job or running a business, this book will repay its modest price thousands of times over.

GETTING STARTED ON LINKEDIN

Begin by selecting who you want to include in your LinkedIn network by importing the names of people you already know who are in your browser contact list or from Facebook. Whenever you meet someone at a conference or while on the job, get their business card and follow up with a note and invitation to connect on LinkedIn.

Signing up for and participating in Groups is another great way to build your list of contacts. Thousands of LinkedIn Groups cover every career and interest subject imaginable. Participating in these groups enables you to get exposure beyond your core network and demonstrates your knowledge in front of peers and potential employers. The groups are also a great way to stay on top of new developments and differing opinions in your profession.

Check the connections of your connections to see if there are people you would like to reach out to and include in your circle of contacts. Over time these people will often transition from being "cold" unknown contacts into lifelong personal or professional friendships as you become known to each other—much like if you had actually met the person. Nearly half of our personal friendships began this way. In many markets, there are frequent LinkedIn networking events where you can meet your connections and make new ones.

Do these things diligently and consistently and soon you'll have a list of contacts numbering in the hundreds. These contacts will put you just one or two degrees away from tens of thousands of other potential contacts.

"Your network is your net worth."

—Porter Gale, author of *Your Network is Your Net Worth:*
Unlock the Hidden Power of Connections
for Wealth, Success, and Happiness in the Digital Age

While many LinkedIn members prefer to connect only with people they've met or done business with, there are others who connect with anyone. "Top linked" and LION (LinkedIn Open Network) members may have thousands of contacts, although they will personally know only a fraction of these connections. There are pros and cons to either linking strategy. Our own linking strategy is a hybrid—about 60% of our connections are people we know and the others are people we would like to know or who want to connect with us for professional reasons.

As we've said, these days it's not only who you know but who knows you that leads to success. Your network is your net worth.

YOUR LINKEDIN PROFILE

> *"LinkedIn is an electronic business card that can be seen by more than 600 million professionals, so you want a complete up-to-date Profile."*
>
> —Ted Prodromou, author
> of *The Ultimate Guide to LinkedIn for Business*

The "hub" around which everything else on LinkedIn depends is your personal Profile. Your Profile must stand out and be keyword search friendly so potential employers, recruiters, and others interested in doing business with you can find you easily. To find out which keywords are most powerful and will be tagged by searches most often, look at what keywords others in your field are using, scan job descriptions, and check out industry websites.

TEN TIPS TO BUILDING A STRONG PROFILE

The key to building a strong Profile on LinkedIn (and get found by Recruiters) is to think of yourself as a brand. Brands build trust by using an authentic voice and telling a believable story to connect with the target audience. Here are ten tips to help you do the same:

1. **Sign up for Premium level use.** The cost is currently $29.95 a month and provides several advantages over the free level, including a greater number of InMail messages you can send to other members. You'll also be able to brand your Profile with a customizable visual background header behind your photo. If you have a singular message encompassing your career, this is a where to do it.

2. **Your Headline and Job Title.** LinkedIn's algorithms weigh the Headline and Job Title heavily in their search parameters. This is also what recruiters look at first. You have 120 characters to build your Headline with, although a little-known trick to get an extra 100 characters is to use the LinkedIn smartphone app to create it.

For some reason known only to LinkedIn you can only get these additional 100 characters if you do it this way. Here's how:

- Download the LinkedIn app to your iOS or Android device.

- Open the app and click on your photo (located in the top right-hand corner).

- Click the pencil to the right of your photo on your Profile page.

- Add up to an additional 100 characters of copy (total 220 characters, including spaces).

- Click Save.

Your new, and significantly longer, Headline will now be visible on your mobile app and desktop.

Our advice is to use as many characters as possible. Start with a clear Title description. Hopefully, you weren't given the title of Guru of Customer Happiness but Customer Relations Director (which LinkedIn's algorithm will find more easily). Then use the remaining characters to add descriptors to your role (e.g. ecommerce customer experience).

3. **Considering adding a personal tagline or slogan to your Headline.** The best marketers "tag" their marketing messages with a memorable line that stays with the consumer. Budweiser, the King of Beers; BMW, the Ultimate Driving Machine; and Things Go Better with Coke, are just a few. In the line of text just under your name—the first thing people see on your Profile—write a branding statement, a slogan, for yourself. NOTE: in some cases, your company's brand may be so strong it is all you need, along with your title.

4. **Don't cut and paste your resumé to build your Profile.** Describe your experience and abilities as you would to someone you just met, not in formal "resumé" speak. Your Profile is an acceptable opportunity to expand upon who you are both personally and professionally that you don't have in your resumé. Plus, you can always attach your formal resumé to your LinkedIn account.

5. **Learn from the best advertising copywriters.** Lighten up your Profile with your unique voice, as you would if you were excited about telling a friend about your career and skills. Introduce yourself much as you would at a conference or meeting with a client. Use your authentic voice.

6. **Ensure your Profile headline targets the position you want.** Use keywords and titles that will alert a hiring manager or recruiter of your compatibility with the position they want to fill. This is the first thing they see beneath your name. Your Headline should usually include your current role, expertise, and career path goal. For example: Project Manager | 5 Years Digital Products + eCommerce Experience | Google Analytics Expert. A recent grad with little or no experience might have something like Financial Graduate from Top 10 Business School | Forensic Accounting | Financial Analyst.

   NOTE: If you apply for a job directly through LinkedIn, the amount of information you can share is limited to your name, the headline under your name, current job and past titles (but no employment details), only the names of schools you've attended, how many people have recommended you (but no details), the number of connections you have, and your contact information. Our advice is to apply to the company directly with a link back to your LinkedIn Profile embedded in your resumé.

7. **Talk about your skills.** LinkedIn recommends thinking about your Specialties field as your own personal search engine optimizer, a way to refine and target how people find you. This is also where you list your abilities and interests that may make you stand out from the crowd. You can include the personal values you bring to your professional experience—and even add a note of humor or passion, if appropriate. Listing your Skills will generate approximately 13 times more views than a Profile without them. And users who list at least five skills on their Profile receive up to 17 times more views.

8. **Describe your experience.** Help the person reviewing your Profile with key points describing what your company does and what you did for them. Use bullet points to point out specific and measurable achievements.

9. **Distinguish yourself from your competition.** Use the Additional information section to round out your Profile with a few key interests—especially those enhancing your overall professional description.

10. **Recommendations are important.** Third-party endorsements go a long way to validating what you say in your LinkedIn Profile. They also give the hiring manager or recruiter a name to follow through on for a reference check. Request recommendations from colleagues and supervisors who will present you at your best. Since nine in ten Profiles don't have any recommendations, you gain an advantage by having them.

11. **Add a website connection, social media or Slideshare presentation** showcasing your abilities. You can supplement your presence here with a Slideshare Professional Journey presentation that adds some visual excitement to your career history. By linking your social media—Twitter, Facebook, Instagram—and your website you can efficiently cross-promote your content.

12. **Edit the default "My Website" label** to promote click-throughs to increase your Google page rankings.

13. **Location.** Be sure the location you've set is correct. Recruiters often conduct geo-targeted searches in specific locations. They know that often the closer a candidate is to their client's business, the greater chance she will be interested in the position. Clients also don't usually want employees who must travel long distances to work.

    You can indicate which cities you are willing to relocate to in your Career Interests settings. Click on Jobs in the top navigation bar, then Career Interests under the search bar to update your location preference.

14. **Add awards received, trade associations you belong to, and interest groups you have joined** to show your professional engagement. Many of these include a visual icon you can post next to the item.

15. **List courses taken online** at sites like Hubspot, Coursera, Khan University, and Udemy to show your continued involvement in learning to enhance your professional education and differentiate

yourself from competitors. You can add (or LinkedIn will do it automatically) the icon of the course or educational source to promote your continuing education. For example, an icon from Harvard or Johns Hopkins University will catch the eye of employers looking for people with educational credentials from top-tier schools.

Use LinkedIn Learning as a resource to gain valuable skills you can promote on your Profile. When LinkedIn purchased the online learning site Lynda in 2015, it added a wealth of educational courses to its functionality.

16. **List any books you've written with an image of the cover.** If you've written a book demonstrating expertise in your field, guess who will usually get the job offer when you are competing with an equally qualified applicant? If you literally "wrote the book" on your area of expertise, you will be viewed as the expert vis-a-vis others in your field. LinkedIn now links your books back to Amazon with just a click, so people can more easily order as well.

17. **Join Groups that reach the target groups you want to connect with most.** Belonging to a group in an industry or interest area in alignment with your career goals is one of the best ways to reach people with similar interests. It's also an excellent method to expand your list of contacts since you can directly invite other group members to be part of your network. In Groups you can ask a question about something you want to know or look for expertise in an unfamiliar area and receive great advice from experts in a matter of minutes. Don't forget to set aside some time each week to participate in the discussions. This is a great opportunity to engage with others in your field or area of interest.

18. **Build your LinkedIn Connections.** Connections are at the heart of using LinkedIn successfully. People are naturally judged by the people they associate with professionally and personally. It reflects on the quality of your personal brand. When someone scans your Profile and notices you are both connected to the same contact, your stock soars. If people reviewing your Profile see you are connected to many others in your field, or your contacts show you associate with influencers in your industry, your value increases.

The more common connections you have with a recruiter or hiring manager, the higher your Profile will be in their search results and the more 2nd Degree connections you will have with them, which increases your likelihood of being found.

We recommend creating a LinkedIn networking plan. Decide who are the people you want to meet in specific segments of your career area of interest, then build connections in those areas in advance. Don't just connect with anyone who requests to connect with you. And beware of connecting with people with no Profile information or from sketchy parts of the world.

19. **Create your "vanity" LinkedIn URL** and use it on your resumé. It shows you are a savvy LinkedIn user. Here's an example: linkedin. com/in/ericwentworth.

20. **Add your Contact information to your Profile.** Just as you would do when meeting someone at a live networking event, share your email and telephone number so that your connections can easily reach you.

21. **List your company website address.** When entering your website URL, choose OTHER and enter your company name or keyword phrases in the box titled Type (OTHER). This enables your company name and phrases to be clickable links to a website or blog.

22. **Subscribe to content that increases your knowledge and presence on LinkedIn.** The content you subscribe to now appears in your newsfeed. You can subscribe to industry-related content, articles from Influencers (e.g. Bill Gates, Tim Ferriss, Richard Branson), and posts from other members of your network.

23. **Use Notifications to "ping" your connections.** Through its Notification feature, LinkedIn automatically prompts you with messages about members of your network who have a birthday, work anniversary, or who have started a new job. You can choose one of the suggested messages to congratulate a connection or create your own to "ping" to respond to the notification. This is a mindful way of creating top-of-mind awareness among your connections. Another way to subtlety "ping" a connection is to simply look at their Profile.

Unless they've turned it off in their settings, they will see that you looked at their Profile. Often it is enough of a reminder to warrant reaching out.

24. **Add your social media accounts.** Add your Twitter, Facebook, and Instagram accounts. There's a popup box instructing you how to do this when you set up your LinkedIn account. Now visitors to your Profile can see what you are posting on your social media with just one click.

25. **Add the Volunteer Experience special Profile** section (assuming you have some) to show that you participate in community or charitable activities.

It's easy to see your LinkedIn activity by clicking on ME from the main menu. Go to Posts and Activity and Views of Your Posts to view a complete listing of your LinkedIn activity.

You can also see a percentage breakdown by profession of who has looked at your Profile as well as a trend graph displaying how well your Profile and activity has performed over time.

YOUR PROFILE HEADLINE

Your Headline is the most important element of a successful LinkedIn Profile. It is the "hook" that will snag the attention of the people you want to attract.

Your Profile Headline is the first thing people—including recruiters/hiring managers—see when they:

- ✓ review your Profile.
- ✓ see your Status Updates.
- ✓ see comments you've made when sharing other member's Status Updates.
- ✓ see you in their list of People Who Viewed My Profile.
- ✓ look at Group discussions you have participated in.
- ✓ search for a University page.
- ✓ look for you in Advanced People Search.

✓   see you among the members in their list of People You May Know.

Add a headline that calls attention to something that sets you apart. LinkedIn trainer Viveka von Rosen includes "LinkedIn Expert & Author | International Keynote Speaker | Forbes Top 20 Most Influential | Digital Sales & Personal Branding Expert | Vengresso CVO" in her Profile Headline. As a result, her LinkedIn Profile is the top organic search result out of 370 million searches for the words "LinkedIn expert."

So, don't be shy about promoting your special talents or skills.

YOUR LINKEDIN HEADSHOT PHOTO

Unlike on your resumé, where a photo will weigh against you, the opposite is true on LinkedIn. Profiles without a headshot are reviewed far fewer times than those with a good photo. Some studies show that a Profile with a photo is viewed 14 to 21 times more on average than one without a photo. They also receive 36 times more messages.

It's important your photo is professional. Why people continue to use snapshots taken by their cousin or on a smartphone for their "professional" online image is hard to understand. If your photo says "geek" or "unprofessional" then perhaps it's time to consider putting your best face forward.

We don't recommend getting a Photoshopped "studio" photo bearing only a faint resemblance to the real you, or one taken 15 years (and 30 pounds) ago. You don't want people to hardly recognize you when you finally meet. But using a bad snapshot to promote your career is just naïve. LinkedIn recommends, when appropriate, having a professional photo taken in your working environment. If that isn't possible, a headshot photo that shows your authentic self in the most flattering way is also ideal.

Your photo is very important to your success on LinkedIn; invest in doing it well.

SCIENCE-BASED HACKS TO CREATE THE BEST HEADSHOT PHOTO

You won't likely find this advice in any other career management book. There are several tweaks you can make to your professional photograph to significantly boost your brand image. These tips come from Robert Dooley, who writes books and blogs about neuromarketing. Dooley says, "Being seen as smart is usually desirable, and it turns out you can influence your perceived intelligence with your Profile picture."

Remember, your first impression can be formed in milliseconds (and can be stubbornly resistant to change). Your smile is what activates your first positive impression. People universally respond well to a person with a genuine smile. Here are a few other tips to creating a positive headshot photo.

1. For centuries artists have preferred to show the left side of the face in their portraits. This is especially true for women (78%) and slightly true for men (56%). Wake Forest University researchers found a preference for images showing the left side of the subject's face. Their findings indicate the left side of the face expresses more emotion. For men, the right side of the face may show less emotion but project higher dominance and self-control.

    • A left-side photo may also make you slightly more attractive and approachable. In any case, nearly everyone has a "good" side that photographs more attractively. Keep this in mind when having a professional photo taken.

2. Most studies on the subject find a confident smile is a good indicator of trust. An authentic smiling face was determined to be more trustworthy than a neutral or stern face.

3. Direct eye contact with the camera is best, showing confidence and a willingness to connect.

4. Having an alcoholic drink prior to your photo shoot can help you look more relaxed and more confident, according to research, although you might not want to drive yourself to the photoshoot.

5. "Model" the emotion you want to project. Your mind will process the image and reflect it on your face.

6. Don't overlook the lighting; it is essential to projecting the right image. Have the photographer experiment with a few different lighting styles. But make sure the lighting of the photo reproduces well online.

7. Avoid busy backgrounds. Keep it simple.

8. Dress to impress. The clothes you wear have an immediate impact on how you are perceived. Business casual works best for most people.

9. Include your face and shoulders only—no full body photos.

10. New York photographer Peter Hurley (PeterHurley.com) suggests doing a "squinch" to make your headshot more photogenic. He says that squinting your eyes slightly creates a photo that "oozes confidence and self-assuredness, as opposed to staring wide-eyed which projects fear and anxiety." He also has some tips on creating the "perfect jawline" in your photo.

11. Choose the correct image size: 8MB and pixel size of 400 x 400 size high quality image or 800 X 800 (which can be sized down a bit for a crisp, sharp final image). JPG, GIF or PNG files are okay.

12. For fun—and to get some feedback on your photo—go to Snappr Photo Analyzer. Your photo can be evaluated for a number of criteria using the latest research and evolving algorithm, combined with image recognition and machine learning technologies to judge your photo on your face composition and editing. Or go to PhotoFeeler and have lots of complete strangers provide respectful feedback on your photo in three areas: Competence, Likeable, and Influential.

A meta-analysis of LinkedIn headshot photos found that those who have better photos also have more connections.

Remember, your photo is the first thing anyone will see when they access your Profile. Make sure it's a good one.

LINKEDIN TOOLS

There are several valuable career management tools on LinkedIn.

- You can tell LinkedIn what types of jobs you are interested in and receive notifications when they become available. Then you can apply for those jobs through LinkedIn. There are several search parameters enabling you to drill down to exactly what you are looking for in a job.

- It's possible to "follow" companies of interest to you. There are nearly 4 million company pages on LinkedIn (2017). Each includes information about the company and shows how you are connected to its employees and former employees. You can find out the address of the company, how many people work there, and when it was founded. You can see how many other LinkedIn members are following the company. Often there are links to websites, blogs, updates on company activities, and listings of products or services. By reviewing the Profiles of people who work at the company you can gain valuable insights into what they are looking for in an employee. LinkedIn lists other similar companies, as well as the companies people who viewed the page have also searched, to provide you with a wider search field.

- Status Updates enables you to share articles or updates from other users with your connections. Choose these strategically, you want them to enhance your personal brand or connect you to information about your profession. Here are a few examples:

  ✓ Articles, blog posts, white papers you have written

  ✓ Comments on Updates by other connections

  ✓ An event or seminar you are hosting

  ✓ A new project you have launched

  ✓ A promotion or new assignment

  ✓ A new job

  ✓ A repost of an article you've read that relates to your industry

  ✓ A new professional certification

  ✓ A comment on a relevant post or article that demonstrates your subject expertise

  ✓ Changes to your Profile

- LinkedIn is the largest publishing platform on the internet. More than 100,000 articles and videos are shared every day on LinkedIn. It's a great way for you to get noticed and display your expertise; increase your online presence via Google, Bing, and Yahoo! search results; and gain valuable credibility. When you share content— an article, status update, or video—you can also control who sees it by using the drop-down menu that appears below your name as you type your update. You can select Public, Public + Twitter, or Connections.

We suggest writing valuable content and then sharing it via LinkedIn and in other iterations on Medium and Quora. If you create enough great content you'll be seen as an industry leader—one of the "Influencers" in your field.

- Every day you are alerted to who has viewed your Profile and the person who took an interest in you. If a hiring manager has looked at your Profile you will know. LinkedIn provides a cool graph showing the total views and the last three months activity. Below this graph is the number of times you have appeared in LinkedIn Search and the percentage you are trending (up 3%, for example).

- The What People Are Talking About Now newsfeed on the right column of your Homepage displays trending national and international news. You can often gain more exposure by commenting on these stories. If you write articles related to breaking news you can often piggyback of the interest on the story.

- Post your Slideshare Professional Journey to your Profile. It's a great way to set yourself apart from most other candidates and visually demonstrate your career path, skills, accomplishments, and education. You can also post slide decks, infographics, PDFs, and documents.

- A box will appear daily on the right side of your news feed that highlights a different company. Clicking on the box takes you to more information about the company, including jobs available and their hiring history.

- LinkedIn Hashtag Communities increases your chance of being discovered. You can follow people and the type of content you prefer in your Newsfeed. Click on the pencil icon next to Your Communities and pin your favorite hashtags by clicking on the pencil icon. You can see the full list of topics at linkedin.com/directory/topics.

- You can now upload native video to LinkedIn. Native video is video you have created yourself. Our recruiting firm is the only one in the world to produce a video to support every job search we conduct.

We use the Promo platform to create our videos. It's simple to use and inexpensive. To upload a video just click on the Video button in the Status Update box.

LinkedIn also now makes it possible to upload live video broadcasts from your smartphone on the LinkedIn mobile app. It works just like Facebook Live Videos.

- You can save most articles you may want to review later by clicking on the little banner icon in the story.

YOUR VISIBILITY MENU

- You have four choices under the visibility menu: Your Connections, Your Network, All LinkedIn Members, and Public (where people who are not members of LinkedIn can find you through search engines like Google). We recommend selecting the Public option.

THE ALUMNI CONNECTION

- The Alumni feature enables you to find members who have attended the same school as you did. Graduates of the same school share a kind of bond that can help you get introduced to important connections, opportunities at companies, and alumni networking events.

LINKEDIN JOBS

The Jobs section of LinkedIn has evolved more robustly than any other feature. In Jobs you can:

- ✓ Search for jobs by job title and location.
- ✓ See jobs based on your Profile and career interests.
- ✓ Track the jobs you are interested in or have applied to
- ✓ See how you rate among other applicants for a job you are interested in.

✓   See suggested jobs like the one you are interested in.

✓   Find Remote jobs.

Click on LinkedIn Salary and see what the average salary by location is for popular job titles. You'll see a handy graph of the salary range from lowest to highest with the Median Salary highlighted. Also, you can check out what several companies pay for jobs by title in your area.

In the Jobs section LinkedIn also currently lists ProFinder resources to help rewrite your resumé to make it more professional and impactful. You can find other job search tips in LinkedIn Learning.

SHARE YOUR CAREER INTERESTS WITH RECRUITERS ANONYMOUSLY

LinkedIn introduced a new feature in October 2016 making it much easier to get on the "radar screen" of recruiters. LinkedIn eliminates the problem of alerting recruiters that you are seeking new opportunities, something you can't easily do if you are employed. Now you can share your career interests anonymously with recruiters only.

It's also a boon for recruiters, who sometimes find it hard to search "passive" candidates who already have a job.

To share your career interests from the **Settings & Privacy** page:

1.   Click on the **Me** icon at the top of your LinkedIn homepage.

2.   Select **Privacy and Settings** from the dropdown.

3.   Click the **Privacy** tab at the top of the page.

4.   Under **Job seeking preferences** section, click **Change** next to **Let Recruiters know you're open to opportunities.**

5.   Switch the toggle to **Yes** to share that you are open and appear in recruiter searches matching your career interests. Or switch the toggle to **No** to stop sharing career interests with recruiters.

6.   The changes will be saved automatically.

Go to the Career Interests page to edit additional settings such as job titles you are considering, the kinds of jobs you are open to, and more.

LINKEDIN PROFINDER

Another feature added in 2016 is LinkedIn ProFinder. With ProFinder, employers can post freelance and project jobs and receive bids from LinkedIn members who work part-time, on contract, freelance or are in between full-time jobs.

Companies looking for a specific skill can create a ProFinder request. If you are interested and have the requested skill, you can submit a proposal. You can register on ProFinder by going to linkedin.com/ profinder.

LINKEDIN'S COMMITMENT TO RECRUITERS

In 2017 LinkedIn introduced LinkedIn Career Pages enabling executive search firms to better engage with both their clients and job candidates. This is one of several features—such as Contractor Search, Pipeline Builder, and Commute Time—LinkedIn provides to the recruiting and staffing industry to support their efforts.

Job seekers aren't generally aware of these LinkedIn features, but they are more reasons why it is important to establish an ongoing relationship with a good recruiter or staffing firm. Recruiters pay thousands of dollars every year to have tools at their disposal that simply aren't there for job seekers to help you in your search or manage your career.

LINKEDIN SALES NAVIGATOR

If you plan to go into sales, Sales Navigator is LinkedIn powered by rocket fuel. It does for sales professionals what LinkedIn Recruiter does for recruiters, providing deep access and special tools designed to help them pinpoint and manage ideal prospects. Navigator currently costs $64.95 a month on an annual subscription.

LINKEDIN SMARTPHONE APPS

More than 60% of members access LinkedIn on their mobile app. On the app, you can do on your smartphone much of what you can do on LinkedIn using your computer, including leaving a voice message.

In 2017 a revamp of the app designed to concentrate on the core user experiences has made it much easier to use.

Ted Prodromou, author of *The Ultimate Guide to LinkedIn for Business,* writes, "Since two-thirds of LinkedIn's revenue comes from job postings and recruiter's subscriptions, of course it has an app to help you find a job." LinkedIn Job Search enables you to review jobs, see who you know at the company, and apply in one click using data from your LinkedIn Profile.

Slideshare is also included among the LinkedIn mobile apps. Premium apps available on mobile include LinkedIn Recruiter (for professional recruiters), LinkedIn Sales Navigator (for sales professionals), and LinkedIn Elevate (for large companies that create a lot of content on social media).

Since members use their smartphones and the LinkedIn apps so frequently, you can bet that by the time you read this there will be further enhancements available.

LINKEDIN LEARNING

As we mentioned earlier, LinkedIn is constantly evolving—especially so now that they have the "deep pockets" of Microsoft to both pay for new feature development and provide additional technical resources to make it happen. LinkedIn is so critical to effective career management that we advise everyone to stay educated about how to use it well.

LinkedIn Learning offers dozens of courses to help you learn how to use LinkedIn, as well as how to increase your career skills. At LinkedIn Learning you can take short instructional classes or sign up for a LinkedIn Learning Path for a full course in a subject. For example, the course to become a Front-End Web Developer is 41 hours long. Access LinkedIn Learning by clicking on the box in the upper far right corner of your page feed.

LINKEDIN SKILL ASSESSMENTS

Another important new feature added in September 2019 is LinkedIn Skill Assessments. According to LinkedIn, "Each Skill Assessment, whether it's Adobe Photoshop to showcase your design skills or Java to land a developer role, is constructed through a rigorous content creation and review process in partnership with LinkedIn Learning industry and subject matter experts. Once candidates have completed an assessment, a badge will be displayed on their Profile in LinkedIn Recruiter and LinkedIn Jobs, so hirers are able to quickly identify and verify skill proficiency."

LinkedIn plans to add non-tech Skill Assessments in the future. This is valuable for executive recruiters who now spend a great deal of time vetting the claims of potential job candidates.

Also, once you have passed a Skill Assessment, LinkedIn will send relevant job recommendations to you as soon as they are posted. LinkedIn says that early results show that "candidates who complete LinkedIn Skill Assessments are significantly more likely (~30%) to get hired."

Here's how it works. Scroll to the Skills section of your Profile and choose one of the available Skill Assessments you would like to validate. If you pass in the 70th percentile or above, you have the option of adding a Verified Skill badge to your Profile. If you didn't pass, your score is kept anonymous and you can always take the test again three months later. You'll also need to retake the tests every year to keep your badges and credentials current.

LinkedIn is cross-promoting their LinkedIn Learning courses to help you improve your career skills. When you complete these courses, you can also add them to your Profile. LinkedIn Learning (which was previously Lynda.com) offers hundreds of high quality online technical and business courses. You'll pay to enroll in most of these courses, but if you have a library card (and your library is a subscriber to Lynda.com) you may be able to take the courses for free.

LINKEDIN PROFESSIONAL COACHING

If you want to become a LinkedIn pro you can't go wrong with these expert LinkedIn trainers who have been in the game for years:

- ✓ Coach Ron Nash, Founder, Get Hired Now! Master LinkedIn Profinder, career success coach and mindset strategist, author of *Jumpstart Your Career with LinkedIn*

- ✓ Mike O'Neil, President, Integrated Alliances (integratedalliances. com), author of *Rock the World with Your Online Presence: Your Ticket to a Multi-Platinum Online Profile*

✓ Ted Prodromou, LinkedIn coach, executive coach, certified CPCC professional coach, author of *The Ultimate Guide to LinkedIn for Business,* provides a wealth of LinkedIn training services, as well as social media and sales support education. Go to (tedprodromou.com) for more information

✓ Wayne Breitbarth, LinkedIn trainer, coach and strategy consultant, author of *The Power Formula for LinkedIn Success* (PowerFormula.net)

✓ Rhonda Sher, LinkedIn consultant and trainer, author of *Get LinkedIn or Get Left Out* (RhondaSher.com)

✓ Neal Schaffer, author of *Maximizing LinkedIn for Sales and Social Media Marketing* (nealschaffer.com)

✓ Hanna Morgan (CareerSherpa.net)

Other highly rated LinkedIn trainers are Nathan Kievman, Viveka von Rosen, Kristina Jaramillo, and Melonie Dodaro. You can find them all, of course, on LinkedIn.

At Wentworth Executive Recruiting we also offer a range of career services, including personal career coaching and LinkedIn Profile consulting/writing. We normally conduct career coaching online and by phone. If you live in the San Francisco Bay Area, we are happy to arrange a personal meeting as well. We also offer resumé writing support. You can see an example of one of the resumés we revamped in the 2018 edition of Dick Bolles' bestselling career book *What Color is Your Parachute?*

To find out more about availability and cost, email a request to CarolAnn@WentworthExecutiveRecruiting.co.

LINKEDIN IS ALWAYS EVOLVING

LinkedIn is always adding (and sometimes dropping) features to fine-tune their service so that it remains the top career management website. Use LinkedIn regularly to stay current.

Fun facts about LinkedIn:

✓ A new user joins every two seconds.

✓ 50% of college graduates in the U.S. are LinkedIn users, but only 9% of high school graduates use LinkedIn

- ✓ Hubspot found that LinkedIn is 277% more effective at genererating leads than Facebook and Twitter.

- ✓ In 2019 there were 14 million open jobs listed on LinkedIn

- ✓ 122 million people received an interview invitation through LinkedIn in 2018

- ✓ LinkedIn drives 50% of social traffic to B2B sites—and is considered the most credible source of content

- ✓ LinkedIn is considered the most effective platform for B2B lead generation—80% vs 13% for Twitter and 7% for Facebook.

- ✓ LinkedIn is the #1 channel to distribute content.

Mindful Career Rules: LinkedIn is the premier career management tool. Learn to use it effectively.

Chapter 20

Social Media and Your Job Search

A surprising number of jobs are the result of social media, either as a direct lead, information about a company, connection with someone who can help get an interview, or a job listing.

Twitter

Twitter is now a popular job search tool as more recruiters, employers, and human resources departments use it to post job opportunities, network, and research companies.

To search for jobs, use hashtags, the little # preceding key words and phrases enabling pinpointed search and expanded reach on Twitter. You can also search for people and subjects of interest in the search box of your Twitter Profile, and Twitter will generate a list of all the recent tweets posted with that specific hashtag.

As with all internet search, the more specific you are the better your results. Some popular hashtags are #jobs, #nowhiring, #hotjobs, #greenjobs, #NewYorkJobs, #advertisingjobs, and so on. Check out TweetMyJobs and sign up for the free services. You can list the job titles you're interested in pursuing, and the locations where you are willing to work, and these will be tweeted to you as they become available.

Twitter is also an effective networking tool. You can join in the discussions at #jobhuntchat and #careerchat, just two of many career-related Twitter locales. Follow leaders in your field and executives at the companies you are interested in. You can often create a relationship via Twitter that can lead to a job opportunity. You can use Twitter to help become known as a leader or expert in your field. Companies often seek out these individuals first for key positions. Follow key journalists and influencers, nearly all are active on Twitter.

> *"44 percent of employers say they've found content*
> *on a social networking site that caused them to hire*
> *a candidate."*
>
> *—CareerBuilder*

Twitter is also ideal to conduct company research. According to Jobscan, "The information hasn't been groomed the way it is on other channels." Follow companies that interest you, even when they don't have job openings at the time. You can learn a lot from their tweets.

Twitter is evolving rapidly and related support apps and sites are being added almost every week, so it's important to spend some time researching how best to use this important job search tool. For a good introduction to using Twitter for your job search, check out *The Ultimate Guide to Twitter for Business* by Ted Prodromou.

Facebook

Facebook is the largest—2.4 billion members—and most used social network. After LinkedIn, recruiters use Facebook more than any other social media source. Employers and recruiters are using Facebook to help evaluate potential hires. This can work for or against you. Many people have lost (or gained) a job opportunity based upon what was on their Facebook page.

It's hard to believe, but every day thousands of people post stupid, embarrassing, or damaging comments and photos on their page. Conversely, Facebook posts can also validate, or even improve, your stature. So, decide upon a strategy and goals for your Facebook presence—then stick to it.

Most companies now have their own Facebook page. Here's a wonderful opportunity to find out the latest info, including job openings, on the company by "liking" and following them. With both Facebook and Twitter, you can learn a lot about the company culture. Also, jobs are frequently posted on these sites before other venues.

Jobs on Facebook lists available jobs in the location you desire, by company, job type, and by industry category. Recruiters also frequently post jobs they are seeking to fill.

In Facebook Groups you can discuss and post news about a particular subject, industry or interest. Connect with people who may be in a position to facilitate a job opportunity.

Facebook as a career management tool can be a bit dicey. It's hard to control what your friends post, and often you'll be judged by the company you keep. It also enables companies to have a much closer look into your personal life than ever before. You'll need to decide if you want your Facebook presence to remain social among friends and family or let potential employers into your private life.

Here's some tips to maximize your Facebook presence with potential hiring managers and recruiters:

✓ Check your Privacy Settings and decide who you want to allow to view your page.

✓ Complete your Profile.

✓ Learn about Facebook status and update settings.

✓ Understand how to use Facebook Jobs.

✓ If you are looking for a job, let your Friends know.

✓ Follow people and companies of interest.

✓ Stay professional at all times.

✓ Post good Profile pictures.

✓ Choose a Cover photo that enhances your personal brand.

✓ Fill out the About section so that it reflects well on you and syncs with your other online personal information.

Instagram

With 1 billion Instagram accounts—120 million in the U.S.—posting more than 100 million photos and videos *every day* in the U.S. (2019), both companies and job seekers are discovering they can connect through this popular social media site. Companies are increasingly promoting their culture on Instagram, and many are posting job opportunities as well. Just search on Google by entering (name of company) and Instagram.

Here's another way to use Instagram. First, go to LinkedIn or the company's Team page to find the names of a few key employees. Then Google search the employee + Instagram. Look for work-related shots and the names of other employees following them.

The Muse (themuse.com) related how GrubHub uploaded a photo of an April Fool's prank at their headquarters and set the geotagged location to GrubHub World Headquarters. By clicking on the geotag, you can see all the photos taken in their office. This provides you with an inside peek into the GrubHub company culture. Okay, while this may be seen by some as borderline stalking, we prefer to label it as doing your research.

For some professions (mostly entertainment) the number of Instagram followers marks you as an "influencer" and can lead to a job or endorsement deal. Influencers can make millions of dollars if they have enough followers.

Also remember, as with all social media what you post reflects upon your personal "brand." Make your story personal and compelling, but don't do anything stupid (no photos of you throwing up after a drunken night on the town). It's a great place to show off the things you are passionate about—that make you who you are. Employers love getting to know your personal side.

There are more than 25 million businesses on Instagram. You can use Instagram to engage with companies by following them. Like their photos, participate in their contests, and get involved with their brand. Tag your own photos relating to their brand or company with a hashtag. Engage with your target company's key influencers. Instagram can also enable you to get a feel for the company culture and activities.

Instagram is also an ideal place to showcase your creativity. Upload samples of your photographs, ads you've created, or a screenshot of a popular Tweet or Pinterest board. Think of Instagram (and the other social media sites) as extensions of your professional portfolio.

Pinterest

Pinterest is the fourth most popular social media platform in America, with more than 80 million users in the U.S. More than a million businesses have a Pinterest account. Nearly three in ten global marketers use Pinterest for promotion.

When you are conducting research on a company you are interested in working for, Pinterest can provide information and insights you won't easily find elsewhere.

The visuals (Pinterest is heavy on infographics and photos) and links to more information are a great research tool. Need to come up to speed quickly on social media marketing basics? There are dozens of infographics explaining it, along with links to more detailed information. Need to find out more about a company, their competitors, or their products? You'll usually find a wealth of great information you can use to educate yourself about a company—and help you standout during interviews.

You can also create a personal account to include boards of your creative work. It's an easy way to create an online portfolio extension. For artists, photographers, architects, advertising designers and copywriters, clothing designers, and other creatives, Pinterest provides an easy way to showcase your work. You can even sell your work on Pinterest. Link this to your personal website and other social media accounts for extra viral exposure.

Many people use Pinterest as virtual Vision Boards to help them visualize the success they want to achieve.

If nothing else, Pinterest can help promote your personal brand. Your boards and interests give dimension to your overall personality. Since potential employers and others may check you out on Pinterest, your content should always support the image you want to project.

Pinterest is a frequently overlooked site for job seekers and career management. Add it to your list of resources.

YouTube

YouTube is a highly searchable online platform to promote yourself, display your creativity, and build your personal brand.

YouTube as an educational resource is one of its major uses. For job seekers, there are several channels to consider following:

1. **Job Hunting Secrets.** Ideal for job seekers just starting their search.

2. **Speed Up My Job Search.** Great details on job hunting.

3. **Andrew LaCivita.** Our friend Andrew covers a wide range of career management topics.

4. **Self Made Millennial.** Fun and insightful career and job search advice.

5. **Happen to Your Career.** Scott Anthony Barlow offers loads of "take action" content.

6. **Job Hunting Secrets.** Ideal for job hunters just starting out in the job search.

7. **JobSearchTV.com.** Hiring advice and job search counseling.

Mindful Career Rules: When you create your personal Job Search or Career Management Plan, be sure to include use of social media platforms. You never know where your next job will come from in the new world of work.

Chapter 21

Networking. It's Not Who You Know, It's Who Knows You

> *"Networking is the No. 1 unwritten rule of success in business."*
>
> —Sallie Krawcheck, CEO and Co-Founder, Ellevest, author of *Own It: The Power of Women at Work*

One stumbling block to career success that we often see, especially in younger tech-driven people, is a lack of understanding about networking and its importance to your career (and life) success. It's easy to hide behind a computer or cell phone screen instead of meeting people in person. Texting and email have largely replaced personal interaction.

While LinkedIn and social media provide a solid base for building a professional network, it's also important to engage in "old school" personal networking. And that means getting out to meet people face-to-face.

Virtually every opportunity you are presented in life will happen because of another person's support. So, the more people you meet, the more opportunities will come your way.

> *"The currency of real networking is not greed but generosity."*
>
> —Keith Ferrazzi, author of *Never Eat Alone*

YOUR "METWORK"

One highly successful businessman we know (we'll call him Len) credits his success to his extensive network. He does something we have never encountered before—he treats every person he meets as someone to add to his network, which he calls his "Metwork." It can be the mechanic who works on his car, the lady at the grocery store who checks his groceries, chance encounters on airplanes, the waiter at a restaurant. He engages them all, showing genuine interest in their lives.

When he returns home or to his office, Len writes down their name and a few facts about the person, like their birthday or the name of their dog. This helps him remember the person should he meet them again. If this seems like a waste of time, the thousands of people in Len's "Metwork" have affected his life in surprising and often beneficial ways.

One time the hostess at a restaurant he frequents told him about a conversation she overheard between two men who were looking for a partner for a deal they were putting together. She thought Len might like to know about it. She had written down their names, and Len followed up with a friendly call, saying he had "heard through the grapevine" about their deal. He briefly described how he could help. This led to a meeting, which in turn led to a partnership that eventually earned Len millions of dollars.

If Len had not taken the time to get to know the waitress, learn a little about her children and personal life, and remembered her birthday, the opportunity would likely never have happened. Len's mindful approach to his network enriches his life and those he interacts with in profound and meaningful ways.

The point is this: you never know where you will find opportunities. But you can always count on it involving another human being.

Treat your network like gold, because it is the most valuable ingredient in a successful and fulfilling life.

INDUSTRY EVENTS, TRADE SHOWS, CONFERENCES

Attending industry events and other networking venues, such as BNI and Meetups, has the potential to expand your network substantially. Personally, both Eric and I have had several career- and life-changing encounters in this way. If we had not gone to these events, we would be leading completely different lives in completely different ways (and would never have met each other). We met the president of one of our oldest and largest clients at a trade show. And the industry knowledge we have gained at conventions and trade shows has expanded our knowledge of our clients' industries.

In a chance encounter at an industry conference when he lived in Denver, Eric met someone who offered him a job in San Francisco. It changed the direction of the rest of his life. And the fellow who provided the opportunity became a lifelong friend.

Attending a trade show can be extremely valuable—or not. It depends on the level of involvement on your part. Many people go to a trade show and do a lot of standing around, accomplishing very little. Here are some tips to maximize the benefit of attending a trade show or convention:

1. Get the attendee list in advance.

2. Go to LinkedIn and make notes about the people/companies you plan to meet.

3. Create a plan to see your top prospects and develop questions to ask.

4. Prepare a 30-second "elevator pitch" describing what you do.

5. Schedule meetings with key people you want to meet.

6. Arrive early and stay late.

7. Adopt an approachable attitude—and smile.

8. Include some time for visiting exhibitors who aren't on your target list.

9. Bring a bag so you can pick up literature to review later.

10. Don't forget to bring plenty of business cards, a notepad, and a pen.

11. Schedule some time to participate in social activities.

12. Follow-up with the people you meet a few days after the show.

13. Ask to connect on LinkedIn.

There's an energy and casualness about interactions at networking venues that doesn't exist in typical job search scenarios. You'll find it much easier to engage with key contacts at these events than almost anywhere else.

Mindful Career Rules: Your network is your net worth. Develop, curate, and manage it mindfully, with an attitude of generosity. It will become the most important contributor to the success you achieve in life.

Chapter 22

The Brand Called You

> *"Personal branding is how we define ourselves*
> *in the workspace while at the same time incorporating*
> *the personal elements that make us who we are."*
>
> —Dawn Rasmussen, Pathfinder Writing and Career Services

Film stars and politicians have long understood the importance of managing and directing their personal image to support their career goals. For example, there is only one known photograph of Franklin D. Roosevelt in a wheelchair during his presidency. Celebrities know the value of personal branding. Kim Kardashian is a celebrity because of her successful personal branding. Now, it's just as important for you to do the same.

In the 21st century, your personal brand image is important to your success. Dan Schwabel (danschwabel.com), personal branding expert and author of *Back to Human: How Great Leaders Create Connection in the Age of Isolation* and *Me 2.0: Build a Powerful Brand for Career Success,* makes the case that every person must create a unique, memorable, value-driven identity.

Competition is fierce in the marketplace. Sometimes there are hundreds, even thousands, of people who want what you want.

So how do you stand out from the crowd? By developing:

1. a unique set of valuable skills.

2. a memorable persona.

3. and a public presence.

THE BUSINESS OF YOU

Business scientist Edward Deming advised people to do as corporations do—write a Mission Statement. Make your mission statement broad enough to encompass your general life goals and branding, but specific enough (with action steps) to create a path to achieving your goals.

To build a personal brand, you must consistently do things leading steadily toward your mission, like placing one brick after another until finally you have a path. While people are willing to overlook and forgive the occasional misstep, if you make too many, then that becomes your reputation. You are what you do consistently.

Reid Hoffman, co-founder of LinkedIn and author of *The Startup of You: Adapt to the Future, Invest in Yourself, and Transform Your Career,* believes it's important in today's world to think of yourself as a startup business. Your life and career are in permanent beta. You are the product. The product must offer value to consumers (e.g. employers or customers). Your product (you) will have many competitors, so you'll need to develop a competitive advantage (skills). That product needs to be attractively packaged (fit, healthy, well dressed, poised). You'll need a strong support team and network (friends, family, professional colleagues, LinkedIn connections). Revenue must be managed well (your income, cash flow, and investments). And then you need to market and promote the business of you (social media, content creation, event participation).

PERCEPTION IS REALITY

"Be your message."

—Mahatma Gandhi

Perception often becomes reality. Once you've decided how you want to be perceived by others, you've got to do what is necessary to promote that brand. Perhaps it's a blog or a book. Maybe it's with specialized training or a degree. It could be through volunteer or extracurricular activities. Some people engage in public speaking. Others do special projects at work that are highly visible. Perhaps a personal "makeover" will set you apart or reinforce the kind of image you want to present. The key is to find things that support your personal brand and be consistent with it. Whatever you do, always be authentic.

Mindful Career Rules: Be aware that YOU are your "brand" in the 21st century. Your personal brand is a compilation of all that you do, how you think, what you say, and how you present yourself to the world. Be consistent. Be authentic. And be mindful that every thought and action should define who you are—and who you want to be.

Chapter 23

Visualize Success

"Go confidently in the direction of your dreams.
Live the life you have imagined."

—Henry David Thoreau, American essayist, author of *Walden*

There's ample evidence that your mind has an amazing amount of influence over your actions, your success, and even your health. Decades ago Wallace Wattles, in *The Science of Success,* said, "Whatever you habitually think yourself to be, that you are." There is scientific support for this belief.

Dr. Lynn Joseph (drlynnjoseph.com), the author of *The Job-Loss Recovery Guide: A Proven Program to Get Back to Work . . . Fast!,* developed a scientifically controlled program (endorsed by the U.S. Health and Human Services Department) that utilizes "mental imaging technology" to help people who have lost their jobs get back to work in about half the average time. Visualizing success programs your mind to receive success, just as professional athletes perform better when they visualize making the shot or hitting home runs.

"The thing always happens that you really believe in,
and the belief in a thing makes it happen."

—Frank Lloyd Wright, American architect

Brain studies have shown that thoughts produce the same mental instructions to the body as actions. CAT scans have shown areas of the brain that are activated by visualization are the same as actually doing what is visualized. The consequences of visualization, both positive and negative, are apparent. It's important to control your thoughts and mental images since they influence behavior, action—and outcomes.

✓ Visualize your job interview.

✓ Visualize working in your new job.

✓ See yourself fulfilled in your career.

✓ Create a mental picture of what success looks like for you.

✓ Create a "vision board" of all the things you desire
   and want to achieve

For more reading on the subject, start with Wayne Dyer's book *Wishes Fulfilled: Mastering the Art of Manifestation* and *Creative Visualization: Use the Power of Your Imagination to Create What You Want in Your Life* by Shakti Gawain.

> *"I believe that visualization is one of the most powerful means of achieving personal goals."*
> —Harvey Mackay, author of *Dig Your Well Before You're Thirsty: The Only Networking Book You'll Ever Need*

FOCUS

> *"What you focus on expands and when you focus on the goodness in your life, you create more of it."*
> —Oprah Winfrey, author, talk-show host, life coach

There are exponentially more distractions today than just 20 years ago. So, focus is important to getting anything accomplished.

In *The Power of Focus,* a bestseller by Jack Canfield, Mark Victor Hansen, and Les Hewitt, they argue that your habits will determine your quality of life, so you must systematically revise your daily habits by eliminating bad ones and replacing them with habits that work. They also emphasize the importance of prioritizing tasks, dumping what doesn't work and delegating work so you can focus on what you naturally do best. Focus also is enhanced with a realistic, measurable, flexible plan to reach your goals.

Focus requires a singular ability to remove all distractions so that you can work on just one thing to completion. In *Deep Work: Rules for Focused Success in a Distracted World,* author Cal Newport relates how Bill Gates takes "Think Weeks" twice a year, when he isolates himself (often in a lakeside cottage) to do nothing but read and think big thoughts. It was during a 1995 Think Week that he foresaw the range of repercussions of the internet that led to much of Microsoft's ensuing success. Writers often seclude themselves for weeks at a time in order to do the deep focus required to produce their work. Mark Twain wrote *The Adventures of Tom Sawyer* in a shed located on his farm, so focused on his work that his family had to blow a horn to summon him to dinner.

In order to focus on what is important it is essential that you declutter your mind and life. Eliminate thoughts that don't serve you well, including negative thinking and media input. Master your technology so your smartphone, computer, and other devices help you accomplish tasks rather than distract you. And remove anything that distracts from your most important priorities in business and in life. Focus requires mindfulness of a deeper order.

THE POWER OF HABIT

> *"You'll never change your life until you change something you do daily. The secret of your success is found in your daily routine."*
>
> —John C. Maxwell, American author
> of *Developing the Leader Within You.*

In Robin Sharma's book, *The 5 AM Club: Own Your Morning, Elevate Your Life,* he writes that "gargantuan results are much less about your inherited genetics than about your daily habits." He posits that your morning routine determines much of what you accomplish during the rest of the day. "Take care of the front end of your day, and the rest of the day will pretty much take care of itself."

In *The Power of Habit: Why We Do What We Do in Life and Business,* author Charles Duhigg writes, "The difference between who you are and what you want to be is what you do." Is what you are doing today getting you closer to the things that are most important to your success and happiness? As Brian Tracy, motivational speaker and author of *Million Dollar Habits,* says," Successful people are simply those with successful habits."

We are what we repeatedly do. Excellence is a habit. This applies to your career as much as it does your life.

Mindful Rules: Visualize the success you want to achieve to achieve the success you visualize. Learn to focus on what is most important. Create positive habits.

Chapter 24

Your Resumé

> *"The primary purpose of a resumé*
> *is to get yourself invited for an interview."*
> —Richard Bolles, author of *What Color is Your Parachute?*

With all the attention given to resumés—and resources available to help write one—it is surprising how often they are poorly conceived. By some estimates, three out of four resumés are considered poorly written. So right from the start, most job-hunters are at a disadvantage. A well-crafted resumé will propel you ahead of your competitors.

While a resumé is seldom the only reason you will get a job, it is often your first impression. It's your calling card, and it sets in motion the cascading perceptions potential employers will have of you. And if you don't make a good first impression, you likely won't get a second chance.

> NOTE: Don't rely on your resumé alone to get a job. In the age of social media, resumés are becoming less important. Networking online (and in person) is how most jobs are found.

Your resumé is also, first and foremost, a sales document. And you are the product. Keep this in mind as you craft and refine your resumé.

Is it just reciting accomplishments or is it selling those accomplishments? Employers don't care all that much about what you've done unless it can show them what you are capable of doing for them. This is the biggest mistake that most people make on their resumés, but there are many others.

Here are common mistakes HR Directors and recruiters find on resumés:

1. **Typos.** If you don't kare enuff to make make sure your rezume is acurate how can a potential employer believe you'll be any diferent on the job? One recent survey indicated that 84% of hiring professionals toss a resumé in the trash can after spotting one or two typographical errors. Typos simply show a lack of conscientiousness and professionalism.

2. **Inappropriate email address.** OneHotSlut@gmail.com will always be viewed less favorably than EmilyAnnCandidate@gmail.com (unless, of course, you are applying for Chief Slut at XXX Productions). C'mon, if you show this much lack of common sense and mindfulness, do you really expect to get hired?

3. **Including non-job related or irrelevant information.** Most hiring executives aren't interested in your hobbies, love of kitties, abilities as a magician (although this might help in the financial services sector) or the last book you read. After reading thousands of resumés (and that's just for the job *you* applied for) HR pros learn to skim resumés and pick out only the information related to the job they are filling. Make sure that's what is on your resumé. There are exceptions to this rule, especially if your extracurricular activities demonstrate leadership or creativity.

4. **Poor structure.** You're lucky if your resumé gets read—at least every word of it. Most HR Directors and recruiters only read the first few lines or, at best, skim resumés. They know what to look for quickly. Some resumés aren't even looked at by humans (and yes, hiring managers are human, at least in theory). A computer programmed with a specific algorithm will review your resumé for keywords pertinent to the job. The best thing you can do is make your resumé easy to read and scannable. Stay away from neon-colored

paper, resumés carved in wood or pheromone-scented cover letters designed to excite the HR Director (unless you want a date with one).

5. **There's no "I" in resumé.** Keep your resumé in the accepted formal style eschewing personal pronouns. Don't say "I created a new widget that boosted sales 1500% in one year." Instead, say "Created new widget that boosted sales 1500% in one year." The place to be more personal is in your LinkedIn Profile.

6. **Boasting.** Statements like "You will never meet a widget genius like me," or "It would be impossible to find a better-qualified widget designer!" seem obnoxiously arrogant and amateurish. It's better to list honors and awards separately as simple statements. "Won 2013 Cannes Lion Gold Award for Acme Widget TV commercial that increased widget sales by 10000%," for example.

7. **Not customizing each resumé you send out.** Include the same keywords that are in the job description. Limit your resumé to only the accomplishments that pertain to the job you are seeking. Lead with your strengths. If you have a bunch of awards and commendations, consider listing them separately.

8. **weird Typefaces.** Use a typeface that is easy to read—a standard type (e.g. Times Roman or Microsoft Sans Serif) and large enough to read (usually 10–12 point).

9. **Not focusing on your achievements—and how you monetized them.** Many resumés focus incorrectly on responsibilities instead of achievements. Always write your resumé to appeal to the company's selfish interests—what you can do for them. Achieving sales growth, increasing efficiency, cutting costs or retaining a higher number of customers is much more impressive than the fact that you were a VP. Tell how your actions resulted in increased sales and then put a number to it. "Created new CAD-based Widget design program that resulted in 190% more production and $240 million in annual sales."

10. **Hiding your skills.** Put your skills up front where they will attract the attention of the hiring manager. And always lead with the skills that are most relevant to the job you are seeking.

11. **Listing references on your resumé.** In fact, don't put the common "Excellent references on request" line on your resumé either. It's assumed that you will provide references if asked.

12. **Trying to put everything on your resumé.** You may have more experience than any other person in your field of work, but don't feel obligated to put it all on your resumé. While it may seem contradictory, less is more—even in resumés. Research shows that longer resumés are read less than shorter ones. Zero in on only the golden nuggets from your career and leave out everything else. You can always talk about what else you've done during your interview.

13. **Using resumé creators.** These are difficult to work with if reformatting is needed. Make it easy to view your resumé.

14. **Failing to use bullet points** instead of long paragraphs to describe your accomplishments.

15. **Cramming too much text onto the page.** Use "white space" to make your resumé more attractive and easier to read. Declutter your resumé to create good "feng shui."

Mindful Career Rules: Your resumé is the single most important document in your job search. While a resumé won't get you a job on its own, invest the time to create one that will get an invitation to interview.

Chapter 25

Applicant Tracking Systems and Resumés

> "Research shows that you only have a 2% chance of landing an interview when you apply online."

While there's a good chance your resumé will be looked at by a human being at small and mid-sized companies, most (90%) larger firms now use applicant tracking software systems to analyze the thousands of resumés they receive. These sophisticated software programs search for keywords and phrases to match up applicants with individual job requirements. If your resumé doesn't get tagged by the ATS parameters, it will be automatically discarded. It doesn't matter if you're the next Steve Jobs. If the all-knowing (and slightly Orwellian) ATS doesn't select you as worthy, you are nothing. Your carefully crafted resumé will disappear into a computerized black hole.

It's ironic, but ATS systems work against companies finding the best people. According to headhunter Nick Corcodilos (asktheheadhunter. com), the out-of-the-box creative thinking companies claim they want is weeded out automatically. If you don't fill out a "required box," your creative thinking is rejected. Creative types are naturally square peg in a round hole people, so you see the dilemma.

Employers shoot themselves in the foot with ATS systems. They need creative thinkers. They need people who don't do the job like the last person in the job—which is what job descriptions are usually based upon.

> **ATS systems don't account for personal and social skills . . . the "soft skills" that are the most important ingredient in job success.**

What companies (and you) need to do is meet promising job candidates face-to-face, preferably in a non-interview setting, to really determine if the potential employee (or employer) is right. We once had to practically resort to hypnotism with one of our clients to get them to hire the person who we knew was right for the job—and is now in line to someday take over the company. They didn't immediately see his potential. People are multifaceted creatures with many of their best attributes often undetectable by a machine, even one powered by artificial intelligence.

ONLY 5 OF EVERY 1,000 RESUMÉS WILL MAKE IT TO THE HIRING MANAGER

Recruiters estimate that 50% of all resumés submitted for open jobs are from people who are unqualified for the position. Hence, we have the dreaded ATS system.

Since HR departments are overwhelmed by resumés from desperate job seekers, they use these systems to help them cope with the deluge. Or at least that's what they say. If you run a business the way most HR departments are run, you'd be out of business in no time. The fact is that many HR departments are staffed with people who have little or no actual business experience who like to say "no" a lot.

According to Career Confidential CEO Peggy McKee, only about 5 of every 1,000 online applications will survive the often confusing and inflexible ATS application process. And those might not result in an interview. These are some pathetic odds, resulting in millions of hours of wasted time. Even if you are the perfect candidate, there are any number of minor mishaps that can kick you out of consideration.

If you suspect your resumé will be scanned by ATS software, you'll need to dial back on the creativity in your resumé and match the requirements of the software. Our advice is to do everything in your power to circumvent the archaic hiring system by making a personal contact.

MAKE A VERSION OF YOUR RESUMÉ THAT IS KEYWORD/ATS FRIENDLY

If you can't avoid applying for a job through an applicant tracking system, one of the versions of your resumé should be keyword and ATS friendly to facilitate the requirements of the process.

Your potential value to a company must be communicated quickly by your resumé's keywords to distinguish you from all the other applicants. The ATS software will rank your resumé and depending upon how well you fare against the other job seekers, you'll either get a call or not. If the company you applied at has decided to only see the top five candidates, and you are number six in the ranking, you lose. It doesn't matter if you have a 185 IQ, graduated with honors from Stanford and Harvard, have most of the requirements of the job (and you're a natural born charismatic leader). If the other five in front of you had all that too as determined by a software program, tough luck. Your incredible leadership abilities likely weren't quantifiable by the algorithm and didn't count in your favor.

Besides keywords, there are other factors that can affect your resumé's ranking, so it's important to apply them all if you want to come out on top.

1. **KISS.** Keep any resumé you know will be reviewed by an ATS as simple as possible. Fancy colors and shading and "creative" layouts mess with the ATS algorithms and can get your resumé rejected before it even gets reviewed. Use a sans-serif type font such as Verdana, Tahoma, or Calibri. Even popular serif fonts such as Times New Roman may be too elaborate for some ATS systems.

2. **Resumé Formats.** Most ATS software is programmed to read only the reverse chronological resumé. Write the name of your employers first, followed by your title, then dates.

3. **Use bullet points.** Use concise bullet points instead of paragraphs wherever possible. They are easier to scan.

4. **Include your address.** It's popular now to show only a name, email, and phone number on resumés. But a surprising number of ATS will pass on resumés that only include this information. They may be programmed to search for a candidate who lives within a certain distance. In some cases, the employer may need to send you something in the mail. The downside is that your address can be prejudicial. Some neighborhoods and towns are seen as upscale or downscale and may reflect upon you as a person.

   Today your address is more than where you physically live, you also have "addresses" online. Besides your name, street address, city, state, zip code, and telephone numbers, include your email address and your customized LinkedIn address.

5. **Mimic the job description keywords.** It's important to customize your resumé for every job application. The best way to do this is to highlight the keywords, phrases, and qualification requirements of the job description as created by the company itself, then mimic these as closely as possible as they apply to your own experience, skills, and expertise.

6. **Keyword placement.** The placing and density of your keywords (obtained by carefully reviewing the job description and pulling the most important descriptive terms) are important in how well you score with most ATS programs. Without being obvious and heavy-handed about it, populate your top keywords into the resumé as high in the document as possible.

7. **One page or two?** There are trends in job-seeking. One recent trend that seems counter-intuitive is the single-page resumé. In recent years, job-hunters struggled to put their entire career onto one page. While this worked well for recent grads with no experience, it didn't work for people with twenty or thirty years of work history. A one-page resumé is like reading only the headlines of a newspaper. While shorter is generally preferred, two and even three-page resumés are acceptable now because companies want to see the details of your career.

8. **If your objective is to get noticed, don't use the heading "Objective."** Many ATS systems don't pick up resumés that start with "Objective." Always remember, when searching for a job, it's not about you . . .

it's about the needs of the company. Your resumé should start with "Summary" or "Profile Summary" or "Overview" and include the exact title of the position you seek.

9. **Opening Statement.** The opening statement (Overview, Summary, Profile Summary) is the most important part of your resumé. It's much like the headline in an ad; if it doesn't get noticed, the rest won't be read. Your opening statement must begin with a strong, attention-getting value proposition. In advertising, this is called the USP, the unique selling proposition. It's what summarizes what you can do for the employer, and why you are the most qualified to do it.

   The opening statement is also the place where you can add a personal branding description that highlights what makes you unique among the job applicants.

   Tailor your opening statement to the targeted job description. Include a few keywords that the ATS system can lock in on.

10. **Don't put your contact information in the headers or footers.** Your resumé likely won't get read.

11. **Qualifications, skills, and competencies.** Skills statements are picked up by the ATS software keyword search and demonstrate that you have the skills needed by the employer. Highlight the key skills in the job description from the employer and include them on your resumé (assuming you have them). These will be picked up by the ATS. Assuming you have grabbed their attention with your opening statement, this is where you back up your claims with specific skills.

12. **Backup proof statements.** Linking each skill to a successful outcome completes the value proposition. Show specific examples of how your skills translated as a clear benefit to your past employers.

13. **Experience.** Potential employers are interested in your experience only as it relates to their needs. So, keep this in mind as you describe your experience and accomplishments at each job you've held.

   Also, for ATS software to pick up this section of your resumé, it must be headed with the word EXPERIENCE. Be sure to provide an accurate description of each company. For example, instead of saying Sony, you'll need to say Sony Corporation of America. Always include the Inc., Corporation, or LLC as it applies to each company you've worked at so that the ATS software can recognize the name of your former employer.

Use what's called the Harvard Format: a brief paragraph describing your roles and responsibilities, followed by bullet point statements of results and achievements. This is an easily scannable and readable format.

Use the CAR method to format each section: the Challenge, your Actions and, in bullet points, the Results of your actions. The CAR method will drive home (pun intended) your accomplishments.

14. **Education.** You don't need to go into detail in the Education section of your resumé. Simply state the name of the educational institution, the location, your major, and degree. If you are an older worker, you may want to leave off the dates of your education to avoid age discrimination.

Career guru Marc Cenedella, Founder and Executive Chairman of the professional career site Ladders (theladders.com), goes so far as to recommend that older job seekers wipe their career history clean of anything dating back to the 20th century. "Don't list any career dates before the year 2000," he says. Of course, this would apply to your LinkedIn Profile as well. So much for having a LONG and illustrious career.

Age bias exists. And the first person to read your resumé is likely in his or her twenties. With the discrediting of experience and the rapid introduction of new technologies, most young people think that older workers aren't savvy enough and will be more of a hindrance than a help.

Sometimes ATS programs are designed to include only top educational institutions or Ivy League schools. If you didn't attend one, your resumé will be rejected automatically. A way around this is to take an online course (many are free) affiliated with one of these schools. Coursera offers courses from schools such as Yale and Wharton, for example. An online course in computer science at

MIT provides a legitimate reason to insert that school's name into your resumé. This will, at the least, get your foot in the door with companies who want to only see candidates from top schools.

Online education providers include: Coursera, FutureLearn, Edx, Udemy, Khan Academy, and Udacity. Many will allow you to place the icon of the school on your LinkedIn Profile.

15. **Affiliations.** Include only affiliations that pertain to the job you are seeking. The Acme Widget Corporation isn't impressed that you belong to the Indiana Beekeepers Association. Avoid listing political or religious organizations.

16. **Testimonials.** A third-party endorsement from someone who you've previously worked with is a powerful statement. Consider including one or two in your resumé, perhaps in the opening statement. The ideal testimonial is, of course, one from a former supervisor or client. The next best are from co-workers and direct reports.

Analyze every sentence of your resumé to determine if it supports your value proposition. Make sure it is keyword intensive. Check your grammar, spelling (SpellCheck), and punctuation (Grammarly). We know one highly-qualified person who lost out on a job because she typed 2013 as 3013. Not a big deal? Well, it was to a financial services firm, where numbers are important (a simple typo could cost millions).

Our advice is to circumvent the ATS process if possible. The odds are too great that you are simply wasting your time. It would be better to spend that time finding a way to do an end-run around the ATS system so that you go directly to the hiring manager. This is often much easier than you would guess, especially if you are fully up to speed on LinkedIn.

HOW TO SUPERCHARGE YOUR RESUMÉ

Psychologists have examined what works (and doesn't work) with employers when they review resumés of prospective hires, and here's what they found:

1. **It's important to quantify your accomplishments.** Just saying you achieved a goal isn't the same as showing how what you did created a specific sales increase (with the numbers to prove it) or how your

efforts increased revenue (with actual dollar amounts). Always frame your achievements with quantifiable results.

Example:

STRONG

"Created partnership program with key clients (e.g. Oracle, Salesforce) that increased revenue by 100% in the first six months from $2 million to $4 million.

POOR

"Created partner sales program that added new revenue to the company."

2. **Show some personality** (even oddball) in your resumé. Although we generally don't recommend it, if you're going to include Interests in your resumé, make them as interesting as possible. Everyone likes movies, sports, and travel. However, it doesn't belong on a resumé. But if you volunteered to help artificially inseminate endangered sea turtles on the Galapagos . . . you will get noticed. And if the CEO of your prospective company is a die-hard entrepreneur, a mention of your membership in a startup group will likely help move you to the head of the line of consideration.

   Interests are opportunities to show some unique personality, stand out from the crowd, or provide bonding possibilities with key hiring deciders.

3. **Show off your accomplishments.** If you were accepted for a Fulbright Scholarship, don't just mention that you were, show how many others competed for it. According to *Forbes Magazine,* psychologist Robert Cialdini, author of *Influence: The Psychology of Persuasion,* says that social proof is one of the most powerful forms of influence. Showing how you beat out significant competition powerfully demonstrates just how special your accomplishments are.

4. **Connect with an employee at the company you want to work at.** A personal relationship with a potential future colleague can be powerful. It's relatively easy to connect with someone on LinkedIn. And since LinkedIn members support each other's career goals, don't

be shy about asking your new connection to give you some feedback on your resumé as it applies to the company and position—then use that feedback to customize your resumé for the company and job. If you form a strong enough connection, that employee may even put in a good word for you with the hiring manager. At the very least, when the HR folks check your LinkedIn Profile, they will see that you are already connected to one of their employees.

5. **Namedrop.** While working with startups is popular now, nothing gets a hiring manager's attention more than Big Brand identification. A resumé that includes Google, Amazon, IDEO, and Apple (as previous/current companies you've worked at or as strategic partners) will always get more attention than unknown companies or startups. It's just how people are wired. Knowing that you worked with the top tier companies provides instant credibility and authority—even if your work was more important at a lesser known "brand." If you're trying to set yourself up for success after college, try to score an internship at one of the major brand name companies. It's an instant "foot in the door" later.

6. **Follow "The Rule of Seven."** If you've done the hard work of creating a personal brand that resonates with your values, goals, and abilities you need to convey that brand to potential employers. Do this by following the Rule of Seven. It's an old (but proven) concept known to ad agencies—customers must see an advertisement seven times before most will take action. Pepper your resumé with words, phrases, and accomplishments that reinforce your brand. If you want one or two of your strongest attributes or accomplishments to be remembered, find seven ways to communicate it in your resumé.

When looking at a prospective employer, find keywords on the company's website, annual report, or social media and include these in your resumé. This strategy is called "mirroring." It subconsciously makes the other party feel in alignment and comfortable with you. These buzzwords should also align with your own brand. And it must be authentic. If not, perhaps this isn't the right company for you.

7. **Make sure your LinkedIn Profile and resumé are in sync.** Potential employers will check both your resumé and LinkedIn Profile carefully. Be sure the information in each syncs up with the other. Any discrepancy will raise questions.

WHAT RESUMÉS AREN'T

Resumés are only a "foot in the door." It's the job seeker's calling card. A first impression. But a resumé alone will seldom land a job. To do that you need to get personal. Don't be afraid to show initiative. Find out who works at the company you want to work at and contact one or two key people (on LinkedIn it's easy; you can "follow" companies and see many of their employees). We can guarantee that 90% of the people you contact, whether you know them or not, will help you. It's a great way to find out insider information about the company and the job—which will give you an advantage over other candidates.

If this is uncomfortable for you, at least you can check out the backgrounds of the people you may be working with so that you can find some common ground when meeting them.

Follow-up on your resumé submission to ensure it gets seen. Make sure you contact the person with the authority to hire or direct the hire, even if that person is the CEO. Doing this shows you are comfortable dealing with C-level executives and immediately sets you apart from many other applicants.

Have a contact plan. Know what you are going to say in advance, even if you have to write out a rough script. Offer new information about yourself—that's not included in your resumé or cover letter—that adds more value to your qualifications.

Stand up when making the call. It will help you project more enthusiasm and energy into your voice.

SEND A HARD COPY TOO

Consider sending a hard copy of your resumé as a backup to your online submission. Yes, it's "old school," but these days you'll stand out just for doing it. And even HR Directors are human—a beautiful resumé on fine quality paper is impressive. In some places (like Silicon Valley) and industries dominated by Millennials, this might be considered déclassé or very "last century," so choose your target company wisely.

Also, an electronic resumé can print out poorly—or not at all if there's a glitch. Always email your resumé and other attachments first to a secondary email address, or the address of a friend with a different computer platform, to see how it will look to others. We like to send our candidates' resumés in both Word and PDF format, just in case.

Mindful Career Rules: Your resumé is usually your first contact with a hiring manager. It should make a good first impression so that you are invited for an interview. While it focuses on skills and experience, a great resumé also includes some information about your personality and soft skills. A carefully honed resumé is lean and efficient, easy to read, accurate, meets the requirements of ATS systems, or is customized to the company and position.

Chapter 26

The Interview

"The interview process itself is broken."

—Liz Ryan, CEO/Founder, Human Workplace,
author of *Reinvention Roadmap*

The way that interviews are conducted is one of the most unmindful areas of the hiring process. Ideally, people get to know each other after having natural conversations or doing something socially together. But the job interview has barely changed in the past 50 years. It's still frequently confrontational, akin to being grilled by the FBI instead of trying to discover if there is a mutually rewarding match of personality and skills. Also, the people interviewing you are seldom skilled at doing an interview and revert to what they think is the way it should be done. As Liz Ryan, CEO/Founder of Human Workplace, says, "It's easier to keep doing things—even pointless and destructive ones—that you have been doing forever than to stop." In other words, interviewers are often woefully stuck in the past.

But it is what it is—and you will have to learn to jump through the hoops and play the game well to reach your ultimate goal, which should be to determine if YOU want the job. Remember, although most job seekers adopt the mindset of the supplicant, trying their best to impress the interviewer, it is *you* who really holds the power in the dialogue. The company needs top talent to be successful. If you are that top talent, then you should be interviewing them to see if they are good enough for you to commit a big chunk of your life to them for the next several years. Even if you are a recent grad it's valuable to adopt the mindset that your potential value to the company is important to them, which it is.

Until things change, the job interview is where you will either be voted off the island or selected to stay. *In Fearless Resumés: The Proven Method for Getting a Great Job Fast,* author Marky Stein points out that the interview is not just important to getting the job but getting the job *well.* First impressions and the salary you negotiate follow you long after the interview. So, it's critical that you understand the interview process and master how to take advantage of it.

START BY DOING YOUR RESEARCH

You'll be ahead of most competitors for a job when you do a deep dive in researching the company and the position before you interview. Here's a handy checklist to help you prepare for your interviews and make the right decision about the company and job.

1. **Location.** Be sure the job is located where you want to work. If taking the job requires a move to a new city you must evaluate the impact of making the physical move, finding a place to live, making new friends, weather, political climate, and adjusting to the personality of the new locale (every place has its own unique style).

   If the job is local, you should determine if the commute is one you are willing to do every day. Factor in transportation costs in time (an hour a day commute adds up to a month of eight-hour days every year) and money ($5 a day in fuel cost adds up to $1,200 a year and a $6 toll or train ticket adds up to $1,440 a year).

   Also, some companies have a standalone office and others are in high-rises. Companies may be in a vibrant part of town while another may be in a suburban office park. Consider this location factor when you are weighing the desirability of a company versus your own preferences.

2. **Company culture.** Glassdoor writes, "Does the company have the free-flowing ethos of a startup, or does it hold a rigid corporate culture? Are employees treated more like peers or subordinates?" Knowing what the company culture is like and how it resonates with your personality is vitally important to your success and happiness in your new job.

    Since you will be spending at least eight hours a day, if not more, among a group of people who have evolved a definable culture, you better be comfortable with it. Ultimately, every job involves interacting with people. These people influence your opportunities and shape the person you are—and aspire to become. As Reid Hoffman of LinkedIn writes, "The fastest way to change yourself is to hang out with people who are already the way you want to be." Be mindful of who you will be working with—are these the kind of people you want to surround yourself with every day?"

    Culture varies widely from one company to another. Some are highly toxic, while others make it a joy to go to work every day. To find out as much as possible about a company's culture, check out the reviews on Glassdoor or The Muse, contact past employees (who you can find on LinkedIn), check out current employees' Instagram posts relating to the company, and be especially aware during your visits of how employees interact and how the offices are decorated. It's like going to someone's home for the first time. Do the family members show love, kindness, and respect? Is the house clean and neat—or look as if hoarders live there?

3. **Values.** Values are important. It's always a mistake to focus on salary and benefits and the job description and ignore the company culture and values. Some companies are highly successful and considered "hip" by users but are sorely lacking in values. Poor values are usually a reflection of the character of upper management that trickle down to everyone at the company.

    Ask current employees what they think about the values of their company. Look at the company's Mission Statement. Does the company have an inclusive and diverse staff, a commitment to sustainability, a track record of charitable contributions? And most important of all . . . do these values sync with your own?

4. **History.** Check out the history of the company. Are there scandals and bankruptcies? Have any of the management gotten into trouble? Conversely, does the company have achievements that are noteworthy? And finally, how has the company evolved over time?

    Does the company have work that inspires you, that you will be good at, and that can make a difference? Who will you be reporting to? Is this person someone who is an inspirational leader? Someone who mentors new team members? Is she a "catapult," a boss who can fast-forward your growth? Always remember, the person you work directly for will have an enormous influence on the success and direction of your career. People often quit jobs—about 14%— because of bad bosses (bossholes!).

5. **Finances.** Companies come and go all too quickly these days. Remember Netscape? Kodak? It pays to check out the company's financial stability and future prospects. You can start by looking at the company Annual Report, if they have one. Otherwise, do an online search for articles on the company and their products. Unless it's a startup you'll be able to quickly get an idea of the company's soundness.

6. **Competitors.** Another way to find out about the strength and viability of a company is to check out their competitors. This will also provide a broader picture of the overall market and industry in which the company competes. For example, you can learn a lot about Lyft by examining what Uber and other shared use companies are doing.

7. **Compensation.** What is the salary—including commissions, bonuses, and equity? Try to find out what this is before getting deeply involved in the discussion. It may be so low that it's a deal killer and you can save yourself a lot of time and effort. Most companies will just provide a salary range, leaving some "wiggle room" open for negotiation.

    In February 2018, LinkedIn introduced Salary Insights. Enter your job description and location and their algorithm will produce an average salary for the position, as well as a range. It's a good place to start in determining where you are in the salary discussion. This feature also appears with LinkedIn job postings and is based on data from their nearly 600 million members and employer provided information. Salary.com is another resource to determine the salary ranges in your occupation and job.

If you're working with a good recruiter, she will try to get you the top of the acceptable salary range with her client, but not more. You must remember that she is doing a delicate balancing act between the best interests of the people who are paying her fee and her candidates, always striving for a "win/win" arrangement.

8. **Benefits.** Your benefits package can make up an important part of your entire compensation package. While some benefits are non-negotiable, other benefits may be more flexible. If for example, you can't get a company to budge on the salary, perhaps more vacation time or flexible working hours can be bargained for. We structure these kinds of deals with our clients all the time.

The basic benefits these days usually include health, dental, and vision insurance. Typically, these are not up for discussion other than the plan you choose. Some companies pay the entire amount for you and your family, others just you. 401k plans are often included, but these vary widely in quality. The best 401k plans include a company match of funding. Vacation time is often flexible . . . how much, when it is available, and what the future allocation will be.

Fun perks such as yoga classes, dog-friendly offices, company outings, free meals, employee discounts, and health club memberships are often available too. If these things are important to you, then include them in your overall evaluation of the benefits package.

Your total benefits package can add up to a significant amount of money, so always factor it into your compensation package.

9. **Hours.** These days Americans are being asked to work longer hours than they signed up for when accepting a job. Try to get an idea of how the company views this. Are they going to expect you to work 60-hour work weeks? Is there any flexibility? Will you be compensated? Can you work from home sometimes? Will you be expected to always be available, even during your off hours?

10. **Your role at the company.** What will you be doing? Will you supervise others? How important is the role to the company? Is it a high-visibility job? Who do you report to? A poor manager is the #1 reason people leave a company. What are the long-term prospects for your position?

11. **What does the company do?** Amazingly, a survey of CEOs found that 47% of job candidates had little or no knowledge of their company. It's hard to believe that anyone would apply for a job without knowing what the company does.

    What product or service does the company produce? And do you care about it? The most satisfied employees are those who work for a company that is producing something that makes our world a better place, working with people they respect, who are guided by a mindful vision of the organization's cultural relevance.

A FEW TIPS FOR A SUCCESSFUL INTERVIEW

Be prepared to address any qualification or expertise needed in the job description. Know what you are going to say before the question is asked. "Winging" it just doesn't fly in the crowded airspace of 21st century employment.

Here are some tips for a successful interview:

- Don't say "generic" things about yourself. Always link comments to the job in some way. It's important to reinforce how you would add value to the company. If asked to describe yourself (a favorite interview question), tell how you are by nature a creative or energetic or organized person and then tell a story about how this admirable trait helped you increase the Acme Widget Corporation's sales by 1000% (just an example, don't actually say this).

- People who listen well are judged more positively than those who speak well. Focus on truly hearing what the interviewer is saying, not what you intend to say next. Studies show that people only retain 50% of what they hear. In an interview, this could be disastrous. Your interviewer is likely providing many pieces of information that are important for you to respond to correctly. So, listen intently and ask clarification questions, if necessary, so that you understand completely what is being said to you. Take notes.

- Don't feel as if you need to respond immediately. Take a moment to gather your thoughts . . . it shows respect for what the interviewer has said and indicates that you are giving some thought to it. Most importantly, if the interviewer wants to talk a lot . . . let her. In fact, encourage her to talk. Don't, under any circumstances, take up more than 60% of the conversation load.

- In *Just Listen: Discovering the Secret to Getting Through to Anyone*, author Mark Goulston advises putting yourself in the other's shoes during a conversation. You'll be surprised at how the barriers to communication come tumbling down. Another tip from his book is to put PEP in your conversation: passion, enthusiasm, and pride.

- Don't talk about your woes. Maybe you're down to your last pennies, there's an eviction notice tacked to your door, and you're on food stamps, but do your best to channel Jeff Bezos instead. Be confident, positive, and upbeat.

- Keep negativity out of the conversation. Even if your last boss was Donald Trump, don't talk trash about any of your previous employers or colleagues.

- Ask smart questions. This means you will need to do some research on the company you are interviewing at (always a good idea). The stories HR managers tell about candidates who knew little or nothing about their company are incredible. One HR director told us about a candidate who thought he was interviewing for another company. When informed of his error he replied, "Hmmm. Well, do you have any jobs for someone like me?" Not likely.

- Always have a question or two prepared to ask when the interviewer inevitably asks, "Do you have any questions we can answer for you?" If you say no your chances of the interview ending well go down substantially.

- Don't get caught not knowing something on your resumé, especially dates.

Preparing for the interview will increase your confidence and performance. Here's a last-minute checklist:

THE MORNING OF THE INTERVIEW

✓ On the morning of your interview, eat a light nutritious breakfast and limit your caffeine intake to one or two cups. Chances are you will be feeling a little jittery about the interview, so don't exacerbate the problem with too much coffee.

✓ If possible, call a friend for a quick conversation, preferably someone upbeat and positive. It will prep you for having a conversation later in the interview, much like singers practice their scales prior to a concert.

✓ Some people like to run or walk in the morning to get the juices flowing.

✓ Arrive at the interview ten minutes in advance.

✓ Bring a slim black leather portfolio, a pen, and an extra copy of your resumé.

✓ Take a small bag with a mirror, makeup, mints.

✓ Use the restroom prior to the interview. Check your appearance.

✓ Pump up your energy and enthusiasm level. Some people find energetic music helps, others strike a pose (hands on hips, legs spread, or arms upraised Rocky-style has been shown to create a temporary boost in testosterone and confidence). Just don't do this in the reception area.

✓ Be sure to bring a water bottle so you stay hydrated. When you get to the interview, accept any drink offered to you by the receptionist.

✓ Immediately before entering the interview take a few deep breaths and exhale slowly. Deep breathing can ease your anxiety.

✓ Finally, smile. The simple act of smiling ups your serotonin levels and puts you in a more positive mood.

It's important to remember that job interviews are about what you can do for the company—and what they can do for you. Think of it as a first date. If all you talk about is how wonderful you are to impress your date, don't expect a second date. It's the same with interviewing.

THE FIRST IMPRESSION LASTS

> According to Stanford Graduate School of Business Professor Deborah Gruenfeld, research shows that "people decide how competent you are in 100 milliseconds."

Always remember that your first impression is likely the one that will last. Numerous research studies have proven that most people make up their minds about someone within the first five seconds of meeting. What's just as interesting is that in about 90% of the cases the first impression later held up as being accurate.

OPENING REMARKS

Stride into the interview room confidently. Smile. Shake hands firmly (but not bone-crushing). Say something brief like "It's nice to finally meet you in person." Take a seat with your legs uncrossed, shoulders back.

Now you are ready.

If you are comfortable with it, engage in a little light opening conversation. Avoid potentially harmful comments like "Boy, the Widget Corporation makes the last place I worked at look like a Siberian work camp." If you've done your homework you could say, "Mr. Roberts, thank you for seeing me today. I realize how busy everyone must be with the introduction of the Super Widget." This is a nice lead-in to an opening conversation and demonstrates you've done your homework about their company.

If you have a chance to scan the room quickly, you can often pick up on a common area of interest to establish a personal rapport. If the interviewer has a photo on the wall showing him during his glory days playing football at Stanford, this could provide an opening. If you also went to Stanford or played football, a comment like, "I noticed you played football at Stanford? Why that's where I got my Ph.D. in widget design." You've just scored an interview touchdown. If you were also a halfback at Stanford, start thinking about your office decorations.

Of course, you should have already done a significant amount of background research on every person who will be interviewing you using internet search resources such as a Google search, the company directory and website, LinkedIn, and Facebook. You want to know as much as possible about who you meet. We like to know where people grew up, who they are married to, where they live, how much they make, the schools they attended, hobbies and interests, and where they have worked previously. It's probably the kind of research they will do on you, so be sure to level the playing field. By doing that kind of in-depth research, you'll feel more in control of wherever the interview process takes you.

PERCEPTION IS YOUR REALITY

"Chemistry is a huge factor in deciding who gets the job."
—Kenneth A. Heinzel, author of *Private Notes of a Headhunter:*
Proven Job Search and Interviewing Techniques
for College Students and Recent Grads

An interesting finding from Stanford research is the proportionate weight three key variables play in how you will be perceived.

1. The factor that influences your perception the *least* is words. Just 7% of the impression you make is a result of what you say and how you say it.

2. Presentation. How you look, dress, and carry yourself makes up 38% of your first impression.

3. And surprisingly, 55% of how competent you are perceived is a result of body language. Body language communicates non-verbally your power, status, and how approachable you may be.

A 2010 survey of 2,500 hiring managers discovered that many job applicants blow their interview with poor body language. This finding was also supported in a survey of 2,000 CEOs in 2011. Here is what they said helped doom a job candidate.

- ✓ 33% said they knew in the first 90 seconds if they would hire a job candidate by their presence, style, and personality—their first impression.

- ✓ 67% failed to make eye contact.

- ✓ 47% had little knowledge of the company.

- ✓ 38% didn't smile.

- ✓ 33% fidgeted.

- ✓ 33% had noticeably poor posture.

- ✓ 26% had a weak handshake.

- ✓ 21% crossed their arms over their chest.

- ✓ 21% played with their hair.

You'll also be judged quickly on weight, beauty, fingernails, height . . . even your hairstyle!

Hiring managers also say these things have an impact on your first impression:

- ✓ 70% say they don't want job applicants to be "overly fashionable" or "trendy" in how they dress.

- ✓ 65% say the way a person is dressed can be a deciding factor between two equally-qualified candidates.

The bottom-line is this: Likability is the #1 reason why you will get hired . . . or not. And being likeable is a combination of several things, most of which you can control.

TOP INTERVIEW MISTAKES

1. Over-explaining why you left your last job

2. Showing that you aren't over your last job

3. Exaggerating or "massaging" the truth

4. Lacking humor

5. A lack of enthusiasm or interest

6. A weak handshake

7. Inadequate knowledge of the company

8. Concentrating too much on what you want and not what you can do for the company

9. Trying to be all things to all people

10. "Winging it" in the interview

11. Not asking questions during and at the end of the interview

12. Failing to set yourself apart from other candidates for the job

13. Failing to ask for the job

14. Asking about what perks are available

15. Asking about salary in the first interview

16. Name dropping

17. Criticizing former companies, bosses, or colleagues

18. Airing personal problems

19. Dressing inappropriately

20. Poor personal hygiene

21. Wearing too much perfume/cologne and makeup

22. Bringing a phone to the interview

23. Being late

24. Fidgeting

25. Poor body language

26. Avoiding eye contact

THE MOST COMMON QUESTIONS ASKED IN A JOB INTERVIEW

1. **Tell me about yourself.** If you only prepare for one question, then this is the one you want to ace. 80% of all interviews start out with this deceptively innocent question. If you are not prepared to answer it well, you will likely fail to go any further in the hiring process.

   This question is a favorite with interviewers. It's open-ended and allows the interviewer to get some early insights into your personality. It shows how well and succinctly you organize your thoughts. And it provides some clues about how well you would fit into the company organization.

   Best Answer Strategy: First, be sure to do your due diligence on the company, industry, competition, job qualifications, and the needs of the person you will be working for. Start by summarizing your career highlights and accomplishments. saying why you are well-qualified for the job. Match up your expertise with the job description as best you can. Remember, they are the buyer and you are the seller. You must be what they want to buy.

   It's usually good to weave into your answer some personal information, including outside interests. If they relate to the job, all the better. Keep anything that might throw you off track out of your answer. "I like breeding cobras in my spare time" won't score you any points, unless the CEO breeds them too. "I mentor kids from broken homes about finances and healthy living" is good.

   Ask for a fuller description of what the position entails and their expectations for it. You could say, "I've been fortunate enough to have a number of accomplishments in my career that I can tell you about, but first would you mind telling me more about the expectations for this position?" Once you understand more completely what they are looking for you can tailor your response accordingly. Telling a story or two that speaks to your career path, successes, responsibilities, and what you've learned in the past 5–10 years is the most effective way to tell the interviewer about yourself.

2. **Why should we hire you?** Here's where you want to have your personal sales pitch prepared and rehearsed. First, demonstrate that you have done your homework about their company, products, and competitors. If you've identified a clear challenge the company faces, bring that up with a couple of initial thoughts about how to address it. You can't answer incorrectly here because the interviewer knows that you don't have a total picture of the problem. But the fact that you see it—and have some creative ideas about how to solve it—will win points.

   Be sure to talk about how you can fulfill the responsibilities of the job. Try to identify the most urgent job requirements and address those. But don't ramble; keep it under two minutes. And never speak negatively about your former (or current) employer.

3. **Tell me about a challenge/success/failure and how you handled it.** Hopefully, the question will be about a success and not a failure you have experienced. In this case, you want to describe what you did to create the success (but don't leave out the contributions of others—you want to be seen as a leader or team player). Be specific and measurable. Make it a story with a beginning, a middle, and a successful ending. And keep it brief.

   Describing a failure is much harder. Despite all the popular talk about how great failure is for your personal development (fail fast, fail forward!), failure still reeks of, well, failure, to many people. If you're describing how you screwed up and took down the most important division of the company with an ill-conceived marketing program, it won't matter how much you learned from the experience . . . no company wants a loser on their team. The best answer is to simply say "I've been fortunate in my career. So far I haven't had that life lesson . . . and I hope I never will!"

4. **What are your greatest strengths/weaknesses?** This is always a tough one. Don't make the mistake of framing a strength as a weakness to make yourself look good. "I'm such a dedicated worker that sometimes I just can't leave the office." The interviewer will see right through it.

   Answering this question mindfully is where emotional intelligence comes into play. As we explored earlier in this book, emotional intelligence is a by-product of self-awareness, which is achieved through honest and thorough introspection, self-reflection, and critical thinking. This isn't so easy for most people in a world that values quick (and often thoughtless) responses to serious issues.

If you have identified through thoughtful examination of yourself and your past actions that you are a people pleaser (we're in that category), you could tell the interviewer about times when this trait has harmed you, like the time you weren't tough enough in a negotiation and paid more as a result. Explain the actions you take now to overcome this trait with specific examples of how it applies in your current work interactions.

You're admitting you aren't perfect (who is?) and showing how your applied emotional intelligence resulted in a successful outcome. A thoughtful and sincere answer like this, combined with examples of how you have overcome this weakness, will be remembered by the interviewer.

If you haven't yet done the inner work to answer this question mindfully, pick something that is genuine and that you are working to improve such as, "I am not satisfied with my organizational abilities. But I recently implemented a new time and task organizational tool that is really helping me prioritize and stay on task. I can see the results already in improved production and less wasted time."

5. **Why do you want to work for us?** This is an important question, and we've seen otherwise excellent candidates blow their chances by answering poorly.

    Demonstrate that you have researched their company, products/ services, market sector, and competition. Talk about how your career goals fit with the company's mission. If you use their product, speak about how much you like it.

    In a job interview for a public relations job with LinkedIn you could say, "I was an early adopter of LinkedIn and use it every day. I feel like I really understand the company and its mission. My 15 years of experience working in public relations, especially my years working at startups, is an ideal background for the PR Manager position. From what I know, I think I can contribute to LinkedIn's continued success as well as fit the culture of the company." This answer wraps up all the important questions and puts a bow on it.

Some other typical questions:

1. What motivates you?

2. Where would you like to be in five years?

3. Aren't you overqualified for this position?

4. Why have you been out of work so long?

5. Tell me about the strengths and weaknesses of your boss.

6. Tell me about a situation where your work was criticized?

7. Here is our biggest challenge. How would you address it?

8. What makes you angry?

9. How do you feel about reporting to a younger person (woman, minority)?

10. Why aren't you earning more money at this point in your career?

11. Why have you had so many jobs?

12. What are your salary expectations?

13. Is there anything you would like to ask us?

Thinking of answers to these typical questions will have the added benefit of consolidating your own thoughts about the job and company.

THE IMPORTANCE OF "SOFT" SKILLS

"Soft" skills and emotional intelligence are increasingly becoming important to companies as they realize that these attributes often determine the long-term success and viability of an employee. Emotional intelligence also impacts company culture. So, you may encounter questions specifically designed to determine your EI strengths and soft skills such as these:

1. **Who inspires you and why?** This provides a clue to who you pattern yourself after and the role models you emulate.

2. **If this was your company, what top three values would you instill in it?** This question can tell the interviewer a lot about your priorities.

3. **Did you build lasting relationships while working at your previous companies?** Building long-term relationships with colleagues show that you care about people more than just being a cog in a company wheel.

4. **Can you teach me something that I probably don't know?** The candidate who takes time to consider this question and answer it forthrightly and intelligently can make a memorable impact during the interview.

5. **What are the top three reasons for your success?** With this question, it's wise to remember that there is no "I" in team. Companies look for team players.

6. **What motivates you to come to work every day?** Companies are looking for people who are passionate about what they do, have an endless curiosity to learn more, and like working with other people to solve problems. Frame your answer in this context, if you can.

7. **From what you know about our company, what do you like and dislike about our business? How would you promote what you like? How would you change what you don't like?** This question is asked more frequently these days because it reveals several important clues to how you would work and fit in with the culture of the organization. You'll want to talk about solutions. If you prepare for and answer this one well, it could be the clincher that gets you the job.

8. **Which book are you reading currently?** We've heard poor advice from HR pros who say you should only talk about a book that relates to improving your skills. But that paints you as a one-dimensional person. We think the best response is to say something like, "Well, I'm currently reading two books, *Work Rules,* a fascinating look at how insights from Google can transform how you work and lead, and I'm re-reading *Heart of Darkness* by Joseph Conrad. It's amazing how differently you interpret Conrad's message at this age compared to when I was in college." This shows you are a well-rounded person.

9. **What is the one thing you've accomplished in your career that you are most proud of . . . and why?** We've been asked this question ourselves from time to time when pitching for new clients or interviewing for a job. Answer this one well and the job is probably yours.

Of course, there is an infinite number of questions you could be asked. It's almost impossible to remember intelligent answers to them all. The best course of action is to prepare diligently. Don't try to "wing it" or you may blow a terrific career opportunity.

Keep in mind that every answer should relate back to the job description and show how you can fill the position successfully. For more information, read *301 Smart Answers to Tough Interview Questions* by Vicki Oliver or *101 Answers to the Toughest Interview Questions* by Ron Fry.

Also, critically important is your enthusiasm for the job. It's generally a mistake to be coy during an interview and play "hard to get." We have seen many CEO's and hiring executives choose the candidate who demonstrated he or she wanted the job the most. Enthusiasm goes a long way.

QUESTIONS TO ASK IN A JOB INTERVIEW

Most hiring managers are simply looking for a combination of skills, experience, and "cultural" fit. They have one goal—to choose the best match from a field of applicants. To get hired, your job is to make this process easy for them. Remember, their job is on the line if they screw up. A bad choice could cost their company tens of thousands of dollars.

It's safer for the hiring manager to reject candidates than to take a chance on one. So, try to look at the process through their eyes and make their job easier. Look for the win/win resolution. The mindful course of action is for either party to walk away from a deal if it isn't right for one of them.

John Kador, author of *201 Best Questions to Ask on Your Interview,* says because of the internet, there's really no reason to ask questions about the company. You should already know. It's better to put into the form of questions statements about who you are and what you can do. This is the way to advance your value as an employee.

If you ask questions, they should relate directly to your job performance at Acme Widget. In Inc. magazine, columnist Jeff Haden lists three questions great job candidates ask.

1. **What do you expect me to accomplish in the next 60 to 90 days?** It shows you want to hit the ground running . . . and that they won't have to invest months in training you while you get up to speed.

2. **What are the common attributes of your top performers?** The answer will help you determine if you're a good fit, and let the company know you intend to be a top performer.

3. **What are a few things that drive results for the company?** Great employees are those who know they must help their company succeed. Asking this question lets the interviewer know that you will contribute much more to their bottom-line than they are paying you (which makes them very happy).

Frame the questions you ask in ways that demonstrate that you are a serious candidate who wants to drill down to what it will take to help their company succeed. Next, transition your questions so they promote your strengths in the context of how you are valuable to the company.

"What are some of the problems the company needs to solve in this position?"

"By what criteria will you select the ideal candidate for this position?"

"In my last assignment, I supervised 20 people. How would this skill translate to the requirements of this position?"

Questions like these put you in control of the interview—now you are asking the questions and the interviewer is responding with important information that will help you determine how to frame your responses. When you get close to an offer, and you know you want the job, begin pressing for a positive response.

"Is there anything standing in the way of us coming to an agreement?"

"This position sounds like what I'd like to do. Is there a fit here?"

"I'm very interested in this position and I realize your support is the key to getting it. Do I have your endorsement?"

For many job seekers, these questions may seem too bold and aggressive. But if there are two candidates equally qualified for the job and one asks great questions and the other doesn't, or one asks for the job and the other doesn't, who would you choose if you were the interviewer?

TAKE NOTES

> *"I take notes like some people take drugs.*
> *There is an eight-foot stretch of shelves in my house*
> *containing nothing but full notebooks."*
> —Tim Ferriss, author of *The 4-Hour Workweek*

Throughout the hiring process—and especially during the interview—be sure to take notes. It's very easy to overlook or forget important details, especially during live interviews, because your mind is working so feverishly to say the right things and make a good impression. Note taking during an interview, done judiciously, can show you are listening actively.

Note-taking and journaling are two often overlooked processes that can make a significant difference in your life over time. When you keep a journal, you can go back to conversations or actions you took from years ago and refresh your memory of the event. It's always impressive during a conversation when you can say, "Remember when we agreed on May 3 last year, it was a Thursday, on the Furbisher expansion project? Furbisher said if we got back to him in a year, we could begin a discussion about working together on the new infrastructure project in Oakland. Then you said . . ." You'll look like a genius. In an extended job interview process your notes can be invaluable in later discussions.

Journaling also enables you to think out over time about your goals, thoughts on your life and its journey, and ideas you may want to follow up on. Tim Ferriss attributes much of his career success in life to journaling. There's magic in putting your thoughts down on paper (or in a computer file).

QUESTIONS TO ASK YOURSELF AFTER THE INTERVIEW

Before you proceed further in the interview process, ask yourself what you have learned, do you want the job, and do you like the company.

Ask yourself:

1. Does my experience and personality mesh with the job and company culture?

2. Is this work I feel good about—is it worthwhile and meaningful to me?

3. Can I show up for work every day with my whole authentic self?

4. Is there a viable future for me at this company in this position?

It's easy to get caught up in the excitement of the interviewing process and neglect to ask yourself these important questions.

PRACTICE MAKES PERFECT

Ask a friend to do a practice interview, with typical questions. If possible, video yourself so you can check your voice, posture, diction, and answers so you can smooth out your delivery and responses.

Or you can check out one of the online job interview simulators. Here are a few sites and apps: Interview4, Interview Simulation, InterviewStream Prep, Monster.com Interviews (on iTunes), or My Interview Simulator. We guarantee taking this step will improve your interview 100%.

THE PHONE INTERVIEW

These days the face-to-face interview is often preceded by a phone interview or a teleconference via Skype or Zoom. We aren't fans of the phone interview since it's a poor substitute for meeting with someone in person and often leads to great candidates being overlooked. And we don't like Skype interviews either. Only the truly genetically blessed look good on Skype. But until companies realize this and find another way to sift through the hundreds of resumés they receive for job openings (working with a competent recruiter would be one way . . . hint, hint) then you must prepare to get through it as best you can.

Our firm meets personally with most candidates, but often this simply isn't possible. So, we conduct phone interviews several times a week. We also use either Facetime or Zoom to conduct online interviews.

Here are a few tips to survive this round of the hiring process.

1. **Research the company, its products/services, the industry, and the competition.** There's no substitute for preparation. If you do your homework diligently, you'll be able to ask intelligent questions, relate your expertise and accomplishments to the qualifications of the position and goals of the company, and feel more confident. Keep the focus of your conversation on the employer and what you can do for them. Keep notes at hand you can refer to during the call.

2. **Make sure the place you conduct your phone interview is a good environment.** I once tried to do a phone interview from my car. While it wasn't in motion, the distractions of passersby, nearby road noise, and fumbling for my notes on the front seat led to a less than stellar conversation. I didn't get past the phone interview.

   I also blew an interview with a top consumer products company in a Skype conversation. I could see what I looked like on my laptop screen . . . and it wasn't flattering. More like the creature from the black lagoon. It didn't do much for my self-confidence. And I didn't get any further with that company either.

   If you must do a video interview make sure you look your best, the lighting is good, the background is neutral (or at least attractive), and you know how to use Skype, Zoom, or Facetime to your best advantage.

   During a phone interview find a quiet place where you won't be distracted, your voice will be heard clearly, and you can spread out all your notes for easy access. Keep a copy of your resumé and the job description in view. If possible, you should have your computer up and running with the company website online or the person's LinkedIn Profile to view (it makes it easier to "see" who you are speaking with). And keep a glass of water nearby (in case you get nervous dry mouth).

3. **Pump yourself up.** There's solid research that if you precede your interview with a few moments of power posing (e.g. arms outstretched in a "Rocky" pose), take some deep breaths or a brisk walk (before the interview, not during), smile while you're talking, and stand rather than sit, you'll sound more authoritative and confident. One person

I know plays the *William Tell Overture* (the Lone Ranger theme) to get fired up before making important phone calls. Amy Cuddy, Harvard Business School professor and author of *Presence: Bringing Your Boldest Self to Your Biggest Challenges*, gave a now famous TED Talk about the benefits of power posing to make you feel confident. She posits that our power poses create a "self-nudge" that activates a more confident mindset. Her advice is to study and mimic the body language of powerful, confident people. Hey, it can't hurt.

4. **Make a memorable impression.** Being prepared and speaking confidently will by themselves likely set you apart from the other terrible phone interviews. But if you can find a way to leave the interviewer with something they can't forget (something memorable *and* positive—not that you just graduated from your prison work release program) you'll rise to the top of the candidate list. And don't forget to smile!

5. **Make sure the interviewer knows you are the right person for the job.** A former boss from when I worked in the advertising business told me how to sell people: "Tell them what you're going to tell them. Tell them. Tell them what you told them. Tell them again." People tend to not listen, forget, or have memory spans measured in seconds.

   Match your key qualifications with those of the job. Align your professional style with the company culture. And let them know in no uncertain terms that you can do the job the way they want it to be done. Repeat until successful.

6. **Let them know you are very interested in the job.** Don't be wishy-washy, aloof or ambivalent about the job. While you don't want to seem overeager, especially in your initial interview, you also want to show some enthusiasm and genuine interest in the position. It's a fine line to walk, but keep in mind that if you err on the side of showing clearly that you want the job, it might not be an error at all.

7. **Send a thank you note.** A thank you note is often overlooked at the phone interview stage. But you'll show class, thoughtfulness, and set yourself apart by sending one. We recommend sending both an email thank you and a snail mail card. The email will arrive immediately, so if the company decides to pare down the candidate list right away at

least they have your thank you to consider. If the process takes longer, then your card will arrive in the mail a few days after the interview and you simply have a second opportunity to make an impression. Send a handwritten thank you card. Keep it brief. Reiterate your interest in the company and job. And add an important reason why you are a prime candidate for the position.

Of course, as we've said previously, all these points apply to the personal interview as well.

THE PERFECT THANK YOU LETTER AFTER THE INTERVIEW

> *"Over 75% of candidates do not send a thank you note after an interview. And for 30% of those, no follow up meant no further steps for the candidate."*
>
> —Amy Segelin, President/Owner of Chaloner,
> an executive search firm, in *Fortune*

BusinessInsider.com ran a post by Dr. Deborah Good about the ideal interview "thank-you" letter that is worth repeating (with a few additions by the authors).

Dear Ms. NAME,

I want to take a moment to thank you again for the time you spent with me this afternoon discussing the (JOB TITLE) position. Interviews can be stressful, so I am grateful for how comfortable you made me feel throughout the process, and how professionally you conducted the interview. Your willingness to provide me with additional information about the position convinces me that I would enjoy working for (COMPANY), as well as my ability to be successful and make a valuable contribution.

- Next add a comment about something specific you learned, such as "It was helpful to understand how your compensations assistant duties are similar to tasks I fulfilled during my tenure at (NAME OF PREVIOUS COMPANY).

- Then add a note that likely wasn't discussed that would add to your qualifications, such as "As a native of (TOWN), the opportunity to work close to home is exciting to me."

You mentioned that a decision will be made next week. I look forward to hearing from you. In the meantime, if there is any additional information you need from me, I'll be happy to promptly provide it to you.

Sincerely,

Jane Doe (PUT YOUR REAL NAME HERE)

There are any number of permutations of this kind of follow-up letter. Just be sure it is attention-getting, professional in tone, direct, polite, helpful—and includes some additional information about why the company should hire you.

DARWINIAN JOB INTERVIEW BLUNDERS

Interviewer: "Why did you leave your last job?"

Job Applicant: "It was something my boss said."

Interviewer: "What did he say?"

Job Applicant: "You're fired!"

Time for a few minutes of comic relief. Here are some of the world's dumbest interviewees. If you recognize yourself in any of these—well, thank God McDonald's is still hiring.

- The well-dressed, attractive job candidate who—in mid-interview— jumped up and ran out, realizing she was at the wrong company.

- The candidate who asked me to hurry up because she left her child in the car. Wow! Hey, it was only 97 degrees outside. Call 911!!

- The guy who brought his mother to the interview to negotiate salary (she was good too).

Here are a couple from former HR Manager and career advisor Liz Ryan, writing for Bloomberg News.

- The applicant took a drink of water, swished it around in his mouth and then spit into a plant sitting on the hiring manager's desk. The bad news is the manager ended the interview then and there. The good news is that the manager didn't have to water his plant that day.

- During a phone interview, the manager heard the distinct sound of a toilet flushing and couldn't stop himself from asking the applicant if he had just done his business. The applicant replied, "Yeah, Dude." Talk about a crappy interview.

And finally, these classics.

- The applicant challenged me to arm wrestle for the job.

- The job applicant announced she was starving and hadn't eaten lunch, then proceeded to eat a hamburger and fries in the HR Director's office.

- The candidate stretched out on the floor to fill out the job application.

- One guy forgot to wear dark socks with his suit, so he colored his ankles with a black felt-tip marker. At least give him credit for being resourceful.

- When I asked the applicant what person they would most like to meet, living or dead, her response was, "The living one."

Ever hurd of spel-chek?

- We had a job applicant whose resumé said he was looking for *"a party-time position with potential for advancement."*

- Another said, *"I am a perfectionist and rarely if if ever miss anny details."* This must have been one of those rare times.

- Still, another said he was *"instrumental in ruining an entire operation for a midwest chain store."* Did he work for Sears?

- One self-employed person promoted himself to President within two years, which was a company record he said. He must be a graduate of Trump University.

- Another listed his qualifications as *"I have guts, drive, ambition, and heart, which is probably more than a lot of the drones you have working for you.*" Give him a couple points for being honest about his feelings.

- Yet another listed the reason for leaving her last job: *"Maturity leave."* Duly noted.

- One of our most embarrassing moments happened when a candidate we recommended used the word "motherf%#*er" during his job interview. Thankfully, our client had a sense of humor about it. But the job candidate didn't get a second interview. Just two weeks after this incident another job candidate dropped the "F Bomb" several times during an interview. She didn't get the job either.

NOTE: it may be trendy now among young people to frequently use the "F" word, but it is still considered declassé to use it during a job interview. This applies to your social media posts too (More than 80% of recruiters and 1/3 of companies review a job candidate's social media). Most have rejected job candidates based on what they found.

It's hard enough to get a job if you have it all together. Don't blow it by making dumb mistakes. Be mindful.

"GHOSTS" CAN BE SCARY

"Ghosting" is a practice recruiters and companies are encountering more often now than ever before. If you're not familiar with the term, it refers to job candidates who begin a conversation about a new position but then simply vanish without any explanation. In dating, it's the guy or gal who goes out with you a couple of times and then doesn't respond to calls or texts and simply vanishes, never to be heard from again. Nearly every recruiter has been "ghosted" a few times. It can be infuriating.

Even worse is a new hire who accepts a position and doesn't show up for work or walks out after a few days on the job without informing anyone they aren't returning. Ghosting is not mindful and it's not helpful to your career to engage in it.

Besides being rude, people who ghost recruiters or companies get a reputation for unprofessional conduct, narcissistic behavior, and flakiness that can follow them for years. With all the communication channels now available to anyone, it's easy for word to spread about your character and behavior.

If you are speaking with a recruiter, have the courtesy, mindfulness, and maturity to continue the conversation to a logical conclusion. If you aren't interested in a job opportunity, simply say so. If you agree to follow-up in some way, do it. Or tell the recruiter why you aren't going to go further in the process. Be honest and authentic.

If you are interviewing for other jobs or working with another recruiter, say so. Recruiters have learned (the hard way) to always begin a conversation with an active job candidate with "Has anything changed since we last spoke?" They have been "played" by far too many job candidates who weren't mindful in the process and hid critical information.

Don't use the recruiter to leverage a better negotiating position with another company you are interviewing with (but conveniently forgot to mention). Recruiters work long hours and invest in expensive software and marketing to find and place top talent for their clients. Wasting their time is the same as stealing. Plus, they have carefully cultivated relationships with their clients that your despicable behavior may jeopardize.

You may never know when someone you interact with will return in the future and be influential in your life. Therefore, always treating everyone the way you would want them to treat you is smart.

Mindful Career Rules: The interview is critically important. Carefully review the questions you may be asked. Prepare questions for the interviewers you would like answered. Take notes. Take a moment to ask yourself if the job and company is right for you.

Don't make dumb mistakes. Be smart, authentic, mindful, and respectful with everyone involved in your job interview process. NEVER "ghost" a recruiter or employer.

Chapter 27

Negotiating Salary

> *"Most companies will be impressed if you negotiate."*
>
> —Salary.com

For many people, negotiating a salary is the most difficult part of the hiring process. No one wants to screw up a job offer, and fear of doing that keeps many new hires from getting the best compensation deal. So, nearly 1 in 5 don't negotiate at all when discussing a potential new job. Remember, you're going to have to live with the deal you make for some time; better to start off with a good deal.

A 2013 study in the *Journal of Organizational Behavior* determined that not negotiating a strong initial job offer could mean missing out on as much as $634,000 in salary over the course of a 40-year career. According to a CareerBuilder survey, 41% of all applicants make this mistake during their career.

- ✓ 73% of employers are willing to negotiate on salary, but 44% of job seekers don't ask for more.

- ✓ If a company really wants you, they will be willing to pay fair market value. If they aren't willing to do so, then perhaps this isn't the company or the job for you.

If you want to find out what the value of your intended position is, and what the company pays, you may be able to find this information at (glassdoor.com), (salary.com), or (payscale.com). LinkedIn also recently added salary information. These sites provide information on salary ranges for a variety of jobs in various industries and even at specific companies. Armed with this information, you are in a better position to bargain for an appropriate salary.

If you've gotten this far, they probably want to hire you and a little money won't stop them. Asking for more money might even make you more attractive as a candidate; it shows you aren't desperate like 90% of the others (even if you are). Psychologically, it makes you a more appealing candidate because human nature wants what it can't have easily. Start your salary negotiation on the high end of your pay range. You can always come down, but it's not so easy getting more once you've stated your price.

Remember, recruiters and hiring managers expect you to counter their salary offer. In a 2019 *Inc.* magazine article, speaker and coach Karen Catlin advises job seekers to use this one-sentence tactic to secure both a higher salary and the job: "If you can get me X, I'll accept the offer right away." This shows you really want the job, and it gives the hiring manager something tangible to respond to. It eliminates the back-and-forth salary discussion, shows confidence, and it demonstrates enthusiasm for the job and company. Depending on the position, you're safe to ask for between 5% and 10% more than the initial offer. If the salary is fixed, as it is with some companies, ask for some other added compensation such as an extra week of paid vacation or a promise of a salary review after six months.

Another effective salary negotiation tactic is to let the hiring manager know you have a couple of other potential offers (or are interviewing at other companies). This can help move the negotiation process along faster, especially if you are speaking with one of their competitors. Of course, to be mindful, you must actually be in discussions with other companies. Beginning a relationship with a lie is never a good idea.

There are dozens of books on the art of negotiating, but the core of negotiation is presenting overwhelming evidence of why you are so damn valuable to the company that what you are asking for in compensation seems to be a bargain any fool would take. Hiring is always a value proposition for a company. Two recommended books are *Negotiating Your Salary: How to Make $1,000 a Minute* by Jack Chapman, and *Salary Tutor: Learn the Salary Negotiation Secrets No One Ever Taught You* by Jim Hopkinson.

SHOULD YOU REVEAL YOUR PREVIOUS SALARY?

The short answer, in our opinion, is NO. By revealing your current or previous salary you seriously limit any negotiating power in the discussion. It limits your ability to negotiate a higher salary.

There are many legitimate reasons for wanting a job that pays less than your previous salary. For older workers who have increased their income over decades of work, it makes sense to lower expectations to compete with younger workers who often are willing to accept lower pay in return for the experience or opportunity. You don't want to price yourself out of the workplace market.

Another reason for accepting less money is when changing careers, as most people will do several times during their working life. If you earned $120,000 as a marketing executive, you don't want that to prevent you from taking a position as a sales manager for $100,000. No one can realistically expect that you will earn the same salary as your previous career position when starting off in a new direction.

Another reason for accepting a smaller salary is when moving from a high-priced market like New York or San Francisco to one where the living costs are much lower, such as Des Moines or Boise.

Finally, identical jobs may pay differently from one industry to another. Typically, private and public for-profit companies pay more than non-profit or charitable organizations.

If it's unavoidable to move forward in the discussion about a new job without revealing your prior salary, try to provide the company with a salary range in which you are comfortable.

THE GENDER GAP AND SALARY

Sad to say, but even in 2019 women are paid less than men for identical jobs, all other factors being equal or considered in the equation, according to a study by the National Bureau of Economic Research. In 2015, women working full-time earned 81% of what men earn on average, according to the U.S. Bureau of Labor Statistics. The good news is that this is changing, albeit slowly. Also, there are some professions and markets where the salary disparity is either negligible or non-existent. Women are now paid more than men in some professions in markets like New York or San Francisco.

Don't hinder your job discussion by subconsciously thinking that it's normal to accept a lower salary than a man. Your mindset is critically important in empowering your overall attitude, body language, and confidence.

Our recruiting firm always takes a gender-blind approach to salary, advising our clients to evaluate job candidates independent of gender . . . as well as ethnicity and age. When speaking with an executive recruiter, discuss their approach to this issue. While recruiters represent their clients, the best ones will also be in your corner during the process in order to create a mutually rewarding placement.

DON'T BE BLINDED BY THE MONEY

We always negotiate the highest salary we know our clients are willing to pay for a job candidate. You never want to sell yourself short. We also know that new hires who feel they are being compensated fairly approach their new responsibilities with a more positive attitude—and that is beneficial to our clients.

In general, it's better for your future career prospects to earn as much as you can. BUT, money isn't everything in a job, especially when you are managing your career for the long-term (as you should).

Be mindful of how a job impacts your future growth and development. And what that means to your career happiness and future compensation. Sometimes money can blind you to making the right choice since we Americans so often equate money with value .

As we write this, our company just lost a job placement for an excellent position with a company whose growth is skyrocketing. The candidate told us he wanted to continue his career in renewable energy because he likes the industry's future potential and he wants to do something that "helps improve the planet."

The position and compensation package we negotiated for him was excellent. He would work directly with the company CEO. The company was a 20-minute commute from his home. There was very little travel involved, so he could spend quality time with his wife and children—something he told us was a top priority. It was a senior management position. The job was all he dreamed of . . . and more. He signed the acceptance letter.

Then, at the last moment, the candidate was offered a LOT of money from a company in a completely different industry, working in a middle management position. The job required extensive travel, so he would frequently be away from his family . And the company was located more than an hour commute from his home. But the money won out. He took the job.

These are the things that drive executive recruiters to drink. We know he made a poor decision for the wrong reasons. And while we wish him well, his lack of mindfulness about his career will likely haunt him in the future.

In a *New York Times* article in *The Future of Work* series, Pulitzer Prize winning author Charles Duhigg *(The Power of Habit)* found that a surprisingly large number of his fellow Harvard Business School graduates felt extreme disappointment in their career—even those earning a million dollars or more a year. As one said, "If you spend 12 hours a day doing work you hate, at some point it doesn't matter what your paycheck says."

This is difficult to understand because now we have decades of solid research about what people want and need in their jobs. It just isn't being integrated into the workplace or in the consciousness of America's workers. As in Mazlov's hierarchy of needs, once you can earn enough to provide for yourself and your family, additional salary and benefits don't contribute much to overall career satisfaction. What does matter to people is the knowledge that they are doing something meaningful.

In the *New York Times* article, one person, who earns $1.2 million a year, said "I'm jealous of everyone who had the balls to do something that made them happy." Another person recounted how he had been passed up on several opportunities and had to scramble to begin his career. "I was saved from the temptation of easy riches. I've been thankful ever since, grateful that my bad luck made it easier to choose a profession that I've loved."

A MAGICAL LESSON

The great basketball player Earvin "Magic" Johnson tells about a costly mistake he made because he focused on the money and not the future. When Nike's founder, Phil Knight, offered Magic an equity stake in Nike—when it was a relatively new company—in lieu of money as compensation for work done to promote the brand, Johnson focused solely on the money. That lack of foresight, he says, cost him hundreds of millions of dollars in stock gains later.

Never let short-term satisfaction (money) cloud your mind about the potential to earn more later. If a job offers slightly less in compensation than you desire, but is more in alignment with your long-range goals, offers an opportunity to grow and learn, and allows you to live a balanced life, always take the lower-paying job.

Mindful Career Rules: Remember, 90% of employers will pay more than the stated salary for a position . . . often significantly more (if they want and need you). Give yourself a nice raise before your first day of work . . . negotiate. However, don't be blinded by the money. While more compensation than your last job is generally better, there are times when an opportunity warrants accepting a lower salary. Never choose a career for money alone.

Chapter 28

Referrals

At some point in the hiring process you will be asked to provide referrals from people who know you, especially former employers.

If you stormed out of your last job after trashing the office and vowing revenge on your boss, a good referral may be problematic. These things tend to follow you around throughout your career like a mangy stray dog. The fact is, referrals can make or break your chances to land the job you want (so never burn your bridges).

If you've managed your career mindfully, you will have stayed in contact with former colleagues and bosses who know what you are capable of on the job. And you have cultivated a few close, long-term personal relationships who can vouch for your character and personality traits. If you are getting close to a job offer, contact your potential referrals and ask for their help.

Here's how:

1. **Describe the job and the company.** Tell them what the job title is and what you will likely be doing at the company. Send them a copy of the job description.

2. **Tell why you want the job.** Describe why you think you are a good fit for the job and company.

3. **Explain why the skills you possess match the qualifications of the job.** Frankly, most of your former colleagues and bosses will not readily recall exactly what you accomplished or what your career strengths are—unless it was something that made a major impact on the business (if that is the case, you're in luck). Gently remind them of what you contributed when you were working together.

4. **Ask for contact information and the best time to call.** Tell your referrals the time frame in which they may be contacted. Ask referrals to provide the best times to call and the number to contact them.

Provide your professional and personal references with as much information as possible. If you sense any hesitancy on the part of the person you have asked to be a referral, you probably don't want to include them among the list of references you provide the recruiter or hiring manager.

Finally, express gratitude and appreciation for their support before and after you land the job.

It's when you need a referral that the value of building and maintaining a strong professional and personal network will be evident.

Mindful Career Rules: Don't overlook cultivating and preparing key former colleagues and supervisors, as well as friends, to vouch for your job qualifications and character traits. Referrals can make or break your chance to secure the job.

Chapter 29

What You Wish You'd Done Before You Said "Yes" to the Job

> *"Patience is the art of concealing your impatience."*
> —Guy Kawasaki, author, entrepreneur

"People are often so eager to land the job—and fearful they may jeopardize the hiring process—that they neglect to find out important information they later wish they had known. It's better to fully know the good, the bad, and the ugly before you commit a major portion of your life to a new company and job.

1. **Get it in writing.** Ask for a written job offer that includes your job title, salary, benefits, and any other items you negotiated during the hiring process. Discuss your responsibilities and expected performance for the first year. If possible, get this in writing in a signed document that outlines your specific responsibilities and deliverables.

2. **Find out the history behind the job.** How does this job fit into the corporate structure? What happened to the person who was previously in the job? How many people have held the position in the past five years? If there's been significant turnover in the position, ask why. It could be a bad boss. Or it could be a fast track

to advancement. If it's a new position, ask why there is a need for it, how well is it supported, what are the expectations for the job, and who will you be reporting to.

3. **Meet the people you will be working with.** Ask to meet your boss's direct reports. Then ask each of them what they like about their job and what they would change if they could. Find out what attributes contribute to successful employment at the company. Is there transparency at the company or do the people you are speaking with seem reluctant to answer your questions openly? Meet as many people at the company as possible to get as accurate a picture of what it is like to work there.

4. **Use social media to do your due diligence.** It's always a good idea to do some investigating before your first interview or taking a new job. In the 21st century, that is easier than ever through social media. At the very least you should check out the company on LinkedIn. If they don't have a LinkedIn presence, that can tell you a lot in itself—obviously the company and its employees haven't kept up with new technology. If they are represented on LinkedIn, find out how many people at the company are members. Use your common connections to reach out to people and ask them directly what it is like to work for the company.

5. **Check out the company online with a simple Google search.** Look into the backgrounds of key people, including your prospective boss. Look at their Facebook page if you can. See if they have a Pinterest, Instagram or Twitter account (it can tell you a lot about a person's interests). Be an online detective to learn as much about your prospective company and its employees as possible. On its own, this will put you ahead of the approximately 40% of clueless applicants who didn't bother to find out what the company does.

6. **Check out the financial condition of the company.** During your interview ask about the financial health of the company, including its cash position, earnings trends, and forecasts. This will not only show you are an intelligent candidate, you'll also shift the energy of the interview to a more equal status. If the company is public, check out their last 10-K filing with the SEC. Read the Management Discussion

and Analysis where company executives discuss the firm's financial conditions and their future plans.

7. **Should I join a startup?** Many exciting job prospects are with startups. However, the long-term viability of these companies is poor—as any angel investor can tell you. But with great risk can come great reward. Just ask billionaire Sheryl Sandberg who took a chance on working at Facebook. Sandberg enjoyed a high-paying traditional career path at McKinsey & Company when she joined newcomer Google in 2001. Then in 2008, she joined three-year old Facebook as COO. Her current annual salary is reported as $20 million and her net worth is estimated at $1.6 billion, as of April 2017.

Early career experience at a startup can be a terrific steppingstone to a much better position at a top tech company like Google. With a startup, be sure to ask about their business model, the path to profitability, available funds, and their burn rate. You'll get immediate respect from a savvy entrepreneur. It will also help you decide if the startup is viable . . . you don't want a failed company on your resumé if you can avoid it, despite all the talk about how great failure is for you.

Mindful Career Rules: Don't be shy about thoroughly checking out the company and its employees where you are considering working. You will be spending a LOT of time at your job and it will have a major impact on your life—so do your due diligence to be certain it's right for you.

Chapter 30

Human Resources

> *"Few great men could pass Personnel."*
>
> —Paul Goodman, author of *People or Personnel*

HUMAN RESOURCES ENTAILS MUCH MORE THAN HIRING NEW EMPLOYEES

HR Departments have many responsibilities other than hiring—administering employee benefits, training, managing company culture, mediating conflicts, labor relations, onboarding and workforce planning. And hiring may not be what they do best. When HR is done professionally and mindfully it can be the engine that drives a company to further success. But when done poorly it can have the opposite effect.

DIRTY LITTLE HR SECRETS

Like air traffic controllers who take naps on the job, there are some dirty little secrets about these folks that can impact your chances of getting hired. Here are a few confessions from real working Human Resources staffers:

"Is it harder to get a job if you're fat? Absolutely. We don't hire anyone who is overweight."

"A lot of managers don't want to hire people with young kids, and they use all sorts of tricks to find out, illegally."

"If you've got a weak handshake, I make a note of it."

"People assume someone's reading their cover letter. I haven't read one in 11 years."

Oh, it gets worse. Much worse.

"If you are over 40, I won't hire you. My company doesn't care about experience or even your skills. It's all about filling positions at the lowest possible cost."

"Over 60? You have 0% chance of being hired."

"If you have been laid off or fired from your last job, I probably won't consider hiring you."

"My boss only wants me to hire good-looking people. He says it's good feng shui."

"We hardly ever hire a man. Women are cheaper and less aggressive."

"We have two Asians, one African-American, a disabled person, and a real Native American. Our equal opportunity requirements are met. Everyone else will be white."

"If there is one negative comment about you from a reference, you're dead to me."

Yikes!

There are other shocking reasons why you might not get hired, even though your resumé looks like a carbon copy of the job posting qualifications. We once heard of a 26-year old HR Director who said that she looks for candidates with very little career experience, so they aren't "tainted and spoiled" by their previous employment. Why even do a job description then? This stuff makes us want to tear our hair out.

Often job descriptions will go on at great length with a laundry list of requirements and qualifications that no living person on earth could ever match. In this way, the hiring manager can reject the candidates with "only" 95% of the qualifications if she doesn't like them. Age discrimination can be easily hidden this way.

One company regularly runs want ads (without identifying themselves, of course) for grand-sounding jobs at above-market salaries. They ask people to suggest solutions to a "hypothetical" business challenge and then steal the best ideas. Of course, they have no real jobs. Another company admitted to running "blind" ads for positions at their company just to see if any of their own people apply for them. You can imagine the fate of those who do.

There are *many* very dedicated Human Resource professionals—and there are those who are doing it just because it's a job. They aren't passionate or mindful about what they do. Frankly, they are an impediment to the success of their company—and to you.

The average HR Department employee has only been in their job for three years and is about 28 years old. And very few have business experience outside of HR. Any company that relies on a minimally-trained, inexperienced person to be responsible for their most valuable resource—their people—deserves what they get.

If you're over 45 and have felt the job market deck is stacked against you, perhaps it has something to do with the fact that nearly all HR staffers are young and female. Sorry, this is just a fact. If an open job has two candidates, one who is 30 years old, single, and female and the other is 50, married, and male, who do you think usually gets selected for the position? Not the candidate who is as old as the HR Director's parents. Not someone who they can't "relate" to at all. Not the "gray hair" who won't "fit the culture."

The ugly truth is that people hire people like themselves—or who they like. Age discrimination is one of the dirty, overlooked secrets in the job market. That's one reason why you see so many people in the workforce who look as if they just got their driver's license in positions that once required some experience, training, and knowledge. If you are 45 and have been passed over for a job you were certain you would get, perhaps this is why.

THE RECRUITING BUSINESS ISN'T PERFECT EITHER

Most of what we've just said also applies to the recruiting industry. We know some outstanding recruiters (and sometimes we collaborate with them on a search). We are also aware that far too many recruiters are in the business only because they need a job. Many recruiters are young, inexperienced, and have little or no business experience. Worse yet, the firms they work for are frequently driven only by numbers and not a philosophy of creating win/win relationships. They have quotas, outsource their candidate sourcing to firms in the Philippines or India, and throw as many resumés as they can against an open job—hoping that one will stick. If you've done business with one of these recruiters, you likely have a poor impression of the industry and the value a professional recruiter can provide.

What sets Wentworth Executive Recruiting apart from most recruiters is our mindful approach to recruiting and steadfast opposition to "typical" methods. In just the past year we have found excellent, talented people—who our clients love—who are just out of college, over 50, African-American, Muslim, Hispanic, Asian, Indian, gay, males, and females. We embrace diversity because we've seen that it works.

Our recruiting firm doesn't take on just any potential client, even if we could make a lot of money from them. They must meet our standards. Our reputation is too important to us. We have been fortunate to align ourselves with companies who have highly professional HR Directors (and owners) who partner with us to strategize their hiring needs, now and into the future.

When investigating a company, also check out their HR Department. If they seem professional and experienced, don't hesitate to apply for a job through this channel. When working with a recruiting firm, check them out on LinkedIn and get references. When your career is at stake, you only want to work with the best.

Mindful Career Rules: HR employees (as in most professions) come in all levels of proficiency and professionalism. Know the good, the bad, and the ugly when applying for a job through a company's HR Department. Be aware that hiring is only a part of their overall responsibilities.

Chapter 31

About Recruiters

Recruiters are in the business of finding qualified candidates for firms willing to pay to attract top talent. These companies understand that the quality of their people is directly linked to their future success.

Think of recruiters as career matchmakers. It's in their interest—and their client's interest—to make a successful match. No one wants to work at a job or company where they will fail. And if you fail, the recruiter may have to give back all or most of the fee they got for placing you. Since a successful placement can take 80 or more hours of intense work, typically over three months, and a replacement will take the same amount of work, recruiters do everything they can to get it right the first time.

Recruiters have resources and knowledge about the job markets that are invaluable to job candidates. A good recruiter can help prepare you so that you're competitive in the job market. A good recruiter can also be invaluable to a company, literally changing the future success of the firm by adding valuable talent to their staff.

The key word here is "good." Good recruiters are as rare as wild Pandas. It's a profession rife with people who are overworked, underskilled, and unprofessional. Nearly everyone has had a bad experience with a recruiter who only sees you as a number (usually with a dollar sign attached)—not a person. They troll the job boards and throw as many candidates as possible against an open position, hoping that one will work. A good recruiter can change your life. A bad recruiter is a waste of time.

Spend some time on LinkedIn, where hundreds of excellent recruiters are represented, to find a recruiter you can trust—or to check out a recruiter who has approached you about a job.

RECRUITERS ARE ESSENTIAL TO THE JOB MARKET

Most companies simply don't have the time, in-house resources or capabilities to find, vet, and evaluate potential employees. Companies who attempt to do their own talent search invariably suffer from too many poor hiring choices, costing them time, money, and a damaged brand.

Companies are often "too close to the forest to see the trees." They simply bring too many biases and corporate structural limitations to the process of finding top talent. This is where a recruiter can provide the outside perspective needed to help their clients navigate the talent search. The best recruiters have the talent bank, search tools, vetting procedures, candidate counseling knowledge, and recruiting experience needed to root out the best job candidates for the positions they need to fill. The biggest and most successful companies all have ongoing relationships with top recruiters. Facebook, Google, Apple, Twitter—even the Federal Government—build their staffs with the help of outside recruiters.

Recruiters frequently have the specialized industry knowledge and search tools, like LinkedIn Recruiter, that 75% of companies don't have. They are skilled at cold calling, screening talent, and checking references. Unlike most HR staffers, recruiters know how to use tools such as Talent Hook, Zoho Recruit, and Zip Recruiter to support their talent searches. Recruiters are "in the market" every day and have an advantage over companies, even the HR department, because their only job is finding great talent. When the task is given to the CEO or Office Manager, they usually don't have much experience or training in evaluating and onboarding new talent.

Recruiters are also good at finding talent that may be outside of the company's core expertise. High-tech firms are often at a loss when it comes to finding a marketing director or accountant. Our firm, Wentworth Executive Recruiting (wentworthexecutiverecruiting.co), specializes in the renewable energy space, high tech, marketing, sales, and commercial construction industries. However, we have also found talented people who are CEOs, Sales Managers, or PR Directors in other industries.

Some companies have their own dedicated in-house recruiters. There are some advantages to working with a recruiter who is part of a company, fully understands its mission and culture, and understands the internal political environment. The downside is they may not be able to provide the outside perspective and objectivity that an independent recruiting firm can.

RECRUITERS DON'T EXIST TO FIND YOU A JOB

"Integrity is the essence of everything successful."
—R. Buckminster Fuller, American architect,
systems theorist, and author

A common misconception about recruiters is that you can contact one and they will help you find a job. That's not what they do. They are in the business of finding top talent for the companies they represent. While a mindful recruiter also cares about you and your career path, and may provide invaluable assistance to your job search, you are secondary to their clients needs. At our firm we always work toward a win/win relationship for the job candidate and our clients. So, we invest more time in candidate development than most other firms. Just remember, recruiters don't exist to find you a job.

Professional recruiters come in two sizes—retained recruiters who are paid by a company to find specific candidates and contingency recruiters who compete with other recruiters and get paid when they fill a position.

Often you will be sought out by a recruiter who has found you through their personal network—usually on LinkedIn or through one of the employment services to which they subscribe, like ZipRecruiter or Monster. Most recruiters, like our firm, also have a proprietary "bank" of highly-qualified people they have vetted previously but did not fit an available position.

The better recruiters will thoroughly check your background and qualifications, contact your references, even test you on the capabilities you claim to have. Some may coach you and help improve your resumé to set you up for success in the interview process.

Recruiting, like everything else has changed in the past ten years. At the low end of the spectrum are younger, less experienced recruiters who have never learned how to creatively source candidates. They scan the job postings and respond to the "low hanging fruit." Since anyone can do this, it's getting harder for these recruiters to find companies willing to pay them a fee for that kind of recruiting.

There are about 20,000 recruiting firms in the U.S. The average recruiter has been in their profession for three years. There are, as in any profession, some sleazy recruiters who will do almost anything to get a placement and get paid. Some provide poor follow-up. Others do little to provide a thorough description of the job and company. It's "churn and burn" for these types.

There are unscrupulous recruiters who want you to pay a fee or a percentage of your salary (NEVER do this). However, most recruiters are honest, very hard-working professionals. Just be sure to check qualifications. If possible, speak with someone who has worked with the recruiter.

WORKING WITH A RECRUITER FOR MAXIMUM RESULTS

You should be honest and forthright about your job qualifications, salary requirements, and education. Like with an attorney, never lie to a recruiter. Don't ever do an end-run around a recruiter and apply directly for a job, unless you haven't been submitted for some reason. And let the recruiter know if you are working with other recruiters.

Working with a recruiter does not forgo your responsibility in the job search process. You still need to do the work to prepare a great resumé, be knowledgeable about the company you want to work at, be presentable, and, of course, be good at what you do. Recruiters are not miracle workers. They cannot guarantee you a job.

It's your responsibility to make it easy for recruiters to find you. As we've mentioned previously, you should create a rich presence on LinkedIn with an engaging headline, keyword rich description, professional photo, recommendations, testimonials, a job history that syncs up with your resumé and expands upon it, education and credentials, and involvement in groups.

> According to the 2012 *Bullhorn Reach Social Recruiting Activity Report,* the average recruiter has 616 LinkedIn connections—and 28% have a thousand or more. 1 in 5 recruiters has 50 or fewer connections.

You want to work with recruiters who are experienced, well-connected, have a reputation for honesty, and show genuine interest in your career path. If the recruiter has hundreds of LinkedIn connections, it shows he/she values networking—the source of most jobs. We have more than 5,000 connections.

Check out the recruiter's LinkedIn presence. Read the endorsements and testimonials. If they have one, look at their website. Check the recruiter's social media. Make an informed decision before working with any recruiter.

A GOOD RECRUITER CAN AFFECT THE TRAJECTORY OF A COMPANY

> *"There's nothing more important to success than finding the right team."*
>
> —Richard Branson, CEO, Virgin Group

A good recruiter can affect the trajectory of a company, propelling it to greatness with key people who bring energy, creativity, and leadership. Smart companies know better than to leave their #1 asset—their people—to online job boards, Craigslist ads, junior HR staff with little or no business experience, and other employees. Instead, they partner up with a recruiter who acts as a long-term consultant and advisor, providing valuable insight into their operations and helping support their long-term goals.

While it's common practice for most recruiters to spend as little time as necessary with a job candidate, we feel it is important to invest the time to get to know a candidate as much as possible. We've often placed people who were passed up by other recruiters who only spoke to them for two or three minutes on the phone.

We have spoken with potential job candidates for as long as an hour during the initial contact. Unless it is geographically impossible, we meet our candidates in person. We seldom send in a candidate for an interview that we haven't also interviewed personally once or twice. Face-to-face meetings are essential to discovering the essence of a person, in our view. We also don't "ghost" candidates. We stay in frequent communication with the candidates throughout the hiring process. To us, this is the essence of our mindful approach to recruiting.

WHY RETAINED SEARCH IS BETTER

There are two types of search firms: retained search and contingency. In retained search a company hires a recruiting firm to exclusively find their top talent. In contingency search the recruiting firm competes against other recruiting firms. Whoever finds an acceptable candidate for an open position wins the business.

It might seem at first glance that contingency search would result in more candidates. But it's the retained search firm (who knows they have the assignment) that invests more effort into the search. In our case, most of our clients retain only Wentworth Executive Recruiting to find their talent.

Finding the top talent in a highly competitive job market requires the search firm to put in a LOT of effort and expense (for advanced search software, paying recruiters and candidate sourcing specialists, advertising, advanced access to job search boards, overhead expenses, and networking at industry events).

A contingency search firm will not invest as much time or effort into their searches because they never know if they will succeed in placing a candidate or not. Contingency firms also usually don't establish enduring partnerships with companies that results in better hiring strategies.

At our company, we insist on a retained search relationship in order to:

✓ Provide guaranteed successful placement (our one-year employee retention rate is 97%). If a placement falls out within 90 days, we will find a replacement at no additional charge.

✓ Conduct style surveys to determine the right personality match with the company and its unique culture.

✓ Do thorough reference checks.

✓ Rewrite resumés so that they get the attention and respect of potential employers.

✓ Assist the candidate in creating a professional LinkedIn profile.

✓ Conduct salary and benefits negotiations so that both the candidate and our client reach an acceptable compensation package.

✓ Provide job-search and interview coaching.

✓ Offer on-boarding support to facilitate a successful integration into our client's company.

We also provide a service that no other recruiting firm in the world does to support their job searches: We produce a custom video to support our marketing for every search we conduct. This video is distributed across a range of social media, email, job boards, LinkedIn, and our own website.

It pays to hire only the best recruiter or recruiting firm. **Finding the top talent for your company can mean the difference between success or failure.** Ideally, you want a recruiter with the integrity and professionalism to back out of any deal that isn't beneficial to *both* you and their client, even if that means forgoing a commission.

WHAT RECRUITERS LOOK FOR IN JOB CANDIDATES

While we take time to scrutinize resumés more closely than the average recruiter, in most cases you'll only have a few seconds to catch their attention. For recruiters, it can be a time-consuming, laborious job to sift through dozens, or even hundreds of resumés. Good time management requires that a recruiter operate efficiently. There are candidates to contact and interview, companies to reach out to, referrals to check, and a myriad of other important functions that demand adequate time and attention.

DON'T WASTE YOUR TIME (OR THE RECRUITER'S)– READ THE JOB DESCRIPTION

When replying to job posts, don't apply for jobs for which you have no training or experience. It's a waste of time and energy. And it's not being mindful.

The internet is awash with advice. But much of it isn't good advice. One piece of "advice" we've frequently seen tells job seekers to apply for jobs they aren't qualified to do "and once you get the job, figure out how to do it." As a result, we receive thousands of resumés from people who have zero chance of ever getting an interview, much less land the job.

Because they aren't qualified to do the job.

A good recruiter will not present a candidate to their client who isn't an excellent match to the qualifications required to do the job. Doing otherwise would be a fast way to lose clients.

If the job description calls for someone with a BSEE degree, don't apply for the job if you don't have that degree. If the job description clearly states "local candidates only" don't apply if you live in India and the job is in San Francisco. We're using this as an example because we get a LOT of resumés from people in India. You wouldn't have heart surgery by someone who is "figuring it out on the job" or has no training in surgery, right? If you don't have the qualifications, don't waste your time or the time of the recruiter/hiring manager. Again, be mindful.

Mindful Career Rules: Working with recruiters can give you a significant advantage in your job search. Learn how they work and which recruiters are the best. Don't waste the recruiter's time (or yours) responding to job posts for positions you aren't qualified to fill.

Chapter 32

Credit Reports and Background Checks

The way you handle money can also impact your career. As recently as 2017, 25% of HR professionals reported they use credit or financial checks when screening potential hires. About 1 in 20 run credit checks on all top applicants. Unfortunately, it doesn't matter much if your credit score is low because of circumstances largely beyond your control (as millions of Americans learned after the Great Recession). Our recommendation is to be mindful and conscious about repairing your credit score as soon as you can. Taking small steps now will create future success for you. Ironically, no clear correlation between performance and credit history has ever been proven, according to a 2003 study by Eastern Kentucky University. It's unfair—but it is what it is.

Employers check credit scores and do online searches to discover other financial information (such as judgements and liens) and to uncover signs of financial stress or inappropriate handling of money that could indicate poor judgement, fraud or theft. Evidence that shows you mishandle your own finances could be an indication of a poor fit, especially if the job involves being responsible for company funds or consumer data.

Potential employers see a modified version of your credit report, according to Experian (one of the three top credit reporting agencies). It does not include your credit score, account numbers or any information that might violate the equal employment regulations. It does show your payment record, the amount you owe, and your available credit. This information can be enough to show if you are creditworthy.

The credit check is considered a "soft" inquiry, so it won't affect your credit score the way a credit card application could.

Potential employers must notify you if they intend to check your credit and must get your written permission, according to The Fair Credit Reporting Act. Employers must warn you if you are rejected based on the information in your credit report. They are required to send you a "pre-adverse action notice," including a copy of the report and a summary of your rights. The employer is also required to wait a reasonable period before taking action to give you time to explain red flags or correct mistakes on the report. Then, after an action is taken, the employer must follow up with a "post-adverse action" notice, providing the name of the reporting agency, their contact information, and detailing your right to a free copy of the report within 60 days.

Many states and cities now have laws that prevent employers from doing credit checks (including California where our business is located) seeing it as potentially discriminatory. For these reasons, employers now do far fewer credit checks than before—the process is too cumbersome for most companies.

It's always a good idea to maintain a healthy credit history and score by paying your bills on time, using less than 30% of your available credit, and avoiding actions such as liens and bankruptcy. Good financial management practices will have a major impact on your career (and life). So, learn to manage your money and be sure to monitor your credit report regularly. You are entitled by law to one free credit report every 12 months from each of the three major credit bureaus, which means you can check your credit at least three times a year. Just go to AnnualCreditReport. com for your reports. If you detect any discrepancies, correct them using a dispute process offered by each bureau.

BACKGROUND CHECKS

About 1 in 3 background checks will reveal something in your past that will kill your chances of getting the job you applied for.

Here's what the background check picture looked like as of 2010:

Screening method	% of employers using it	Increase in last 5 years
Some form of screening	93%	48%
Background checks	79%	51%
Drug tests	50%	54%

Percent of background checks showing red flags:

Criminal records	29.5%
Employment verification	48.1%
Drug tests	3.3%
Credit checks	42.9%

Companies lose about 5% of their annual revenue—billions annually—to employee fraud, according to the Association of Certified Fraud Examiners. If you look at it through the eyes of employers, you can see why they run checks. In fact, it might be a good idea to run a background check on yourself to see what is reported. If there's negative information or a mistake, have it corrected so it won't affect your career.

Mindful Career Rules: Keep a clean credit, driving, and criminal record. Consider doing a background check on yourself to catch any errors.

Chapter 33

The Dark Side of Job Candidates

*"70 million Americans—or 1 in 3 adults—
have a criminal record."*

—Society for Human Resource Management, 2019

The secrets and lies people tell are sometimes incredible. We recruiters are more aware of human frailties than most because we interact with thousands of people in the course of our work. We also learn a LOT about people, sometimes things we wish we didn't know.

Many have not followed a mindful path in their life and career.

- **People lie on their resumé.** A national survey found several, uh, "discrepancies" on more than a third of resumés when doing background checks on applicants.

- **31% lied about their job or educational qualifications.** Many even made up Ivy League degrees or claimed they worked at companies where they were never hired. Harvard University said that about half the resumés listing Harvard degrees they are asked to verify are false.

- **Nearly 1 in 3 applicants were linked in some way to criminal behavior,** including time spent behind bars for offenses as serious as rape, child molestation, and robbery. If you have a reportable criminal offense in your background, it will likely be found. The good news is nearly 2 out of 3 employers reported they are willing to overlook a substance abuse felony or misdemeanor offense such as shoplifting or vandalism, if the job candidate has led an otherwise exemplary life. One-third of employers said they would even consider a person with a property-related felony such as theft or arson. But if you murdered your previous boss, well, you may want to start your own business.

When employers and recruiters check online, they often find disturbing information.

- **19% bad-mouthed their former employer**—often on social networking sites like Facebook. That's not too encouraging to future employers.

- **19% boasted about drinking or doing drugs** on social networking sites or on their blogs. Perhaps you can land a job at a marijuana dispensary.

- **15% shared confidential information about former employers.** Don't expect any future employers if you do this.

- **11% posted provocative photos of themselves online.** A study from Purdue University reported that 46% of its college age participants had sent someone a naked photograph of themselves. This isn't mindful behavior and it will likely, uh, expose you to future embarrassment.

- **8% used an unprofessional screen name.** Don't expect much traction in the job search if your screen name is OneHotBabe or MrBigD.

Many recruiters and HR pros use a service such as Checkr or Checkster to thoroughly vet all your former jobs, references, education credentials, and other claims. They can find people you've worked with previously that you might prefer they not contact. Checkster's CEO, Yves Lermusi, literally wrote the book on this subject, *Reference Check 2.0: How Digital Social Networking is Transforming the Selection Process*. It provides a wealth of information about how the background check process is conducted.

With so much lying and "enhancing" the truth going on in the competitive workplace, it's no wonder employers are taking their time hiring these days. Their potential liability from a dishonest or criminal employee is enormous—in dollar losses, employee morale, legal costs, and reputation.

EMPLOYERS LIE TOO

In this age of Alternative Truth don't make the mistake of assuming the company to which you are applying for a job is telling the truth—about themselves or the job.

As many as 1 in 5 new employees find that the company and job were misrepresented in the job description, company culture characterization or the financial health of the company. When a job or company isn't what you were told, it can set you back—even derail—your career path.

Employees of companies such as Enron, Circuit City, and Homestore. com—among hundreds of others—found themselves out of a job when the actions of their firms' top execs caused those companies to crash and burn. It's particularly devastating when you've devoted a large chunk of your life to a company, been a valuable employee, and still find yourself on the unemployment line. Just as bad is the guilt by association of working for a dishonest company. It can harm your reputation forever.

While there isn't a 100% foolproof way of determining if a company is engaged in dishonest dealings or has lied about themselves, it is still important for you to do your due diligence and investigate the company and the people you would be working with every day. Often "red flags" will show up that can be an indication of a much larger problem. At the least, do the following:

- ✓ Do an in-depth online search of the company's background and competition. Try searching using the company name + "fraud" or "misconduct."

- ✓ Investigate the background of the key people in management (as well as the people you will be reporting to in your position) on LinkedIn and with a background checking service like Spokeo, Intelius, or PeopleSmart.

- ✓ Check out what former employees and customers think of the company by looking at Glassdoor.com or Yelp.

- ✓ Find former employees of the company on LinkedIn and ask them what they liked and didn't like about the company.

If this seems a bit paranoid to you, think of it as insurance. Your career is important, and a bad move is costly—financially, emotionally, and how it affects your career path. And remember, the company will be checking you out by pulling your credit report (where still legal), hiring a background check service, as well as calling your former supervisors and colleagues. So why shouldn't you do the same?

Your reputation is critically important to your success. You are often evaluated in life by the company you keep. The same is true about the companies you work at. These days you can't be too careful.

HOW INVESTED IS THE COMPANY IN FINDING TOP TALENT?

> *"It's possible for a bad hire to cost up to five times their annual salary, especially for top executives."*
> —Society for Human Resources Management

> *"The average cost of a "bad" hire is about 1/3 of the employee's annual salary."*
> —U.S. Department of Labor Statistics

When a company is serious about finding the best talent, they generally will retain a top recruiter to work with them to find the ideal person. Or they maintain a professional in-house recruiting staff. That isn't to say that jobs listed with a job board, LinkedIn, or from a contingency recruiter are inferior. They may be terrific jobs. But the jobs retained recruiters work on are only jobs considered vitally important to the company—their "critical hires." As a job seeker, wouldn't you choose this kind of company over any other?

Also, retained recruiters aren't the "churn and burn" type of recruiter that populate the talent search industry so pervasively. Retained recruiters operate as consultants, helping companies structure their talent needs to advance their clients' future growth. Retained searches are conducted in greater depth and detail. The company executives are usually involved in the process too, not just HR.

The end result is a better fit with the long-term requirements of the position and the culture of the company. In our case, our placements rarely fall out, while the industry average is 40-50% within the first 18 months. A failed placement can potentially cost a company millions of dollars, lose customers, disrupt its progress, and demoralize the staff. That's why smart companies don't mind paying us 20% (of the employee's first year salary) to find the right person. The cost is well worth it when they know there's a 97% chance that it will work out over the long term. As a job candidate, these are the firms you want to be associated with to manage your career effectively—and mindfully.

Mindful Career Rules: Never lie about your credentials or background. Check out companies you are considering working for to see if they are being truthful. If you can, determine how much value the company places on hiring and keeping its people.

Chapter 34

Job Search Frustrations

> *"Do not be afraid of your difficulty. Turn toward it.*
> *Learn to lean into the wind. Hold your ground."*
>
> —Jack Kornfield, Founder, Spirit Rock Meditation Center

Job search can be difficult and frustrating, fraught with setbacks and disappointments. When asked, job seekers voiced similar frustrations experienced during their search.

38%	"I have the ideal experience for the job, but no one calls me back."
16%	"I don't have the right experience."
15%	"There aren't enough jobs in my location."
9%	"There aren't enough jobs in my niche."
8%	"I'm 'overqualified' for most jobs."
2%	"I can't seem to get past the interview."

WHY YOU DIDN'T GET THE JOB YOU WERE "PERFECT" FOR

Here's something that happens all the time. You apply to a position that seems to be a perfect match for your experience and skills. You research the company, and the culture seems an ideal fit. And it goes nowhere.

If you haven't already figured it out, many job listings include nearly every qualification imaginable in the job description—in order to make it difficult for you. It's unlikely that the actual job would require that you do all of these things. The laundry list of responsibilities is there to make it easy to disqualify you for any reason they want since you don't meet *all* the qualifications of the position.

You've got to ask yourself if you would want to work for any company willing to engage in underhanded tactics like those. The answer should be "no."

If you make it to the interview stage of the hiring process there are many other, frequently irrational, reasons you didn't get the job that seemed like a perfect match for your qualifications.

One CEO told us why he didn't hire the perfect candidate for a VP position he was trying to fill. "The guy looked just like my first business partner—the jerk who ripped me off for $500,000. I knew I couldn't look at him every day without feeling the pain of that experience."

Another person said she couldn't hire the perfect candidate for a job because he looked and acted like her ex-husband. "I could hardly wait to get him out of my office," she admitted.

Yet another CEO confessed that she didn't hire the SuperCandidate (as she called him) because she was afraid this person would make her look bad.

> **According to one study, a fear of hiring someone who is "too talented" is a factor in more than 1 in 5 hiring decisions.**

Perhaps one of the most frustrating experiences is to be told you are "overqualified" for the job. This seems to defy logic. After all, isn't being extremely qualified a good thing? As recruiters, this frustrates us too because we're asked to find the very best people for a job. While we can reason with our clients to advance a highly-qualified candidate, it's not usually an option for the individual job seeker.

Often there is pushback by entrenched employees at the company about a new hire. They fear their comfortable employment status may be disrupted in some way. These days job candidates are frequently asked to interview with several members of the team at a company. Any one of them can "vote you off the island" and ruin your chance to be hired. And if you are hired, you'll need to be constantly aware of employees who may try to sabotage you—at least until you are integrated into the team.

The reasons why great candidates get rejected can range from the truly bizarre to the more mundane (and slightly more understandable) things like living in the wrong zipcode, being seen as a job hopper (or staying too long at a job) or being perceived as "odd" in some way. Often, it's simply a case of poor "chemistry."

Just know that when you are told a "more suitable" candidate was chosen, it doesn't mean you weren't perfectly suited for the job. Also know that when you are told your resumé "will be kept on file" that it won't be.

The point is . . . you may not get the job for the most inane reason imaginable. People are human. And humans often defy logic. Don't take it personally.

Mindful Career Rules: Luckily, most successful bosses are happy to hire people better than themselves—because it makes them look good. But don't take it personally if you seem to be highly-qualified for a position but don't get it.

Chapter 35

The First 90 Days at a New Job

Okay, you prayed to St. Jude (and took our advice) and miraculously found the perfect job. Now what?

Your first 90 days, when everyone will be watching and evaluating your every move, are crucial to your long-term success in your new job. This is a particularly important time to be mindful in thought and actions.

In *The First 90 Days: Critical Success Strategies,* author Michael Watkins points out that "small differences in your actions can have a disproportionate impact on results." The first 90 days are a particularly vulnerable time for a new employee, especially if you have executive decision-making responsibilities. "Failure to create momentum during the first few months," he writes, "virtually guarantees an uphill battle for the rest of your tenure in the job."

Corporate and business life is not the same as real life. You're a player in a game with other players of varying talents and ambitions. There are specific rules to the game that you must learn and follow. Like a soccer player, you must always be on the move, watching the other players—both on the opposing team and your own. Former superstar hockey player Wayne Gretzky says his success is not being where the puck is, but where it's going to be. Think strategically about where you want to be in 90 days, and start your new position with the end goal in mind.

> According to a study of 20,000 searches by executive search firm Heidrick & Struggles, as reported in *The Financial Times*, more than 40% of senior executives leave a new organization or are fired within 18 months.

You cannot assume that, if you were successful in the past, you will be successful in the future. Every organization operates by its own unique set of rules and expectations. Companies become a collective mélange of the people and systems in place. A corporate personality develops over time (their unique "culture") that is often radically different from any company you have worked at in the past.

Often the reason a new hire fails is as simple as a poor cultural fit—something few people evaluate before joining a new company. Whether or not your personality is a good match with the collective personality of the company is something that is hard to determine but important to your future success.

Senior executives are not immune to these pitfalls. According to a recent article in the *Harvard Business Review*, 4 out of 10 top executives who are hired from outside the company are fired within 18 months. These are worse odds than playing Russian Roulette! But if you are mindful, you can beat these odds.

Here are some tips to succeed during your first 90 days:

1. **Familiarize yourself with the company.** Review your interview notes to recall the people you met and what was said. Do a deep dive into the company's media coverage, newsletters, and annual reports. Check out the competition and what they are doing currently. You will feel more comfortable on your first day.

2. **Connect with your colleagues.** Get to know as many people in the organization as possible. Identify those who have positions that are critical to your performance. Ask them to explain what they do so you have a better understanding of how the company functions. Offer to help them with their responsibilities, where appropriate.

3. **Establish your work ethic.** Know when and where to report to work on your first day. Get to work 30 minutes early and leave when most of your co-workers go home. Do extra work when asked without

question to show you are a team player. Focus on getting the job done with little or no distractions (stay off social media and keep personal communication to a minimum). Do not engage in gossip or talk disparagingly about anyone, especially your boss. Share credit with your teammates for work well done.

4. **Pay attention to your appearance.** You will be watched by everyone during your first weeks on the job. Dress tastefully (and slightly above the dress code) and pay attention to your grooming.

5. **Establish credibility.** You may have the urge to bluff your way through some early interactions in your new job. Don't. You'll command more respect if you're honest and forthright. Admit it if you don't know something and ask for advice. People love to give it. And you'll seem more "human." Just be careful. There are some things you'll be expected to know from your first day.

Take extra care during your first 90 days to operate as error-free as possible. A faux pas that would be overlooked later in your career at the company can be deadly now.

6. **Project a positive, confident attitude.** Look and act like you are happy to be joining the company and team. Adopt a relaxed "old shoe" confidence. Remember, your attitude is your altitude.

7. **Create some early wins.** Find some tasks or projects that you can be sure to excel at during your first few weeks on the job. It doesn't have to be a major project. In fact, taking on something big in the beginning is very risky. Hit some singles before you try for a home run.

8. **Build momentum.** Don't rest on your early wins. Keep building upon them. Think of everything you do as concentric circles that keep expanding outward. Stay focused and keep working hard. If you lose momentum it will be hard to get it back. Momentum is critical to your future success at the company.

Michael Watkins also said, that "the overriding goal in a transition is to build momentum by creating virtuous cycles that build credibility and by avoiding getting caught in vicious cycles that damage credibility."

9. **Promote yourself.** Without being tagged as an arrogant braggart, you need to quietly and subtly learn to blow your own horn. There's a real art to doing this well. It can be in the form of congratulating your boss or your team for doing such an outstanding job. In effect, you are also congratulating yourself. Or you can be seen having lunch with the boss or a key client. Another way to raise your profile early on is to get published in the company newsletter or a trade publication.

10. **Accelerate your learning.** There's always a lot to learn at any new organization, much of it tied in with the company culture. Be observant. Study company materials and systems. Become knowledgeable about the company's products and competitors. Not knowing something crucial about your company or its products/services during your first 90 days will telegraph to others that you aren't a company "player."

11. **Communicate with your boss.** Most people who join a new company think they work for that company. Well, yes and no. Technically you work for the company. But in reality you work for your boss. Keeping him/her happy is the key to success. Don't let anyone tell you otherwise. Just like in marriage "a happy wife, a happy life," in business "a happy boss prevents job loss."

    Clarify expectations with your boss and keep him/her advised of your work progress with frequent updates. Take initiative, but do not make major changes without a full buy-in from your boss. Learn to collaborate with his/her work style.

12. **Build your team.** Most people like to work as part of a team, but some don't. Get to know the personalities of your team and don't force them to do something that is against their nature. You are a new entity to them and there may be some initial resistance to your presence. Change isn't easy for many people. Be a clearheaded, logical, persuasive leader. Be mindful and step outside your ego. Most people are willing followers and will support someone who has a logical plan. Get input from team members beforehand. It demonstrates that you value their expertise and enables them to feel "ownership" of your plans. If your team "has your back" your first 90 days will likely be successful.

Some companies like to conduct style surveys to help determine how to integrate the company culture and the disparate personalities of colleagues with the new employees, and the responsibilities of the job itself. One method that has been used for decades is the Birkman method (birkman.com).

Our clients often conduct personal research to help determine how the various personalities of the key people at a company will interact with a job candidate. It's remarkably insightful and has helped us place candidates with a 97% 18-month retention rate.

Note to employers: In selecting a talent recruiting firm to work with, choose one that provides transitional counseling. Studies show that about 4 in 10 senior hires ultimately prove to be a disappointment. A failed placement can be costly to both the company and the recruiting company. It's in everyone's best interests for the new hire to succeed. Our firm provides a free *Successful Onboarding Guide* to help integrate new employees into the company.

13. **Create supportive coalitions.** Get out and about at your new company and develop a mutually supportive relationship with at least one key member in each department. Let them know you are there to help them make their jobs easier and more successful. You want to build credibility and be a catalyst for new levels of operational productivity. Be aware that entrenched and comfortable employees will resist change. You'll need to be diplomatic and inclusive to win over their support. If you can appeal to their self-interest and calm their fear of change, you'll build a support framework that can take the company to new heights.

14. **Support your co-workers.** Support your co-worker's ambitions and you will go a long way toward succeeding at your new company. Make them look good. Be a mentor. Zig Ziglar, the famous motivational speaker, said, "You can get everything you want in life if you help enough other people get what they want."

15. **Stay calm and balanced.** A LOT will be coming at you during your first 90 days. Stay cool and calm at all times. Don't let anyone think you aren't in control. Losing your cool at this stage with the company can be disastrous. In your personal time make sure you get enough

rest, exercise, and good nutrition. This is when you want to be at the top of your game.

The first 90 days on the job should be your launch pad to greater success and fulfillment—if you are mindful. This is the period when you want to show high emotional intelligence, avoid negativity, and not be complacent now that you have the job. Your mantra every day should be a dedication to mindfulness on the job. And always be aware that your co-workers, employees, and clients may not be mindful themselves—so practice mindful understanding and non-reaction.

Mindful Career Rules: You've got a lot to do when you're new. So, you'll need to plan your transition and integration into your new job carefully. Remember, what worked for you before may not work at your new place of employment. If you manage your first 90 days well the rest of your tenure on the job will be much easier. This is the time to be especially mindful of your thoughts and actions.

Chapter 36

How to Be More Mindful at Work

Mindfulness at work can be a game changer in your career, primarily because it helps you with important tools to navigate the stressful, distracted, demanding workplace environment.

FOCUS

Emails, meetings, open offices, and frequent interruptions make it difficult to focus on getting your work done. It's why you arrive at work with a thoughtful "To Do" list for the day and suddenly the day is over and you've accomplished little or nothing.

Two skills that are key to mindfulness at work are focus and awareness—the ability to get the highest priority job completed. To achieve this, you can insist on privacy, take a few minutes throughout the day to meditate and clear distracting thoughts, and spend a few moments doing some deep breathing. These simple mindful actions will make a huge difference in how much you get accomplished.

An analysis of 40 studies on mindfulness suggests that it contributes to stress reduction, decreased anger and conflict, and promotes more positive feelings in the workplace (and elsewhere). Other attributes of mindfulness include better memory, enhanced cognitive ability, and more flexibility. Mindfulness also enables a greater awareness, which also contributes to a successful day at work.

When Salesforce built the tallest building in the West in San Francisco for their new headquarters, they included a meditation room on every floor (at a reported cost of $30 million). Marc Benioff, the Salesforce CEO, understands how important it is to provide employees with the mindfulness support they need to succeed.

BE PRESENT

It's estimated that more than half of workers are either "disengaged" or even "actively disengaged." They are just sleepwalking through the day. Mindfulness is bringing into focus your complete attention in the now. When your mind starts wandering or you feel distracted, bring the focus back to what you are doing.

SLOW DOWN

While it may seem counter-intuitive, slowing down your pace during the day will make you more efficient and productive. It's a healthier way of working too. You'll feel much less stress.

During times of high anxiety or the kind of stress that comes with tight deadlines, slowing down will help you dissipate the negative emotions and you'll make fewer mistakes.

BE IN GRATITUDE

Mindfulness and gratitude go hand-in-hand. We humans have a negativity bias; you're more likely to see the things that went wrong rather than what is going right in your life. Feeling gratitude is the antidote. According to numerous studies, gratitude (even for negative things at times) leads to more creativity, improved health, better relationships with colleagues, and a more positive outlook.

Even in the worst situations (like working for a toxic boss) there is something you can find gratitude in (at least you'll know how not to manage when you are the boss).

DEVELOP HUMILITY

Studies on the effectiveness of business leaders revealed something that seems contradictory—the most successful leaders were those who exhibited the most humility. Their focus was not on themselves but on their company, the welfare and success of their employees, and providing customers with exceptional care in a trusting relationship. They didn't have inflated egos or the need to be recognized for their achievements.

ACCEPTANCE

Mindfulness in the workplace requires acceptance of the present moment as it is. It is also important to accept yourself without the debilitating energy that comes with self-criticism. Acceptance activates clarity of thought, recognition of your strengths and shortcomings (and what to change), and the self-confidence that your contributions matter.

A GROWTH MINDSET

Mindset is your view of the world and everything you do. People either have a fixed mindset or a growth mindset. Having a rigid belief that you don't need to learn and grow, that your current and inherent abilities are enough to succeed, will ultimately lead to failure. But a flexible mindset, combined with mindfulness, a love of learning, grit and determination, perseverance, and curiosity will lead you to both success and fulfillment. This is the mindset to cultivate in whatever work you do.

MINDFULNESS GIVES YOU AN EDGE AT WORK

Major organizations like Google, LinkedIn, and the U.S. Army are conducting mindfulness training to improve the performance and satisfaction of their employees. They're doing it not because it's trendy but because it's becoming mainstream. These organizations invest millions in measuring the effectiveness of mindfully conscious processes and techniques. And they have discovered they work.

So, as you go about your day at work, be mindful in every situation at all times. You'll soon find that mindfulness is the key to career success.

Mindful Career Rules: Mindfulness is the "secret sauce" to success on the job and in life. Be mindful of being mindful throughout your day.

Chapter 37

Working Hard . . . and Smart

"My one skill is that I'll outwork anybody. I'll work harder."

—Matt Damon, actor

The baseline for success is the ability and willingness to work hard. If you aren't willing to put in the work, you likely won't ever be successful.

People who are passionate about their career often work insanely hard—as much as 70 hours a week. Many travel 100 or more days a year on business. Sure, you will hear about some who got rich quickly, with no more effort than the typical factory worker. Mark Zuckerberg, the co-founder of Facebook, became a billionaire before he was 25 and freely admits he hasn't slaved to get there. Still, the truth is that most wealthy people got that way through consistent, focused, hard work.

Malcolm Gladwell, author of *Outliers: The Story of Success,* makes the point that it takes about 10,000 hours of practice to become truly proficient at anything meaningful. The Beatles, considered an "overnight success" by many, played 1,200 gigs before their first hit. Gladwell estimates the Beatles had played about 10,000 hours at that point.

Bill Gates began teaching himself about computer code and programming in 1968 when he was 13 years old. Comedian Jay Leno worked more than 340 days a year for years before he hit it big. Even when he hosted the *Tonight Show*, Leno continued to work more than 100 days a year, doing stand-up comedy on weekends all over the country.

> *"The only time success comes before failure is in the dictionary."*
>
> —Anonymous

What Gladwell also writes about are the other factors to success: environment, being in the right place at the right time in history, and the many accidents of birth that can almost predetermine a greater or lesser opportunity in life. If you don't have a natural talent for something, even 10,000 hours may not be enough to achieve proficiency. If you are tone-deaf, 50,000 hours of practice won't make you a great, or even a good singer. However, it's generally a fact that the more work, the more hours, and the more practice you apply toward a goal, the greater your chances for success.

The great majority of wealthy people will tell you that they got where they are through hard work. What you see are the parties at lavish homes, country club membership, safaris to Africa, and glittering social functions. However, it took a LOT of work in the past for most of these people to get where they are today, not four hours a week as some bestselling authors say is possible.

THE VALUE OF HARD WORK

> *"The first qualification for success is a good work ethic."*
>
> —Henry Ford, Founder, Ford Motor Company

Work shouldn't be your entire life, but if you want to succeed—especially at entrepreneurial ventures—you will likely have to put in more work, time, and effort than you ever imagined.

In the 1970s there was a popular book sold through direct response ads in newspapers all over America called *The Lazy Man's Way to Riches* by Joe Karbo. It was a bestseller because most people (a) want to be rich, and (b) are lazy. Joe got rich but few, if any, who read his book did. By the way, the secret to Joe's lazy man's way to riches is to write a book like *The Lazy Man's Way to Riches*. He sold millions of copies and made millions of dollars.

What Karbo's book, along with lotteries and casinos, proves is that there are a lot of people who want to be rich without working hard for it. Work habits are often instilled by our parents and teachers at an early age. If your work habits are poor, learn to be more efficient with your time, create a plan, make frequent progress checks, and focus on the immediate task at hand. With good habits, you should be able to create the elusive work/life balance.

> *"Talent is cheaper than table salt.*
> *What separates the talented individual*
> *from the successful one is a lot of hard work."*
>
> —Stephen King, American author

The "bibles" for learning good work habits are *Getting Things Done: The Art of Stress-Free Productivity* by David Allen, *First Things First* and *The 7 Habits of Highly Effective People* by the late Stephen Covey.

If you're lazy you won't succeed. Practice, study, visualization, and developing mental fortitude, combined with focused work, will lead to success.

WORK SMARTER

> *"You can't have a million-dollar dream*
> *with a minimum wage work ethic."*
>
> —Stephen C. Hogan, social entrepreneur

Jack Canfield makes a great point in his bestseller, *The Success Principles: How to Get from Where You Are to Where You Want to Be,* when he notes that mindset is a key ingredient in success. If you think you are worth $36,000 a year salary, that's probably the mark you'll hit. For many people this is okay. They really don't want to exert the sustained effort and focus it requires to be a success in life.

For those who want to succeed, the mental aspects of being a winner are perhaps most important. The right mindset about work—the ability to focus and eliminate distractions, a creative viewpoint, strategic delegation, a collaborative win/win attitude, and being able to motivate people—is critical to success.

Yes, success requires hard work, but if your work is not managed properly, it can lead to burnout, something that 23% report experiencing very often and another 44% say they feel sometimes, according to a 2018 Gallup Poll.

Working hard doesn't mean you can't work smart. And if you work smart, you may not have to work so hard. Many highly productive people have figured out how to produce a prodigious amount of meaningful output, yet work five or six hours a day.

Here are six ways to be more productive while working less.

1. **Be prepared.** Time spent preparing your work properly and planning your workflow will pay off in more efficient production. Before you go to sleep, write out what you plan to accomplish the next day. Prioritize your work. Pose a question to yourself that you want answered, and let your sleeping mind search for an answer (it's surprising how well this works).

2. **Take breaks.** Go for a walk. Get up and stretch. Go to a park. You need to put your brain in idle mode now and then to avoid burning out. Scientific research has found that the most a person can focus on one task before the law of diminishing returns sets in is 90 minutes. So, break your day up with small rejuvenation breaks.

3. **Delegate tasks, especially time-consuming work.** Many successful executives say that learning to delegate well was the "secret sauce" of their success. Try to shoot for a minimum of 20% of your work offloaded to someone you trust. Just make sure they are well-informed and have clear directions first or you're doomed to failure. If you are a solopreneur, check out the many personal assistants available now. You can often get time-consuming work done faster and for much less than your own compensation rate.

4. **Check your email before you begin to work.** You need to be up to speed with your colleagues and work team so that you don't

inadvertently become a drag on their productivity. Make a pit stop first in order to be on the same page as everyone else, then start your work. After that, just check two more times, at 2 pm and 4 pm.

5. **Tackle the one "must do" project first.** With as many distractions as there are in a day, and considering the large workload most professionals must carry, it's advisable to choose the one thing on your plate that is most urgent or will have the biggest impact and get that done first. It's too easy to get caught up in minutiae and discover late in the afternoon that you have essentially accomplished nothing of value. By completing one key task you'll feel as if you've accomplished something important. Everything you do during the day after that will be icing on the cake.

6. **Take a nap.** The list of highly successful people who take naps is long. President John Kennedy took a nap every day. President Lyndon Johnson separated his day into two "shifts," one before and the other after his nap. Other fans of naps include Leonardo da Vinci, Winston Churchill, Thomas Edison, Arnold Schwarzenegger, and Eleanor Roosevelt. Napping is backed by science too. It helps clear your brain, refresh your body physically, and diminishes stress. And be sure to take all the vacation time you accrue; it will help improve your productivity when you're back on the job.

Time management is the key to getting things done. Plan your day and your week in advance. Prioritize the work you need to get done. Focus on what matters most.

SUCCESS BEGINS WITH YOUR MINDSET

> *"Too many people operate through fear and scarcity."*
> —Jeff Siebold, professional speaker,
> author of *How Rich People Think*

World-class performers conduct their life through a lens of love and abundant mindfulness. They can see opportunities and act on them consciously.

The differences between successful and unsuccessful people are dramatic.

1. Successful people are passionate about what they do.
   Unsuccessful people drift through life without any passion.

2. Successful people are persistent.
   Unsuccessful people give up easily.

3. Successful people aren't afraid of hard work.
   Unsuccessful people are lazy.

4. Successful people are patient.
   Unsuccessful people want everything immediately.

5. Successful people embrace change.
   Unsuccessful people fear it.

6. Successful people create multiple sources of income.
   Unsuccessful people rely on just one source.

7. Successful people think for themselves.
   Unsuccessful people follow the herd.

8. Successful people have good etiquette.
   Unsuccessful people are unthoughtful.

9. Successful people talk about ideas.
   Unsuccessful people talk about people.

10. Successful people accept responsibility for their failures and learn from them.
    Unsuccessful people blame others.

11. Successful people give others credit for their victories.
    Unsuccessful people take all the credit.

12. Successful people want others to succeed.
    Unsuccessful people hope others fail.

13. Successful people engage in lifelong learning.
    Unsuccessful people "wing it."

14. Successful people ask how they can help others.
    Unsuccessful people ask how they can help themselves.

15. Successful people take risks.
    Unsuccessful people play it safe and are afraid of failing.

16. Successful people ask for what they want.
    Unsuccessful people are afraid of being turned down
    for what they want.

17. Successful people always want to understand themselves better.
    Unsuccessful people are not introspective.

18. Successful people listen to understand.
    Unsuccessful people only want to express their points-of-view.

19. Successful people think of money as a tool.
    Unsuccessful people see money emotionally.

20. Successful people focus on earning.
    Unsuccessful people focus on saving.

21. Successful people are vulnerable and transparent.
    Unsuccessful people are secretive and closed.

22. Successful people are okay with uncertainty.
    Unsuccessful people seek comfort and security.

23. Successful people believe poverty is the root of all evil.
    Unsuccessful people think money is the root of all evil.

24. Successful people dream of a better future.
    Unsuccessful people long for the "good old days."

25. Successful people spend time alone to think.
    Unsuccessful people rarely do.

26. Successful people expect to be successful.
    Unsuccessful people expect to struggle.

27. Successful people keep a positive attitude.
    Unsuccessful people are negative and dour.

28. Successful people show gratitude every day.
    Unsuccessful people aren't grateful for all the good things in their life.

29. Successful people are voracious readers.
    Unsuccessful people watch TV.

30. Successful people set goals and plan.
    Unsuccessful people never set goals or make plans.

31. Successful people despise losing but accept losses and persevere.
    Unsuccessful people think of themselves as victims and losers.

32. Successful people eat a healthy diet and exercise consistently.
    Unsuccessful people eat junk food and never exercise.

33. Successful people think long-term and make sacrifices
    now to achieve success later.
    Unsuccessful people think only of instant gratification and reward.

34. Successful people know how to focus to get things done.
    Unsuccessful people are easily distracted by social media, frivolous
    activities, and multi-tasking.

35. Successful people surround themselves with accomplished people.
    Unsuccessful people have toxic people in their lives.

36. Successful people work to be respected.
    Unsuccessful people only want to be liked.

37. Successful people live below their means.
    Unsuccessful people don't budget and carry high debt
    and credit card balances.

38. Successful people control their emotions and filter what they say.
    Unsuccessful people say whatever comes into their minds.

39. Successful people do more than they are paid for.
    Unsuccessful people have a "it's not my job" attitude.

40. Successful people get up three hours before work begins.
    Unsuccessful people seldom get up early.

41. Successful people have a mentor or coach.
    Unsuccessful people believe they are unnecessary.

Being mindful means being open to changing how you think. Change
your mindset and you can change your life.

NOT BEING MINDFUL CAN HAVE SERIOUS REPERCUSSIONS ON YOUR CAREER

A recent survey by VitalSmarts discovered that 83% of people had experienced seeing someone make a disastrous career blunder—and 69% admitted to having done something that had damaged their own career. One in three said their blunder had cost them a promotion, raise, or job. Another 27% said they had damaged a working relationship by not being mindful. And more than 1 in 10 reported that they had done something that destroyed their reputation.

If you are living a mindful life, you can avoid these disastrous errors in judgment.

TOP 15 CAREER-LIMITING MOVES

It's surprising how many people get a job or embark on a career path and then mess it up by making some very stupid mistakes. Here are 15 of the most common career-limiting moves.

1. **Lack of insight or introspection.** The number of people who have never thought in-depth about themselves or their career is astounding. Without knowing yourself, paying attention to how the world works, or considering the consequences of your actions, you will be flying blind through life. As Frank Zappa said, "A mind is like a parachute. It doesn't work if it isn't open."

2. **Mistaking busywork for accomplishment.** The bottom-line for everything you do should always be measurable results. Being busy without accomplishing much will get you nowhere in life.

3. **Not showing up or showing up late.** Being absent or late, just doing your job, and not contributing anything extra is a sure path to getting nowhere in your career.

4. **Not learning from your mistakes.** When you don't learn from the mistakes you make, you don't grow. If you don't grow, you fall behind. And in the competitive 21st century, you can't afford to fall behind and become irrelevant. Admit your mistakes and then learn from them.

5. **Not fitting in.** Perhaps the #1 reason why new employees don't work out is a poor culture fit. Be sure you share the values and style of the company you join—before you start working there.

6. **Abusing company time with personal tasks.** Shopping online, checking your Instagram page, tweeting your friends, internet porn, non-business calls, and running errands on company time is a form of theft. With more companies monitoring employee activities, you will eventually get caught.

7. **Unreliability.** Few things will knock you down a few notches on the company totem pole as being unreliable, missing commitments and deadlines, and not meeting deadlines. Become known as someone who can be trusted to do what you say you will do.

8. **Lack of creativity.** If you can't be innovative or think "outside the box," you'll take a backseat to those who can. As Steve Jobs famously said, "Think different." Remember, creativity is one thing machines or robots will never match humans in doing.

9. **Believing you are indispensable.** If you operate with a sense of entitlement, believing you are God's gift to the company, you'll find yourself being quickly ostracized. Everyone can be replaced. It's better to be an enthusiastic company advocate, grateful for your job.

10. **A negative attitude.** Gossiping, bad-mouthing your boss, and a sullen disposition will make you as attractive to work with as if you had Ebola. People who are optimistic and positive are more successful, make more money, and get more promotions. If you truly practice mindfulness on a daily basis you can easily avoid the toxicity of negative emotions.

11. **Only doing what you are paid to do.** Often, you'll be asked to do things that aren't in your job description. Some people resist these requests, feeling they are being taken advantage of by their company. This is a mistake. You're being asked because the company (or at least your boss) feels confident you can handle the request well. Assuming it's a legitimate request (e.g. something job-related and not overhauling the transmission of the boss's car or babysitting her kids) turning them down shows you're not ready for more responsibility, that you are perfectly happy working at your current level.

12. **Not learning and growing in your career.** Too many people graduate from college, take whatever training is required, and then stop learning. In the 21st century, you must stay continually involved in self-education just to keep up with the rapid changes in technology and processes.

13. **Not networking beyond your own company.** It's great to build a strong network within the company you work at, but if you want to succeed you must constantly expand and improve your professional network. As we've said before, approximately 85% of all jobs are sourced through your personal network (including a surprising number from friends and family). A strong network will also provide many opportunities to do your job well. Learn to use LinkedIn effectively, get to as many industry events as possible, and stay in contact with your contacts.

14. **Not getting out of your comfort zone.** Getting ahead usually takes you outside your comfort zone. Learn to set stretch goals for yourself, take on ambitious projects, and make every effort to follow through to successful conclusions.

15. **Hiding your talents.** If no one knows what you can do, you can be sure no one will give you anything exceptional to do. It doesn't hurt to display your successes, let people know about your special talents, and promote yourself (without bragging) within the company. Practice humility, but don't hide your talents and successes.

WORK/LIFE BALANCE

Most people are much more productive when they take time to recharge their mental and physical "batteries" with vacations, weekend time, and family time during the week. About a third of all salaried employees work 41 to 50 hours a week, with overtime seldom being compensated. Even worse, Americans, who often only receive a two-week annual vacation, are taking less of their accrued time every year—a total of 577 million unused days (almost 1.6 million years total).

It's no wonder the Europeans call us the "no vacation nation." The French receive five weeks of paid vacation time . . . plus up to 22 days of

RTT (reduction du temps) for employees who choose to work more than 35 hours a week (the limit is 39 hours). In France, if workers take their vacation during the off-season they can earn bonus days of vacation.

✓ The value of all this unused vacation time to corporate America is $67 billion (2012), according to *CNN Money*. When was the last time any corporation gave their employees that much money out of the kindness of their hearts?

✓ According to a University of Pittsburgh study, employees who took vacations suffered less depression, high blood pressure, and had healthier weight levels.

✓ Another study showed that people who take their vacation time are up to eight times less likely to develop heart disease.

✓ According to a Gallup poll, 1 in 3 Americans has suffered from anxiety during their life.

Numerous studies have proven the health benefits—as well as the productivity gains—derived from taking time off to regroup, refocus, recuperate, and re-energize.

> **According to the *Austin Business Journal*,**
> **every $1 invested by companies in employee vacation time**
> **returns $3 in productivity.**

It's simply good business to take time off to rejuvenate. In fact, a comparison of European workers' productivity with American workers' productivity shows they surpassed us for 14 of the 19 years between 1981 and 2000. Yet Europeans take more than twice as much vacation time as Americans.

> *"There is no more fatal blunder than he who consumes the greater part of life getting his living."*
>
> —Henry David Thoreau, American essayist,
> author of *Life Without Principle*

WORK TO LIVE, DON'T LIVE TO WORK

✓ Nearly three-quarters of all working adults say they have little control over their schedule.

✓ Only 29% of employed adults have access to flexible scheduling.

✓ A third of working moms have a schedule that's different from their husband's.

✓ 81% of working parents say work/life balance is more important than pay when looking for a new job AND 70% have thought about leaving a job because it doesn't offer flexibility, according to a Working Parents survey in 2017.

✓ Among Millennials, 69% wish they had chosen a job with better work/life balance, and 44% wish they had chosen a job they enjoyed more, according to a Bank of America 2018 Better Money Habits Millennial Report.

Work is taking over our lives when it should be making our lives better.

LIVE WITHOUT REGRETS

It's instructive to hear the "regrets" that people on their deathbed share about their life. None say they wish they'd spent more time at the office working. But here's what they did say:

"I wish I'd had the courage to live a life true to myself, not the life others expected of me."

This was the #1 regret in life.

"I wish I had worked smarter and not so hard."

Nearly everyone expressed this regret.

"I regret not following my passion in life."

Don't wait until you're dead to begin living.

You will likely have to work hard to reach your professional and personal life goals. But you should learn to work smarter, so your work doesn't harm your life. Be more efficient with your time. Focus on the important tasks. Be ruthless about eliminating distractions. Be constantly mindful of yourself and others, removing as much of the negative intrusions in your daily life as possible and accentuating the positives.

Mindful Career Rules: Don't be afraid to work hard. But also work smart. Do yourself (and your company) a favor and take all your vacation time. Take time to enjoy life, refresh, and recharge. You will come back to work more productively than ever before. Choose a job you enjoy, that provides enough flexibility to create a work/life balance.

Managing a career should be an ongoing effort. Take time regularly to review your goals, progress, and strategy/tactics that can drive you toward future success.

Chapter 38

Think Like an Immigrant

*"No one understands and appreciates the American
Dream of hard work leading to material rewards better
than a non-American."*

—Anthony Bourdain, author, chef, TV personality

In 2017, more than 40% of all Silicon Valley tech companies were founded by immigrants—someone born in a country other than the United States. In 2016, all six of the American Nobel Prize winners were immigrants to the U.S. New business creation skews heavily toward immigrant founders.

If you add second-generation Americans who are successful, like Steve Jobs, son of a Syrian immigrant, the phenomena of immigrant success is profound. So, why is it that people with little or no understanding of American culture, traditions, and language are so successful?

It all comes down to mindset. And mindfulness.

IMMIGRANTS BELIEVE IN THE AMERICAN DREAM

Many Americans see the difficulties and changes of modern society as the end of the American Dream. So, they don't even try. Immigrants believe in the American Dream. It's why they left their country, their friends and family, and their culture to move to a land completely foreign to their way of life.

We know a young Vietnamese woman who had been abandoned and was found by a nun laying in a rice paddy, close to death. She eventually found her way to America, studied hard, earned a degree from Colorado State University, and nearly qualified for the Olympics as a gymnast as well. She learned how our system works and worked her way up to CEO of a Chamber of Commerce in Northern California. She was recruited to another Chamber in Southern California and eventually recruited again to be the first female, foreign-born CEO of the San Francisco Chamber of Commerce.

Stories like this are common with immigrants—because they are mindful of the opportunities that exist in America and aren't afraid to do what it takes to achieve the American Dream.

IMMIGRANTS ARE GRATEFUL TO BE HERE

Americans have gotten complacent and lazy about the opportunities that abound in America. We take our freedoms for granted—40% don't even bother to vote. Many Americans whine constantly about life instead of taking the initiative and creating their lives.

Most other places in the world aren't as bountiful, free, or have as many opportunities as the United States of America. But immigrants still see America as their bright hope for a better future and are thankful to be here. They see America as a boundless land of opportunity.

Gratitude is a powerful ingredient in success.

> *"Give thanks for everything that you are and everything that you have—that's the first step toward discarding a scarcity mentality."*
> —Dr. Wayne Dyer author of *Manifest Your Destiny*

IMMIGRANTS VALUE EDUCATION

Benjamin Franklin famously said, "An investment in knowledge pays the best interest." No one understands this more than an immigrant. If you go to any university in America, you'll see a lot of "foreign" faces. Immigrants know the key to success is knowledge—and they are not afraid to work hard and sacrifice to get it. Too many native-born Americans discredit learning and education. There seems to be a growing distrust of educated people by a large percentage of our population . . . frequently the same people who are angry because they are going nowhere in life.

> "Education is the passport to the future,
> for tomorrow belongs to those who prepare for it today."
>
> —Malcom X, human rights activist

IMMIGRANTS AREN'T AFRAID TO WORK HARD

If you drive from L.A. to San Francisco on Interstate 5, there is a 28-mile section where as far as the eye can see are vineyards. You'll also pass mile upon mile of orchards and farmland. In the 40 years we have lived in California, we have never seen a white person working in these vineyards, orchards, and fields. The work is backbreaking (often literally). And the pay is low. But these immigrants are willing to do this work to live in America and provide their families with a chance for a better life.

This isn't to say that native-born Americans don't work hard. Many do. In fact, our national work ethic is so strong that it can be counter-productive at times. Americans who work spend more time on the job than the famously hard-working Japanese. But America is also home to millions of people who aren't willing to work hard.

> "A dream doesn't become a reality through magic;
> it takes sweat, determination and hard work."
>
> —Colin Powell, American four-star general
> and former Secretary of State

IMMIGRANTS ARE WILLING TO SACRIFICE AND POSTPONE IMMEDIATE GRATIFICATION

Americans are an impatient bunch. We want what we want when we want it. But being willing to give up instant fulfillment to achieve more gratifying long-range objectives is important to genuine success. The old saying that nothing meaningful is easily gained generally holds true.

If you want to create a solid, satisfying future you must be willing to be patient and work steadily toward your goals. When choosing a career or job, don't think of it as a temporary "gig" but plan on staying the course. In all likelihood you'll change direction at some point, but at least go into your job with the intention to provide long-term value.

IMMIGRANTS AREN'T BURDENED BY AMERICAN-BORN HANDICAPS

Being born to American parents and raised in our mostly affluent society (at least compared to 90% of the rest of the world), we are privileged to have many opportunities and luxuries—and some serious handicaps as a result.

In America, things that are unattainable or undreamed of in many nations are an everyday part of our lives: a rich variety of healthy food, new cars, closets full of clothes, big homes. We have more freedom to do what we want (and more opportunity to do it) than anywhere else in the world.

We don't live in mud-floored grass shacks. We aren't terrorized by machete-wielding gangs, repressive governments, or civil war. Our healthcare, while expensive, is better than most countries. There are no debtor's prisons. We spend more money on feeding and caring for our cats and dogs than some countries do for their entire human population.

And although America has its share of problems, from inner city violence to opioid addiction to endemic racism, we are still the "land of opportunity" to most of the world.

Our comfort and affluence have also bred complacency. Not enough Americans are "hungry" to succeed in any significant way. Comfort has killed off initiative and ambition. Try to adopt the mindset of someone who didn't grow up with our advantages. You can start by practicing gratefulness every day of your life,

---

Mindful Career Rules: To be successful, think like an immigrant. Never stop learning. Work hard. Be grateful. And recognize that America provides everyone the opportunity to succeed.

Chapter 39

Become Irreplaceable

"Be so good they can't ignore you."

—Steve Martin, actor, musician

We just love that word "irreplaceable." If you can achieve this in your career you can also achieve your dreams. Few people can honestly say that their company could not easily replace them with another equally skilled and personable employee.

You don't need to be the best salesperson or the top anything to be of high value in your job. There are many ways to create value that far exceeds your cost to the company. Barring unforeseen possibilities such as mergers, sociopath bosses or a global catastrophe, there are several ways to ensure you will be a key player for years to come.

Here, derived from Keven Daum's 2015 article in *Inc.* magazine are 17 ways to become irreplaceable in the workplace:

1. **Don't wait to be asked.** Employees create value when they anticipate what is needed and get it done without any prompting.

2. **Attack the disease, not the symptoms.** Much time is wasted at companies being reactive. Create value by assessing the root cause of the problem and make a systemic change that eliminates it completely.

3. **Be the pressure release, not the pressure builder.** Stress is endemic in the workplace, and uptight people feed off each other. Create value by helping people decompress. Be the cool head when others are losing theirs.

4. **Plan your work, work your plan.** As you might guess, we are big fans of planning. Lazy thinking and random action usually produce mediocre results. Do the thinking, planning, and collaboration to create a sound plan of action.

5. **Do your due diligence.** Research and test ideas before developing a plan of action that can be implemented efficiently and has the best chance of success.

6. **Be forward thinking.** Think beyond the task at hand to the future. What are the consequences of your actions? How can they be augmented for greater success in the future? Like the chess grand masters, develop a strategy and tactics several steps ahead of where you are to get to where you want to go.

7. **Keep the big picture in mind.** Don't work in isolation or on a vertical path. Know what the big picture is for your company, project, and your career. Think of all the ways your actions fit into the bigger picture. Do the mental work required to move beyond the immediate task at hand.

8. **Build bridges, not bombs.** You'll find most work environments are rife with political intrigue as people jockey for advantages in order to get ahead. Stay aloof to office politics. Encourage esprit de corps and a cooperative, collaborative approach.

9. **Cross-train yourself and your colleagues.** When employees understand the jobs of their colleagues, there will be fewer misunderstandings. You and the company will benefit from ideas generated by people with different skills and expertise. An engineer may have a great marketing idea—if she understands the marketing goals of the company. This is the path to utilizing the fullest range of talents from all employees— and yourself.

10. **Be your boss' right or left brain.** No one can know it all. Even top leaders have their knowledge gaps. Bring knowledge or expertise to

your relationship with your boss that helps him perform better. It will benefit him, the company, and you.

11. **Stay ahead of the curve.** The future is arriving faster every day. Change is a constant. Strive to stay knowledgeable about the changes that can impact your company and career. For older workers, who are often assumed to have less knowledge than younger employees, being current—especially with technology—is an effective way to stay relevant.

12. **Create circles of influence.** Inspire others to greatness. Identify potential leaders. Create collaborative relationships with these people to help lead the company in the future.

13. **Communicate clearly to be effective.** Don't be ambiguous in your communication. Be clear and direct. Don't engage in "passive aggressive" communications, muddled thinking or contradictory statements.

14. **Know when to lead and when to follow.** Good leaders know when to lead and when to get out of the way and let others take charge. Be secure in being second in command. Encourage the people you supervise to take the lead to help them grow.

15. **Don't be afraid to fight for what you believe in.** Be pragmatic but stand up for a position you believe is right. Be ready to admit you're wrong if another point of view is superior.

16. **Make your work environment a great place to work.** Stay upbeat and optimistic. Studies prove you'll be more successful if you are. Have a sense of humor. Place everything in context. Follow author Miguel Ruiz' *Four Agreements:*

    1. Be impeccable with your word.
    2. Don't take anything personally.
    3. Don't make assumptions.
    4. Always do your best.

17. **Always be a student.** Don't stop learning and growing. In the 21st century, it is easy to get behind unless you continually upgrade your knowledge.

SKILLS THAT WILL PAY DIVIDENDS FOREVER

Research from Stanford University by Carol Dweck, Ph.D, author of *Mindset: The New Psychology of Success,* and her colleagues showed clearly the power of mindset in job performance and growth. When people were taught that they had the power to personally change their brains and improve, they improved dramatically. All they had to do was believe in themselves to make it happen. The power to learn and grow and improve is in the belief that you can. As Napoleon Hill famously said, "What you believe, you can achieve."

EMOTIONAL INTELLIGENCE

> *"Emotional intelligence (EQ) is a strong predictor of how well people do in life."*
> —Dr. Travis Bradberry, author of *Emotional Intelligence 2.0,* co-founder of TalentSmart

Research from several studies has shown that emotional intelligence is a primary factor determining success in all areas of life. This is especially true in your career success. When TalentSmart tested emotional intelligence against 33 other workplace skills, they found that it is the strongest predictor of performance, a factor in 89% of success in all types of jobs. Dr. Travis Bradberry, found that in the people he studied, "90% of top performers are also high in EQ. On the flip side, just 20% of bottom performers are high in EQ." People with high EQ, he found, make an average of $29,000 more than those with low emotional intelligence. "EQ has twice the power of IQ to predict someone's performance," according to SixSeconds, the emotional intelligence network.

At the core of emotional intelligence is mindfulness.

TIME MANAGEMENT

> *"Until we can manage time, we can manage nothing else."*
> —Peter F. Drucker, educator, author of *The Effective Executive*

Dr. Bradberry also lists time management as a key skill for success. Learning to manage your time by prioritizing your tasks, eliminating time wasting (e.g. surfing the internet, useless meetings), and delegating work is key to controlling your time.

Mindfulness can provide a valuable perspective on utilizing your time well. As Deepak Chopra writes in *The Book of Secrets: Unlocking the Dimensions of Your Life,* "Most of us take for granted that time flies, meaning that it passes too quickly. But in the mindful state, time doesn't really pass at all. There is only a single instant of time that keeps renewing itself over and over with infinite variety."

LISTENING

"When people talk, listen completely. Most people never listen."

—Ernest Hemingway, American author of *The Sun Also Rises*

To truly listen to another person requires focus and mindfulness. Eliminate distractions and hear what the other person is telling you. Don't jump ahead to what you want to say next because this prevents you from understanding what you are being told. Just listen mindfully.

ASKING FOR HELP

"You are never strong enough that you don't need help."

—Cesar Chavez, civil rights activist

It takes a confident and mindful person to ask for help. Dr. Bradberry points out that true leaders aren't afraid to seek support and guidance when they need it.

Sometimes all that is needed to break the barriers to a difficult relationship is to ask for help. Ben Franklin once asked a bitter enemy if he could borrow a book from his extensive library. The man was so surprised by the request that he granted it. Franklin returned the book with thanks a few weeks later. Doing Franklin a favor softened the man and the two eventually became good friends. Franklin was mindful of human emotional responses and used this ploy to defuse the other man's animosity.

GETTING QUALITY SLEEP

"Sleep is the best meditation."

—Dalai Lama, spiritual leader

We've spoken about the importance of high-quality sleep elsewhere in this book. But it bears repeating that sleep can be one of the most important ingredients to success in your career (and life). Dr. Bradberry says that "learning to get high-quality sleep on a regular basis is a difficult skill to master, but it pays massive dividends the next day." Lack of sleep or poor-quality sleep makes it very difficult to focus, think critically, be creative, and master your emotions.

TAKING INITIATIVE

"Success comes from taking the initiative and following up. Persisting."

—Tony Robbins, author of *Awaken the Giant Within*

When you take initiative, you take control. Initiative is the launch pad to success. Don't be afraid to come into your competence, take risks, and drive things forward to a successful conclusion. It's a skill that will take you far in life. Master the grit it takes to succeed.

STAYING POSITIVE

"Believe you can and you're halfway there."

—President Theodore Roosevelt

Being positive isn't being a Pollyanna. It's been proven that positive thoughts actually rewire your brain to help mitigate the natural tendency to find threats in life to defend against. Numerous studies have demonstrated that positive thoughts more often lead to positive outcomes. Positive action combined with positive thinking results in success. Positive thinking is a result of being mindful. You cannot have a positive life and a negative mind.

> *"There are only two ways to live your life.*
> *One is as though nothing is a miracle.*
> *The other is as though everything is a miracle."*
>
> —Albert Einstein

THE TOP 10 SKILLS MOST DESIRED BY EMPLOYERS BY 2020

According to the World Economic Forum, the skills employers are looking for aren't necessarily the skills you have been led to believe are most important. After surveying 350 executives across nine industries in fifteen of the world's largest economies, the WEF issued *The Future of Jobs* report that clearly shows how much and how fast the job market is changing.

Inc. magazine writes, "In a world increasingly dominated by robots, artificial intelligence, and virtual reality, having a firm grasp on what employers will be looking for is smart. Interestingly, more than 33% of the skill sets listed are not yet considered important by many employers. They may not be on their radar now—but they will be. Here are the findings from the WEF report:

10. **Cognitive flexibility.** This involves creativity, logical reasoning, and problem sensitivity. It also means being able to adapt how you communicate based on who you're talking to. Employers want to know you don't just say the same thing to everyone -- that you think critically about who you're talking to, deeply listen, and tailor communication to that person.

9. **Negotiation skills.** This will be in especially high demand in computer and math jobs, such as data analysis and software development. It will also be critical in the arts and design (including commercial and industrial designers).

8. **Service orientation.** This was defined as actively seeking ways to help others. How much do you assist those on your team, your superiors, and people across your industry? How much are you known for that?

7. **Judgment and decision-making.** As organizations collect more and more data, there will be an even greater need for workers who can analyze it and use it to make intelligent decisions. Good judgment also involves knowing how to get buy-in from a colleague, or making a strong suggestion to a manager (even if it might not make you popular).

6. **Emotional intelligence.** Robots can do a lot, but they still can't read people the way other humans can (at least not yet). Employers will place a strong emphasis on hiring those who are aware of others' reactions, as well as their own impact on others.

5. **Coordinating with others.** Again, this falls under the social skills umbrella (sensing a trend?). It involves being able to collaborate, adjust in relation to others, and be sensitive to the needs of others.

4. **People management.** In the report, people management included being able to motivate people, develop the talents and skills of employees, and choosing the most talented people for a job.

3. **Creativity.** In 2015, creativity ranked 10th on the list. It's now one of the top three skills employers will seek. Why? Because as we're bombarded by new technologies, employers want creative people who can apply that technology to new products and services.

2. **Critical thinking.** As automation increases, the need for humans who can employ logic and reasoning increases. This is, in part, because machines must be directed ethically and optimally. Employers want people with critical minds who can evaluate the uses or abuses of the power of technology, and use them to benefit the company, the people in it, and the future.

1. **Complex problem-solving.** Technology can make life easier, but it can also make things more complicated. For example, you could use wearables to help map the walking patterns of nurses and doctors in a hospital to see how to make things more efficient. But without

a human being analyzing those results while *also* having intelligent conversations with nurses, doctors, and patients, you will likely end up with a wrong or even dangerous result. One report shows that 36% of all jobs across all industries will require complex problem-solving abilities as a core skill by 2020.

SOCIAL SKILLS

Most studies measuring what employers and the marketplace deem important to success in the future have one underlying, recurring thread—the importance of social skills. A 2015 NBER working paper, *The Growing Importance of Social Skills in the Labor Market,* points out that most job growth since 1980 has been in occupations that are social-skill intensive. They go on to say that "high-skilled, hard to automate jobs will increasingly demand social adeptness." A 2015 *Harvard Business Review* of studies on the subject found that people who have higher social skills make more money, even after controlling for education, cognitive skills, and type of job.

Mindful Rules: Be the person who would be impossible to replace through mindful performance on the job. Pay attention to developing your social skills. Be aware of what employers deem important.

Chapter 40

The 50+ Career Reinvention

*"The lack of respect for experience is a reality
that older workers have to swallow."*

—Penelope Trunk, author of *The New Rules for Success*

When you are over 50 and looking for a job for the first time in years, it can be a shock. Phone calls that aren't returned, resumés that disappear into the HR "black hole," and being "overqualified" for jobs you would love to have (even with the reduced pay) are the new norm in the workplace. At times you'll despair of ever getting a job. With another 30 years or so left to live, you may wonder how you're going to survive.

Similar complaints by younger, inexperienced workers seem to indicate that your "best" career years are between 30 and 40. While this is not always the case, you will need a plan to navigate the transition of your career into its mature stages.

"The only source of knowledge is experience."

—Albert Einstein

OLDER . . . BUT NOT "OLD"

First, it's important to present yourself as experienced yet relevant, older but not "old," and with professional assets that would be hard, if not impossible, for anyone younger to have acquired. Emphasize the skills and experience that someone who is 26 years old would not likely have, such as advanced training or supervisory experience.

Chip Conley, author of the 2018 book *Wisdom@Work: The Making of a Modern Elder,* argues that "experience is on the brink of a comeback." He writes, "At a time when power is shifting younger, companies are finally waking up to the value of the humility, emotional intelligence, and wisdom that come with age. And while digital skills might have only the shelf life of the latest fad or gadget, the human skills that mid-career workers possess—like good judgement, specialized knowledge, and the ability to collaborate and coach—never expire."

You may feel an impulse to "fit in" with younger workers by trying to be like them. This seldom works and rings false. Act and dress age appropriate but not "stuffy." Adopt an attitude of equal collegiality and you'll usually be treated the same way in return.

One of the unspoken prejudices against older workers (and there are many) is the fear by younger workers of having someone report to them who is as old as their own father or mother. Perhaps the best stance to adopt is that of a trusted older advisor or senior counselor. Be willing to "mentor" younger staff members and support their career goals. If you are seen as someone who is not a direct competitor—or as the guy or gal who they can safely go to for advice—you will not only be welcomed, you could be the office champion.

You'll also need to look and act non-threatening to younger workers. If your co-workers dress down and seem to favor college dorm room garb, you'll probably not want to wear a dark blue suit, white shirt, and tie. However, you would look ridiculous emulating their style. Stylish casual wear appropriate to your age works best.

Socializing with younger workers, who may still be into collegiate style binge drinking and chasing members of the opposite sex, can be problematic. Choose your socializing venues carefully. You don't want to be caught in awkward situations. Neither do you want to appear unsociable.

It's a shame that older workers—and the wisdom their experience can impart—are not valued more in our society. Everyone loses when there isn't a full integration of age, sex, and racial types.

OVERCOMING AGE DISCRIMINATION

Here are a few tips that can help those over 50 stay competitive in the workplace:

1. **Upgrade your tech skills.** If there is one thing that separates the younger workforce from those over 50, it's technical abilities. At the least, invest in basic computer and social media skills. Many older people are resistant to learning these important ingredients in career success. Embrace the challenge and just do it.

2. **Freshen up your look.** If your hairstyle and clothing conveys a "grandpa" look, the younger workforce will tag you as outdated. You don't have to show up at the office in jeans and a college sweatshirt, but try to be current. Also, nothing makes you look "older" as being overweight. Consider engaging in a healthy nutrition program and a gym membership. Plus, regular exercise will give you more energy, increase your confidence, and improve your mind.

3. **Create an online presence.** Today employers almost always check out job applicants online. Make your presence known in a positive way on LinkedIn, Facebook, Twitter, Instagram, and in blog posts. Consider creating your own website (using Wix, Weebly or Wordpress) and blogging regularly. See if your name is available as a URL at GoDaddy. com. Creating your own website to promote your experience and skills will also demonstrate that you are comfortable with contemporary career skills.

4. **Edit your resumé.** Leave off college graduation dates. Only include your last 15 years of experience. While your age information will eventually be known, by removing age from your resumé you decrease your chance of being automatically excluded from consideration. Also, make sure your resumé has a contemporary format and style.

5. **Use your network.** Hopefully, you have created a large network of business and social connections over the years. Now is the time to

use them. Several studies show that a large percentage of jobs are found through networking—between 65% and 85%. This may be the older workers' most reliable source of new opportunities.

6. **Commit to a strong LinkedIn presence.** If you haven't committed to creating a strong LinkedIn presence, do so immediately. Most professionals use LinkedIn to manage their career; it's not just for job search. LinkedIn is the sole platform you *need* to use as part of your overall career strategy. In early 2017, LinkedIn undertook some dramatic revisions in how it looks and works. For most people, it will be much easier to use than the previous version. Take the time to learn how to use it.

7. **Consider working remotely or freelance.** Many companies will hire older workers as long as they don't have to see them personally every day. Really. They may need your skills, but you don't fit their "culture." Also, working remotely, freelance, or as a contract worker are fast-growing areas of employment that will soon represent 1/3 of all workers.

8. **Leverage your experience.** The one key area you should have a decided advantage over younger employees is experience. Make a point to create a powerful story about how your experience and expertise can contribute to the success of the organization interviewing you. Employers want to see how you can help them succeed.

9. **Drop the "attitude."** Coincidentally, as we are writing this Carol Ann has just come back from a counseling session with a woman who is 58 years old and can't find work. Like other age 50+ people we have advised, she is angry and resentful about being unable to find meaningful work. She refuses to use LinkedIn or upgrade her tech skills for "personal" reasons (she thinks it negatively affects her privacy). Her resumé is dated. Her social media skills are almost non-existent and limited to poorly-conceived Facebook posts. She doesn't even have business cards. She projects a tired, "old" image. Until she becomes more "mindful" of her situation there is little hope anything will change. With many years left to live, her future looks bleak.

10. **Expand your consciousness.** This is a good point in your life to become more mindful, more conscious, and more enlightened. Begin meditating. Practice introspection. Read books that will expand your understanding of the world and yourself. Transition to a better version of yourself.

With age often comes rigidity. As Richard Branson, the Virgin Group founder said, "It's more important than ever to keep an open mind and challenge our perceptions, opinions, and subconscious biases. I always try to remember that all of our thoughts and choices are shaped by our own experiences, emotions, and surroundings." Or, as Anaïs Nin said, "We don't see things as they are, we see things as we are." Try to see things differently.

THE GOOD NEWS FOR OLDER WORKERS

The good news for older workers is a result of three employment market dynamics that will likely continue for decades:

1. The first Baby Boomers reached retirement age (65) in 2011 and millions more will retire or cut back their working lives in the next decade.

2. The rapidly falling birth rate hit a 30-year low in 2018 and is shrinking the available workforce. This trend will likely continue for decades.

3. By 2020, the labor pool will barely grow—just 0.4% annually— where it is expected to stay for decades, creating a huge challenge for employers to meet their growing hiring needs.

It's time for older workers to dust off (and update) their resumés, upgrade their skills (especially tech), and get back into the workplace. Older workers will find it more receptive than it has been in modern times.

Mindful Career Rules: Don't let your age define you or allow yourself to develop an age-related mindset. If you've done the work to stay current, developed valuable skills, built a network of professional contacts, and learned how to collaborate well with younger workers, you should have no problem finding meaningful work.

Chapter 41

Why You Should Never Retire

> *"There's this American Dream to put enough away*
> *that you can golf and build a birdhouse or just be*
> *in a Barcalounger watching football all day.*
>
> *I'll never be that guy. And I'm not sure the people*
> *who have that are all that happy."*
>
> —Kevin Bacon, actor

Retirement has had its 15 minutes of fame.

As a concept, retirement was first introduced in Germany in 1889 when Otto von Bismarck set it at age 70 (later reduced to 65 in 1916). This retirement age was adopted by the U.S. in 1935 when the Social Security Act selected it as the age when benefits could be received. Before then, for most of history people worked until they physically were unable to do so—or died.

The idea of working for 40 or 50 years and then quitting—despite the fact that you may have many productive years ahead—to play endless rounds of golf, travel for years, or watch reruns of *Seinfeld* is a zero sum game. You will lose as much as you gain.

Most people need the sense of accomplishment or achievement work provides to be fulfilled. Even worse is leaving normal society to go live in an artificial, adult daycare facility to frolic with other "seniors" in their Golden Years.

Numerous studies have proven that continuing to work, staying mentally and physically active, lengthens life and helps prevent age-related diseases and the decline of mental acuity. Work gives shape and substance to our lives. Americans continue to hang onto the concept of retirement because they simply don't know any better or because they dislike the work they are doing.

Also, today Americans are living longer, healthier lives than ever before—65 is the new 45! Many people can look forward to a long working life after 65. The oldest National Park Ranger now is 97 and still going strong. Nearly 1 in 5 people over 65 are still at work.

OLDER WORKERS ACCOUNT FOR ALL WORKFORCE GROWTH THIS CENTURY

This may come as a surprise to most people, but the entire growth of the workforce since 2000—17 million—has been workers 55 and older, according to a new report by the Federal Reserve (2018). The report predicts that workers 55+ will remain between 23–24% of the overall workforce for the next 20 years.

Since fewer than 1 in 5 people have saved enough to sustain their retirement (and will need to create ongoing income) managing your career mindfully during your "golden" years is important. Also, for demographic reasons, the workforce is expected to be short of skilled workers for several more years. So, don't despair if your hair is gray and you're a card-carrying AARP member. Just upgrade that resumé, expand your skill set, stay current, maintain good health, and look forward to continuing your career well into your eighties, if you want.

RETIREMENT MAY NOT BE AN OPTION IN THE 21ST CENTURY

"34% of older workers don't plan to retire."

—Charles Schwab, American financial executive

The economic meltdown of 2008 and its aftermath have dealt a serious blow to the retirement plans of many Americans. Retirement may no longer be an option for millions of people who have seen their savings and investments decimated.

> **Nearly half of Americans have no savings and cannot meet an unexpected expense of just $400.**
> **Fully 40% of households admit to living paycheck to paycheck.**

One in four households have less than $5,000 saved. Just 25% have $200,000 or more set aside for their retirement years, according to the Northwestern Mutual 2018 Planning and Progress Study. However, if you live 20 years after retiring at 55, you'll likely need $1 million just to survive on a modest $50,000 a year. Most people will live longer than age 75.

It's clear America is in for a huge financial and humanitarian crisis when all these folks reach their "golden" years.

It's baffling that so many people are fixated on the day when they will no longer work. Among many, it's an obsession. Frankly, retirement is outdated, leftover thinking from the 1950s. Very little of it applies to 21st century conditions. Economic instability, changing lifestyles, increased longevity, second families, and new careers are the norm now. The majority of Americans face one or more of these new realities.

Besides the likely necessity of creating additional income in the third part of their lives, most people are happier if they have meaningful work to do. In the last few years, there has been a significant increase in the labor force participation rate among people 55 to 69. It's apparent that many Baby Boomers have a much different view of retirement than their parents. Although many are forced to return to the workplace as a result of the effects of the Great Recession or poor financial planning, many *want* to continue working; it's just a matter of finding work that, well, works.

Your best bet to finding sustainable work when you have "aged out" of the corporate workforce is to create a business or service that you can do until your dying days (which may not come for twenty or more years). The most ideal business is one that provides passive income, a business that once it is established runs automatically with little or no maintenance or input. A classic example is writing a book. Once the book is published it can provide steady revenue, if you market it properly. This is especially true for non-fiction self-help books. An online class is another example of a passive income generating business. Or you might create a product you can sell both online and off that will generate income into the future. Creating income when you are older is usually the result of what we refer to as your Plan B Career, a second source of income you can develop as you are working in your primary career.

THE "PLAN B" CAREER

Everyone should manage their career by creating a second source of income. Ideally, this would come from a hobby that evolves into a side business (or "side hustle" as it is currently referred to among Millennials and Gen Z-ers). In this way you are creating a revenue stream doing something you enjoy. If (or when) your primary career path ends, you can fall back on your secondary source of income and create the Plan B career. This is often the case for retirees.

Sometimes the side hustle is so successful it becomes a primary career path. Perhaps the most famous side hustle that became a big business is Apple. Steve Jobs worked at Atari and Steve Wozniak was employed at Hewlett-Packard. They worked on the personal computer at night and weekends in Jobs' parents' garage. Who could have guessed that, within five years, they would have one of the hottest tech companies in Silicon Valley? Other successful companies began as secondary sources of income, including Groupon, Etsy, Houzz, Under Armour, Craigslist, Twitter, Khan Academy, WeWork, Udemy, Instagram, and hundreds of others.

In our rapidly evolving and changing world it is risky to put all your eggs in one career basket. Develop a side hustle that has the potential to create a secondary income stream and potentially develop into a full-time career.

Mindful Rules: Work defines much of who you are in life. Full retirement may not be good for your health or soul. And if you haven't saved enough for retirement you may need to work—which is why a Plan B Career is important to your survival.

Chapter 42

Freelance, Contract, Temp, and Gig Work

> *"I didn't want an unsatisfying career. And I didn't want to commit to one place—either one company or one location. I wanted to make my own decisions."*
>
> —Rocco Baldasarre, Founder, Zebra Advertisement

The rapid and pervasive restructuring of the American workplace has resulted in a huge increase in the number of workers outside the mainstream of full-time employment. Some might call this "underemployment" but others find working at temp jobs, freelance projects and contract "gigs" to be more attractive than a 40+ hour commitment to one employer. Going solo can be scary but the rewards are often worth the risk.

A report published in 2014 by the Roosevelt Institute and the Kauffman Foundation states that by 2040 the American economy will be "scarcely recognizable." The changes in the U.S. workforce will be wrenching, with opportunities for some and career destruction for others. Both private and public enterprises will be severely impacted.

According to a 2014 survey by Edelman Berland, freelancers already make up 34% of the workforce—55 million people. The shift toward self-employment, entrepreneurship, contract work, temp jobs, and "gigs" will continue to accelerate.

1. Nearly 40% of America's workforce will be freelancers by 2020, according to research by NextSpace (from *The Rise of the Naked Economy* by Jeremy Neumer).

2. Millennials make up the largest share of the freelance workforce. Nearly one-third of Millennials are employed as independent workers.

3. The total freelance market in America earned more than $1 trillion in 2016.

4. 86% of freelancers prefer freelancing more than traditional employment, according to a 2016 Field Nation Freelancer Study.

5. 50% of freelancers would not give up freelancing for ANY amount of money.

6. 19.8% of full-time independent workers earn more than $100,000 annually, according to a State of Independence in America 2017 study.

Soon, nearly everyone will be their own business in some way. You are the CEO of your work life. You are responsible for your own success.

To be successful, you will have to be self-sufficient, resourceful, and entrepreneurial. You'll need to plan your life and career, learn to sell effectively, and educate yourself to stay ahead of the learning curve. The linear corporate career ladders that have become embedded in American life will no longer be there for the most part. For millions of complacent workers, the safe cocoon of corporate life will no longer be an option.

THE ADVANTAGES OF GOING SOLO

First, there's the freedom (most of the time) to control your own schedule. You can work mornings and be with your family in the afternoon. Or work a three-day week. You can work until 3 a.m. if you're a night owl. Want to take a month-long vacation? You can—if you plan.

You also often have the freedom to work on what interests you—not just what you are required to do.

Every study on the subject has found that people are happier and more productive when they work on what they find interesting and meaningful, and helps increase their knowledge.

Second, the financial rewards can be substantial. Many freelancers make more than they did in their previous fixed salary jobs. The sky's the limit on earnings.

Third, you save on commuting, lunches, dry cleaning, clothes and all the other "support" costs of working for a company. This can add up to a substantial amount—thousands of dollars—each year.

Fourth, you are largely untouched by office politics, boring meetings, and abusive bosses. And if any of these things do become a problem—no problem—you simply go on to another "gig" or freelance project. With most temp, contract or freelance work, you are not perceived as a "threat" to anyone. So, there's no one out "to get you." And you usually aren't involved in projects long enough to establish any negative relationships.

> **Since nearly half of all workers say they don't like the company or the boss they work for, freelancing can result in a major improvement in job satisfaction and personal happiness.**

According to Statistica, there are currently 56.7 million people in America who freelance—enough that there is a freelancers union with health care plans and other benefits (Freelancerunion.org).

Upwork, a freelance resource website, discovered in a survey that "Americans are spending 1 billion hours per week freelancing."

The number of freelance websites has grown rapidly to nearly a hundred. Check out these top freelance resources:

(freelance.com), the world's largest online outsourcing resource with more than 2.5 million freelancers and 500,000 businesses registered with the site for web design, data entry, content writers, and other jobs

Upwork.com for freelance work in 3,500 skill categories

(Guru.com) for programmers, web designers, and content writers

(iFreelance.com) for programmers, content writers, data entry, proofreaders, virtual assistants, writers, and web designers

(PeoplePerHour.com) for programmers, content writers, virtual assistants, and graphic artists

(Fiverr.com) freelance jobs start at $5 although most cost more—a good resource to find inexpensive quality freelance work in a variety of skills

(eWorker.com) for writers, graphic artists, and programmers

(logomyway.com) for graphic designers and artists

(99Designs.com) for graphic designers—you can have dozens of designers bid for your job with spec work

(GetACoder.com) for computer coders

(sologig.com) is the place for IT and engineering professionals

(translatorcafe.com) for typing jobs, medical translation, and other work-from-home jobs

(FreelanceWriting.com) for people who can write quality freelance articles

(ProjectSpring.com) for various projects, mostly programmers and web designers

(FreelanceJobSearch.com) for content writers, graphic artists, programmers, and other jobs

A great resource for the fast-growing area of remote working is FlexJobs. com. You can also find part-time, contract, and a few full-time positions (most with some remote work) on this site.

Additional resources: *The Wealthy Freelancer: 12 Secrets to a Great Income and an Enviable Lifestyle* by Steve Slaunwhite, Pete Savage, and Ed Gandia (thewealthyfreelancer.com) or *Creative Inc: The Ultimate Guide to Running a Successful Freelance Business* by Joy Deanqdeelert Cho and Meg Mateo Ilasco.

Mindful Career Rules: Going solo may bring you more happiness and compensation. Plus, you can never be fired or outsourced.

Chapter 43

Start Your Own Business

> *"There are some people who don't belong in a large organization."*
>
> —Peter Drucker, businessman, author of *Managing Oneself*

If the Great Recession taught us anything, it's that job security working for a corporation is a myth. It doesn't exist. So, if you're not going to have any job security, then why not take a shot at the gold ring and start your own business. After all, most millionaires who make it before age 40 did so with their own business.

Paradoxically, more businesses are started in recessions than during good times. Many of these new businesses are born of necessity—people who can't find work, create their own. But many more are a result of the opportunities that arise during any period of change or chaos. One person's hard luck can be another's great fortune.

> *"All you need is ignorance and confidence and the success is sure."*
>
> —Mark Twain

JUMP INTO ENTREPRENEURSHIP
WITH BOTH EYES OPEN

More than a million people will start a business in the next year. Sounds great, doesn't it? The hip new thing, especially among recent college grads, is to be an entrepreneur. Make scads of money and buy an Aston-Martin, a 180-foot yacht, and marry a supermodel. This actually does happen—to three or four people a year.

The reality is that 40% of all new ventures will be out of business before they reach their first anniversary. Within five years, 80% will fail. And of the 20% that make it to the five-year mark, another 80% will fail within the next five years.

Are you okay with those odds? Does it make you want to go running back to a comfy cubicle at the giant Acme Widget Corporation?

HEY, ISN'T FAILURE GOOD FOR YOU?

"Nothing succeeds like success."

—Alexander Dumas, French author of *The Three Musketeers*

Despite all the rah-rah hype about how "good" failing is for you, how it builds character, and teaches you important lessons in life and business, the cold truth is that failure can often be a life-sucking, emotionally devastating, miserable experience that will take years to recover from personally and financially.

Many owners of failed startups are forced into bankruptcy because new businesses are usually backed heavily with the entrepreneur's "skin in the game," which is usually not enough to sustain the business. Now you've got that albatross around your neck for at least seven years. Try to get a loan or a job or start another business and the old BK will come back to haunt you. It's like trying to run while wearing those ankle bracelets you see shackled to prisoners.

If you think failing is good for you, just see how your previously adoring bank treats you if you fail. Or the IRS. Or the BOE. Or the EDD. Or American Express. It doesn't matter if Exxon or Amazon doesn't pay a cent in income taxes, the IRS will look the other way. But if YOU owe them $50 they will track you and hunt you down and harass you and add fines and interest and eventually seize the money from your bank account to get what you owe.

And that goes for creditors too. Especially your creditors. It's okay for them to lose huge amounts of money on bad business decisions or investments that a monkey wouldn't make, but if you owe them money, they don't see it the same way. You OWE them—and they will nag you a hundred times worse than your mom ever did to get their money back.

FAIL FAST, FAIL OFTEN . . . SOMETIMES

> *"It is hard to fail, but it is worse never to have tried to succeed."*
>
> —President Theodore Roosevelt

Embracing the "fail fast, fail often" philosophy so popular now in Silicon Valley is a little irresponsible since failure also harms other people in addition to yourself. Investors lose money, suppliers don't get paid, and employees lose their jobs. Landlords may get stiffed for unpaid rent.

There is no shortage of wise sayings about how much you will learn from your failures. You *will* learn a LOT. Just remember that others may pay dearly for your education.

> *Don't fetishize failure. "Where I come from, people like to succeed. My goal is not to fail fast. My goal is to succeed over the long run. They are not the same thing."*
>
> —Marc Andreessen, legendary Silicon Valley investor, from the book *Tribe of Mentors* by Tim Ferriss

Success—winning—is what the world celebrates. The 1936 United States Olympic rowing team won the gold medal by 6/10ths of a second (less than one foot) after six and a half minutes of a grueling 2,000 meter race. Their win secured them a place in history. Now a bestselling book and movie, *The Boys in the Boat,* celebrates their feat. Who came in second or third? Few people have any idea (it was Italy and Germany, by mere inches). The win changed the lives of everyone on the American team. They remained friends for life. And the victory shaped their lives. No one knows what happened to the other teams.

You can't always succeed in life. But success should always be your goal. And like the 1936 Olympic rowing team, success is frequently only a matter of a little more effort.

SUCCEED FIRST, SUCCEED FAST

> *"It's good to learn from your mistakes.*
> *It's better to learn from other people's mistakes."*
> —Warren Buffett, American investor, billionaire

Failing fast and failing often only works if you are testing out product ideas, debugging software or practicing jump shots . . . just don't embrace the concept in all areas of your life. Yes, failure is an inevitable fact of life. But your first responsibility is to do everything in your power to succeed. "Succeed first, succeed fast" should be your motto. It's a more positive approach.

You need to be mindful about the personal consequences of failure. It could mean bankruptcy and a compromised credit rating. Or you could lose your family and friends' money—and perhaps sour the relationship with these important people in your life. Or you could lose an investors' money—a person who had faith that you would succeed and bet on you—but likely won't again.

Your reputation may be harmed—no matter what people say about the value of failure, they will look at your failure in a negative way. Your confidence will be shaken. And you may feel depressed. Failure exacts a heavy price.

Do you want to know how wonderful failure can be? Just look at the faces of the ballplayers who win the World Series compared to the faces of the losing team. Enough said. Know that you will fail in life, of that you can be certain. But try your best. Put in the hard work and critical thinking to boost your chances of success. Be mindful at every step of the journey of the consequences of success—or failure.

RECOVERING FROM FAILURE

*"Every perceived failure turns out to have a secret success,
and every perceived success has some secret failing in it."*

—Ethan Hawke, actor

Since the near collapse of the economy in 2008, the repercussions have been severe for tens of millions of Americans. "Failure" in its many forms is pervasive—careers ruined, homes lost, credit destroyed, evictions, repossessions, broken marriages, retirements on hold, savings and investments depleted, and dreams of a better future evaporated. With failure comes sleepless nights, stress, and depression. With failure comes fear; fear like you've never known in your life. Fear that causes you to do things you wouldn't ordinarily do. Fear that will make recovery even more difficult.

However, you need to extract whatever positive lessons you can from failure, if for no other reason than to avoid it in the future.

Re-evaluation and re-invention can come from an honest self-analysis of failure. "Sometimes our old self has to die for complete rebirth," says Julie Wainwright, former CEO of the now-defunct Pets.com. "Remember, the best is yet to come." In her book *ReBoot: My Five Life-Changing Mistakes and How I Have Moved On*, Wainwright describes her own journey from public failure to depression to resurrection. She is now the CEO of a highly successful new company The Real Real (therealreal.com) which recently completed a successful IPO.

Realize that failure is simply a part of life—a sucky part, but nonetheless a life experience that nearly everyone will experience. If you've failed in your life personally or professionally (or both), you're not alone. Some of the most successful people in history have had repeated failures: Henry Ford. Walt Disney. Abraham Lincoln.

*"Develop success from failure.
Discouragement and failure are two
of the surest stepping stones to success."*

—Dale Carnegie,
author of *How to Win Friends and Influence People*

According to California Governor Gavin Newsom, "Mistakes are the portals of discovery. I believe in failure in the context of learning from mistakes." Frankly, this is about the only positive feature of failure. You'll learn something—albeit the hard way. Just be forewarned that just because you failed doesn't mean you won't fail again . . . even doing the same thing. It's not easy to change entrenched habits or ways of thinking.

ADVICE ON FAILURE FROM ANN LANDERS–REALLY

The advice columnist Ann Landers once said this about life's "bumps" in the road:

"If I were asked to give what I consider the single most useful bit of advice for all humanity it would be this: Expect trouble as an inevitable part of life and when it comes, hold your head high, look it square in the eye and say, 'I will be bigger than you. You cannot defeat me.'"

After decades of dispensing advice, this is what Ann Landers considered the most important.

FAILING IS A PART OF THE GREAT CIRCLE OF LIFE

It may be difficult to see when you are in the midst of overwhelming trouble or experiencing soul-wrenching failure, but these experiences are a natural—and important—ingredient in your personal growth. Faced with courage, honesty, and resoluteness you will emerge a better, smarter, and more confident person. It's during times of difficulty or crisis that mindfulness is most essential. Be mindful that life is a bumpy ride and focus on handling the present with grace and courage.

> *"If we don't succeed, we run the risk of failure."*
>
> —Anonymous, but often attributed to Yogi Berra

Bernie Siegel (berniesiegelmd.com), the author of *Love, Medicine, and Miracles: Lessons Learned about Self-Healing from a Surgeon's Experience with Exceptional Patients*, talks about the "yin and yang" of life.

"There are cycles of success when things come to you and you thrive, and cycles of failure when they whither or disintegrate and you have to let them go in order to make room for new things to arise, or for transformation to happen. If you cling and resist at that point, it means you are refusing to go with the flow of life, and you will suffer. It is not true that the "up" cycle is good and the "down" cycle bad—except in the mind's judgment."

Eckhart Tolle *(eckharttolle.com),* author of *The Power of Now: A Guide to Spiritual Enlightenment,* believes that dissolution is needed for new growth to happen . . . that one cannot exist without the other. From times of chaos or destruction can come creativity and growth.

> *"You always pass failure on the way to success."*
>
> —Mickey Rooney, actor

We've always liked the inspirational words of President Theodore Roosevelt on failure:

"It is not the critic who counts; or where the doer of deeds could have done them better. The credit belongs to the man who is actually in the arena, whose face is marred by dust and sweat and blood; who strives valiantly; who errs, who comes up short again and again, because there is no effort without error and shortcoming; but who does actually strive to do the deeds; who knows great enthusiasms, the great devotions; who spends himself in a worthy cause, and who at the worst, if he fails, at least fails while daring greatly, so that his place shall never be with those cold and timid souls who neither know victory nor defeat."

The "bad" times, the failures, the disappointments, the rejections, the losses, the inevitable negative stuff that is a natural part of life is an opportunity to change course, do something different, learn, and grow.

> *"I failed my way to success."*
>
> —Thomas Edison, inventor

The life lesson here is that you can learn a lot from success *and* from failure. And failure may be the better teacher.

THINGS TO CONSIDER BEFORE BECOMING AN ENTREPRENEUR

> *"The supreme accomplishment is to blur the line between work and play."*
>
> —Arnold J. Toynbee

Being good at something is great. But that's not the same as building a business to market your product or service. What is important is whether YOU have the smarts, the stamina, the mindset, and the grit to operate and manage a business effectively. The product or service isn't as important to your long-term success as you might think.

Are you the world's best pie maker? Does everyone salivate just thinking of your peach pie? Do your friends tell you all the time that you should start a business selling your wonderful pies?

Then why not offer them to the world and become a pie gazillionaire? Let's go! But wait. Do you enjoy accounting? Ordering and managing inventory? Hiring and firing people? Are you a great promoter? Does it excite you to think about cleaning your ovens? Do you enjoy working at 11 p.m. doing the receipts for the day after everyone else has gone home? Do you mind being frequently exhausted?

Are you okay begging for money from your friendly local banker? Have you ever met one of the charming employees of the Health Department? What about that disgruntled whacko employee who takes you to court in order to extort money out of you to finance their pot-growing operation? And isn't it fun to pay 250 bucks a month to the pest control guy so your pie ingredients don't become infested with cockroaches? How many pies must you sell just to pay for all that?

Did your kid become a juvenile delinquent and you didn't even notice? Your husband says you haven't had sex with him in *how many* months—even though your peach pie scent turns him on? Do you mind spending nearly *every freakin' waking hour making pies?*

Say sayonara to all your important relationships—boyfriend, girlfriend, *friends,* wife, husband, kids, yourself—just about any other human being in your life other than those directly or indirectly involved in your wonderful business, like those employees who goof off half the time and steal from you when your back is turned? Or customers who complain because they think it will get them 10% off their order. Or suppliers who say nasty things because you're a day late paying them.

Do you like to work fourteen-hour days, seven days a week? That's what it will be like. Do you like to take vacations? Play tennis now and then? Read a fiction book? Meet friends for lunch. Forgeddaboutit! If you really believe you can take time off to lead a "balanced" life, then prepare yourself to be one of the above-mentioned business failure statistics.

That is the harsh reality of being an entrepreneur—not the hyped up, trendy blather you hear so much these days about how "sexy" and "in" it is.

PARTNERS

But I'll get a partner you say. We will divvy up the work and it won't be so hard. Let us tell it to you straight—not what you'll be told in your MBA classes or some blah blah blah business book.

You can always fire a CEO or General Manager or anyone who works FOR you if things don't work out. But it's a different story when they work WITH you. The Lone Ranger worked well with Tonto. But we bet it wouldn't have worked out so well if there were two Lone Rangers (Dual Rangers?).

If you do start a business with a partner, at least make sure that every contingency is covered—in writing, witnessed and approved by a competent business attorney, and signed in blood by both of you (the same blood you'll likely be spilling soon). Take the time to talk frankly with your future partner about expectations, how the inevitable disagreements will be resolved, which responsibilities will be exclusive and which shared, how expenses and income will be divided, exit strategies for the business and for the partnership.

Then shake hands, have a celebratory drink or two, and begin the arduous task of building a business together. Hey, maybe it will work for you . . . it did for Hewlett and Packard, Larry Page and Sergey Brin (Google), Ben Cohen and Jerry Greenfield (Ben & Jerry's).

Just remember this, a bad partnership will make you wish you'd never gone into business, likely cost you money, can lead to mental instability, and ruin your life. However, a good partnership can take your business to places you never dreamed it would go. Don't let our gloomy assessment of partnerships deter you from entering one; the statistics show partnerships work out more often than going it alone.

✓ According to the U.S. Small Business Administration, companies with multiple owners are more likely to survive longer than sole proprietorships—and had three times higher average revenues.

✓ A Darden School of Business study found that the single, common thread among successful entrepreneurs is their ability to compensate for their weaknesses by finding the right people to fill in the gaps.

In their book *The Power of 2: How to Make the Most of Your Partnerships at Work and in Life,* authors Rodd Wagner and Gale Muller utilize Gallup research data that shows the important ingredients in a strong partnership: complementary strengths, a common mission, fairness, trust, acceptance, forgiveness, communication, and unselfishness. They provide convincing data that people in mindful, collaborative relationships are happier and more successful in their endeavors. Yet, nearly 1 in 4 reported they had never experienced a great working partnership with anyone in their entire career!

Wagner and Muller also point out the poisoning effects upon an organization when a partnership goes wrong. Partnerships can reap huge rewards, but they're very difficult to get right. The bottom line? Enter a partnership only if you're reasonably certain it will work—and then do the work to make it work. Remember, a partnership is like marriage . . . without the sex. Since marriages *with* sex only work out half the time, ask yourself how many would work if there was NO sex.

NOW THAT WE'VE SCARED THE BEJEEZUS OUT OF YOU

Yes, going into business is terrifying. On the other hand, done mindfully, and with some luck and perseverance, you can create an exciting, satisfying, and financially rewarding career by doing your own thing. Owning your own business is the surest path to wealth in America. Nearly all the top wealthiest 1% of Americans either started their own business or inherited one.

SOME PEOPLE SHOULD OWN THEIR OWN BUSINESS— SOME NOT

As we've demonstrated, not everyone is cut out to own their own business. In fact, most people are happier with jobs where the onerous parts of owning a business are someone else's responsibility.

A business of your own can have many positive rewards though, including:

1. **No psycho boss** from hell —the bosshole—to deal with every day (nearly half of all employees dislike their boss).

2. **Freedom to work when you want** (even if that may be ALL the time).

3. **Freedom to work where you want** (Apple started in a garage and millions of businesses are run out of home offices or shared working spaces).

4. **No commuting.** Many self-employed people work at home or close to their home (commuting is always at the top of the list of what people hate about working).

5. **No annoying colleagues.** Most businesses are one-person operations—which essentially solves the problem of annoying, backstabbing, gossipy, don't-pull-their-weight co-workers. And if you hire someone you can always fire them. Just make sure they are "at will" employees and cover yourself in writing anytime they screw up. One disgruntled employee can ruin your business and years of hard work.

6. **The sky's the limit.** No tedious working your way up the corporate ladder of success for decades—only to get wasted in a corporate downsizing or buyout or bankruptcy. You can leapfrog your way to great success (if you're good, lucky, and the product/service you sell is wanted or needed—hopefully by lots of people).

7. **There are many free or inexpensive resources available for entre-preneurs** to help you learn the ropes. The Small Business Administration (sba.gov) conducts excellent classes (most are free—your tax dollars actually doing something good). SCORE (score.org) can set you up with a retired executive as a mentor. And hundreds of sites

online provide guidance, resources, and support. In major markets, there are dozens of startup and entrepreneur events to attend.

8. **You can do a lot with a little.** Unlike 30 years ago, the computer and internet revolution makes it easy to set up and conduct business. A smartphone (about $500), a few free or low-cost apps ($60), a wi-fi enabled computer ($600 - $2,000) a wireless printer/copier/scanner/ fax (about $200), a business license (about $200), a website you can create in a day from a template (less than $500 at (wix.com) or (squarespace.com) a business URL (about $20 at (godaddy.com), logo design (about $150 at (99designs.com) or (fiverr.com), incorporation (about $200 at (legalzoom.com), social media accounts to promote your business (Facebook, Instagram, Twitter, LinkedIn, Reddit, YouTube), a direct mail account to communicate with current/future customers ($50 a month at (ConstantContact.com) plus setting up a business account at the bank and your wireless phone provider—and a few other incidentals like business cards ($100 at (vistaprint.com) or (moo.com) and, voila, you're in business for about three thousand bucks. Of course, you still must either do (or make) something people will want to buy. Hopefully LOTS of people.

What do real entrepreneurs like about running their own business?

"Being the master of my own fate."
—Randy Hendrick, TRX

"Being able to create something magical and lasting."
—Larry Mindel, Il Fornaio Restaurants

"The freedom to do work I love and work with people I like."
—Suresh Kumar, Green Earth

"One reason to own a small business is the ability to direct the culture of your company."
—Kasey Gahler, Gahler Financial

"I love the pace and the challenges. I haven't had a dull day in six years."
—Christian Yanek, SurveyGizmo

"I can work from anywhere."
—Darin Kraetsch, Flip Flop Shops

"Owning a business challenges me to be the best I can be. My success is entirely my own making. I also like the upside financial potential. Most millionaires own their own business."
—Adam Perl, Co-founder, Arrangr.com

"For me, it was a very conscious choice to make a living doing what I love."
—Trish Breslin Miller, This Little Gallery

"Continuing to learn new things."
—Jesse Lipson, ShareFile

Before you commit to opening a business, find out as much as possible about every aspect of operating a business. Begin by reading some of the excellent books on the market (there are hundreds), business websites, and blogs. Business books are published virtually every week.

Here are a few that come highly recommended:

- *The E-Myth Revisited,* Michael Gerber (e-myth.com)

- *Good to Great: Why Some Companies Make the Leap… and Others Don't,* Jim Collins (jimcollins.com)

- *Influence: The Psychology of Persuasion,* Robert Cialdini (influenceatwork.com)

- *First, Break all the Rules: What the World's Greatest Managers Do Differently,* Marcus Buckingham and Curt Coffman

- *The Start-up of You: Adapt to the Future, Invest in Yourself, and Transform Your Career.* Reid Hoffman and Ben Casnocha (thestartupofyou.com)

- *The Art of the Start: The Time-Tested, Battle-Hardened Guide for Anyone Starting Anything,* Guy Kawasaki (guykawasaki.com)

- *The Lean Startup: How Today's Entrepreneurs Use Continuous Innovation,* Eric Ries (theleanstartup.com)

- *A Whack on the Side of the Head: How You Can Be More Creative,* Roger von Oech

- *Made to Stick: Why Some Ideas Survive and Others Die,* Chip Heath, Dan Heath (heathbrothers.com)
  Also, *Decision: How to Make Better Choices in Life and Work.*

- *The New Leader's 100-Day Action Plan: How to Take Charge, Build Your Team, And Get Immediate Results,* George Bradt, Jayme Check, Jorge Pedraza (primegenesis.com)

- *See You at the Top,* Zig Ziglar (ziglar.com)

- *Awaken the Giant Within,* Anthony Robbins (tonyrobbins.com)

- *EntreLeadership: 20 Years of Practical Business Wisdom from the Trenches,* Dave Ramsey (daveramsey.com)

- *Tribe of Mentors: The Tactics, Routines, and Habits of Billionaires, Icons, and World-Class Performers,* Tim Ferriss

- *Get Backed: Craft Your Story, Build the Perfect Pitch Deck, and Launch the Venture of Your Dreams,* Evan Baehr and Evan Loomis

- *The Startup Owners' Manual: The Step-by-Step Guide for Building a Great Company,* Bog Dorf and Steve Blank

- *The Creator's Code: The Six Essential Skills of Extraordinary Entrepreneurs,* Amy Wilkinson

Read these books before starting a business—they're your learning baseline for success. Check out newly released business books about business creation and entrepreneurship.

If possible, enroll in business courses at the SBA (sba.gov) or your local college. You'll need some understanding of accounting, tax reporting, payroll, marketing, sales and employee management. There are exceptional facilities in most major cities. Many of the resources are free.

Stanford University offers more than 900 free lectures on entrepreneurship by over 100 top thought leaders, including Mark Zuckerberg, Elon Musk, and Reid Hoffman. Listening to these lectures is like getting a Ph.D. in entrepreneurship. You can find many of these lectures online at Udemy (udemy.com). Many other colleges and universities offer programs in entrepreneurship. A simple online search will reveal dozens of schools offering free and credit courses.

In 2018, Y Combinator opened its Startup School to any new venture that meets their basic requirements. This is an excellent way to learn from the top startup incubator in America, as well as network with other entrepreneurs.

> *"Wealth is nothing more than abundance consciousness."*
> —Deepak Chopra, co-author of *SUPER BRAIN:*
> *Releasing the Explosive Power of Your Mind*
> *to Maximize Health, Happiness, and Spiritual Well-being*

It's important to go into business for the right reasons. If it's to only make money you may not do well. Money is a bi-product of providing value to lots of people. It helps to have the right mindset too. A fearful and defensive attitude is counter-productive. Mindfulness in a kind, supportive, collaborative environment is more conducive to success.

LOCATION, LOCATION, LOCATION

Your location may be a factor in your eventual success or failure—especially if you're opening a retail business. As the saying goes, "Location, location, location." Depending upon your business type you may want to consider shared offices or an incubator space. Rent is one of the biggest fixed expenses that you'll need to control. Check out (hq. com), (regus.com), and (wework.com) shared space companies with full-service office spaces available worldwide. Here in the San Francisco Bay Area you can rent a "hot desk" for as little as $450 a month. There are also innovative startup shared spaces in most markets—such as RocketSpace (rocket-space.com) in San Francisco where Zappos and Zaarly got their start.

DON'T SKIMP ON THE LEGAL STUFF

Be sure to have a competent attorney review your business documents—especially leases. And speaking of leases, the lease deal you put together can be one of the most important decisions you'll make. A bad lease can cost you a lot of money down the road. Just one poorly written line in a lease—one drawn up by an attorney—once cost us more than a half-million dollars. So, double-check everything.

As with most things you can get a lot done online at a reasonable cost. Start with LegalZoom (legalzoom.com). But for the really important stuff, get the best attorney you can afford. It will be money well spent.

GET MENTORING

Find a successful businessperson who will help mentor you. A mentored business is five times more likely to succeed. It is invaluable to get advice from someone who has "been there" and can help you avoid painful and costly mistakes. Some businesses will allow you to "shadow" them by working temporarily in their operation. This, and part-time work for a company, is a great way to see if the day-to-day working environment is something that appeals to you—before you jump into it 100%.

You can also learn a lot by joining a business group in your industry or geographical area. Learn "the lay of the land" from others who have gone through it all before you.

A top source for qualified mentoring (for free) is SCORE (score. com). Retired executives give back by helping entrepreneurs get their businesses up and running successfully.

OPERATING CAPITAL

The single most frequent cause of business failure is not having enough capital. It is the lifeblood of business. You'll need money to get started. You'll need money to see you through the first years when income is often low but expenses keep mounting. And you'll need money to make changes after you're in business for a while, as well as to expand. We can't say this strongly enough—make sure you have the capital necessary to establish and grow your business.

Startup capital comes from several sources:

1. **Your own savings.** This is perhaps the best capital because you aren't paying interest on it and you don't have to give up any equity or control. If you do seek out investors at some point, they will be impressed that you have "skin in the game." Bootstrapping your business may be difficult, but if you can create a successful venture without taking outside money, it can pay off handsomely.

2. **Friends and family.** The source of capital for many new businesses. Just make sure they understand the risks—or you risk losing important family relationships and souring long-time friendships. When Jeff Bezos got his parents to invest $245,573 in Amazon in

1995 the investment was eventually worth more than $30 billion. Few people know that Bill Gates Sr. was responsible for helping Howard Schultz buy Starbucks when there were only six stores (he also provided much of the purchase price—and made hundreds of millions on his investment).

3. **Angel investors.** According to the Angel Capital Association, there are more than 300,000 active angel investors in the U.S., some belonging to highly organized investor groups. In 2015 angels helped fund about 71,000 small businesses, many early-stage or start-ups, with a total of almost $23 billion in capital.

   Angels are often former entrepreneurs themselves. They love being "in the game" and provide much-needed mentoring, as well as funds, to new businesses. Angels also make far fewer demands on entrepreneurs than VC's (Venture Capitalists). Source: Jeffrey Sohl, *The Angel Investor Market in 2011: The Recovery Continues.* Center for Venture Research, University of New Hampshire.

4. **Venture capitalists.** Rather than use their own money, VC's invest pooled money from other people. Their investments are usually substantially higher than Angels, starting at $1 million. VC's typically ask for an equity interest and some control over the operation of the companies they invest in. VC's also are reluctant to invest in early-stage companies, preferring to invest in expanding companies. However, there are times when a VC is so certain of the eventual success of a startup they will lock in a strong equity position early in the growth of the business, as Sequoia did with Dropbox. About 1% of companies pitching VC's eventually obtain funding.

5. **Banks.** Ironically, banks are frequently the most difficult sources of start-up capital. As everyone has probably heard by now, banks don't like lending money to people who need it. While they don't seem to be risk-averse to making their own investments with *your* money, they don't like you taking risks with *their* money. However, if you do have a long relationship with a bank, there are some that will take a calculated risk to help you start a new venture. Smaller community bank personnel often know their customers on a first-

name basis, may even attend the same church, or be a neighbor. In these cases, the loan almost becomes a hybrid of Friends and Family and Angels.

RICHARD BRANSON'S TIPS FOR BUSINESS SUCCESS

Richard Branson started his first business at age 16—and dozens more in the years afterward. Now a billionaire, Branson enjoys sharing his wisdom with entrepreneurs.

1. Don't do it if you don't like it.

2. Be visible—sell yourself.

3. Choose your name wisely.

4. You can't run a business without taking risks.

5. First impressions are everything.

6. Perfection is unattainable.

7. The customer is always right (most of the time).

8. Define your brand.

9. Explore uncharted territory.

10. Beware of an "us vs them" environment.

11. Build a corporate comfort zone.

12. Not everyone is suited to be CEO.

13. Seek a second opinion . . . and a third.

14. Be a good listener.

15. Pick up the phone.

16. Be a leader . . . not a boss.

17. With mistakes, bounce back . . . don't fall.

The payoff from an intelligently planned and operated business can be life-changing, and the consequences for doing it poorly can negatively affect your life for years.

If you want more freedom and fulfillment in your career—and a shot at the "brass ring" of success—consider starting your own business.

Mindful Career Rules: Don't get so excited about going into a business that you overlook conducting your due diligence. Owning a business isn't right for everyone, but it may be the best thing you can do for career success and personal happiness.

Chapter 44

Soft Skills—
The Secret Sauce of Career Success

> *"Ultimately, 80% of your success will be the result of your soft skills—your ability to network and form mentoring relationships, strategic partnerships, joint ventures, and political alliances."*
>
> —*Inc.* magazine, 2014

Successful careers are a result of many factors: leadership abilities, education, connections, knowledge, luck, and being in the right place at the right time. But when all else is equal, the secret sauce of success are your "soft" skills.

Jerry Della Femina, the charismatic founder of an ad agency Eric worked at, used to say, "People like to do business with people they like." We once pitched against several top agencies for a big automotive account. Our agency was the only one that didn't spend a lot of time or money on spec creative work. In our pitch, the potential client asked us why we didn't show them any examples of our work or create something to impress them. Jerry replied, "All the agencies pitching for your business are good . . . but so are we and you'll have a lot more fun with us." We got the business.

Many young people make the mistake of thinking that all they need to do is acquire the right college degrees or attend the right school or work really hard to succeed. What they should be doing as well is developing their personality. According to *Inc.* magazine, "ultimately 80% of your success will be the result of your soft skills—your ability to network and form mentoring relationships, strategic partnerships, joint ventures, and political alliances."

In a widely reported 2015 Carnegie Institute of Technology study, and research conducted by Dr. Arthur Poropat of Griffith University, soft skills were ranked highly in future success and happiness—even against IQ and college grade point average. The 2016 World Economic Forum *Future of Jobs* report also listed soft skills as critically important to future employment viability.

Developing your soft skills will get you just as far in life as any Ivy League degree or 80-hour work week. Here's what works:

Adaptability	Persistence
Ability to work well with others	Cooperation
Complex problem solving	Respect
Critical thinking	Open-mindedness
People management	Emotional maturity
Decision making	Dependability
Creativity	Honesty
Cognitive flexibility	Presence
Negotiation	Unflappable under pressure
Emotional intelligence	An "old shoe" easy-to-be-with personality
Service orientation	
Coordinating with others	The ability to work with diverse (and often difficult) personality types
A sense of humor	
Optimism	Charisma
Enthusiasm	

In one survey of CEOs, who were asked about the relative importance of soft skills for their employees, here are the top ten ranked in order of critical importance:

1. Communication   58%

2. Organization skills   57%

3. Team player   56%

4. Punctuality   56%

5. Critical thinking   56%

6. Social skills   56%

7. Creativity   55%

8. Interpersonal communication   55%

9. Adaptability   55%

10. Friendly personality   55%

To maneuver through the enormous change in the workplace in the next few years, and address the changing nature of work itself, we think these soft skills, as well as an adaptable personal approach supported by a well-planned and curated strategic network, will be key to success.

THE SOFT SKILL THAT MAKES ALL THE OTHERS WORK

Perhaps the "soft skill" that will impact your career the most profoundly over time is mindfulness. Being mindful is the medium in which all other soft skills germinate. Every key soft skill cited in surveys of executives and HR professionals has at its core the principles of mindfulness.

Also, if you practice the principles of mindfulness you will largely avoid the negative aspects of working with people who are less enlightened—and learn to intelligently counter the petty, self-interested, and often cruel behavior in the workplace. Learning to be mindful is a powerful tool to deal with the challenges of the workplace—and life.

It isn't easy for a potential employer to assess your soft skills before you start work. So try to make it easy for them. As you write your resumé and online social media profiles, try to incorporate examples that include the use of soft skills as they apply to your past accomplishments. And during your interviews, demonstrate soft skills whenever possible.

85% OF FINANCIAL SUCCESS COMES FROM PEOPLE SKILLS

Too many people believe that all they need to do to succeed financially in their career is to obtain more education and skills. While we aren't suggesting these don't play a role in your financial success, studies have shown that about 85% of your success will largely be a result of your "people" skills.

The eight success factors that determine your financial success more than anything else are:

1. Self-regulation

2. A growth mindset

3. Resilience

4. Passion

5. Empathy

6. Conscientiousness

7. Openness to new experience

8. Social skills

Other studies add to this list Agreeableness, Extraversion, and Emotional Stability.

Again, by adopting mindfulness in your interactions with others, and being mindful about yourself, these soft skills will come naturally.

There is scant evidence that "intelligence" can be taught. We are all born with an intellectual set point (a kind of IQ) that we must work with. But you can become more mindful. You can develop social skills. And you can purge your personality of unlikable or negative traits.

DEVELOP FLEXIBLE SOFT SKILLS

Consider developing skills that allow you to "pivot" as opportunities appear or as your personal interests point you in a new direction. Core skills that will enable you to succeed in nearly any endeavor include:

1. Public speaking

2. Marketing

3. Sales

4. Promotion

5. Computer skills

You can likely "hit the ground running" in nearly any new position with these skills as part of your career repertoire.

Mindful Career Rules: Your career and life success are largely a result of having a range of key "soft skills." Devote as much attention to developing soft skills as the qualifications for your field of endeavor.

Chapter 45

Effective Communication Is a Critical Soft Skill

> *"The one easy way to become worth 50% more than you are now—at least—is to hone your communication skills—both written and verbal."*
>
> —Warren Buffett, American businessman and billionaire

Warren Buffett considers a public speaking course he took as a young man his most valuable degree.

The ability to "communicate" well is cited by most top executives as a core skill for success. Communication takes several forms, including your ability to think clearly and convey those thoughts so that others respond appropriately, as well as your skill at speaking well and with passion. Communications include the ability to write clearly and intelligently so that others can easily understand your message. And communication also involves more subtle things such as body language, how you dress, and your personal style.

Here are a few key tips from career expert Hannah Morgan (careersherpa.net) that can help you become a better communicator:

1. **Know the outcome.** Before you speak, consider what you want the outcome to be. What do you want others to do? What can you say to move them? What are their "hot buttons?"

2. **Build a reputation.** Your reputation is key to success. Always make a good first impression. Be a Boy Scout: trustworthy, loyal, friendly, helpful, kind, brave, clean, and reverent. Help others succeed. Morgan points out that every interaction—from how you greet your colleagues in the morning to how you summarize a status update in an email— eventually will contribute to how you are viewed by others.

3. **Avoid flaunting power and intellect.** Ego is the death of many an otherwise competent person. Avoid being condescending or belittling others who have less talent or knowledge. Share your knowledge mindfully to help your audience learn.

4. **Be confident.** Confidence is the "secret sauce" of success. Speak, move, stand, sit, interact confidently. Here's a tip based on research conducted by Harvard and Columbia Business Schools. There are some "power poses" you can use to increase confidence (it even boosts your testosterone level). Before going into a meeting or giving a talk, stand with your hands on your hips or stretch your arms high in a victory posture for 30 seconds or so. It lowers levels of cortisol, a stress hormone, and will increase your confidence.

5. **Show awareness of others.** Building strong, trusting relationships is a key ingredient of effective communications. When you understand your audience—what they think, feel, and their emotions—you can use that information to tailor your message so that it resonates with your listeners. Former president Bill Clinton is a master at connecting with people, even adversaries. Most people who meet him feel he is truly interested in them and values their connection. His close friends call it "The Clinton Car Wash." They may not like him before they meet him, but they do afterward. When you meet people, forget about your own agenda or self-consciousness about how you come across and simply concentrate on what the other person is saying—really listen. Then ask about the other person with questions that show you genuinely want to know more. Trust us on this one, you will get as much from the interaction as the other person does.

6. **Consider timing.** Choose your time and place carefully to deliver your message. Also, consider the pace with which you communicate.

Sometimes it's important to carefully cultivate your audience over time to build trust and a meaningful relationship with them.

7. **Show that you are listening.** Communication is a two-way street. If you are only talking at someone, you'll never communicate effectively. Being authentically concerned about another person's viewpoint or input will help you gain their respect and admiration—even when you disagree.

8. **Earn respect and trust.** Exceed expectations. Tell the truth. Be helpful even when it doesn't create any personal gain. Be a hard worker. And be consistent.

So, what are some other ways you can develop your communication skills?

✓ Model great communicators. Study great communicators (both the famous ones and people you may know) and emulate what they do.

✓ Learn from mentors. Carefully find mentors along your career path, cultivate your relationship with them, and ask them to give you constructive coaching and feedback.

✓ Watch TED Talks. TED Talks should be a part of your ongoing education for life. We suggest viewing at least one every week. In 18 minutes or less, these videos demonstrate the essentials of good communication. An excellent book that distills the TED Talk experience into "nine public-speaking secrets of the world's top minds" is *Talk Like Ted* by Carmine Gallo.

✓ Speak at Meetups. Meetups are a great way to practice speaking in front of small groups. Offer to speak at a Meetup or create one of your own. For more information, go to (meetups.com).

✓ Join Toastmasters International. This century-old program has helped thousands of people become effective communicators in a "learn-by-doing" environment. Everyone who participates is there solely to help each other improve their communication and leadership skills. For further information, go to (toastmasters.org).

✓ Go to a Dale Carnegie leadership program. You'll learn how to strengthen interpersonal relationships, manage stress, handle fast-changing workplace conditions, develop communications skills, and be a more focused leader. The program can also help you develop a take-charge attitude, build confidence, and create an enthusiastic and passionate persona. (DaleCarnegie.com)

✓ Learn to be an effective writer. You will be judged frequently by the skill of your written communications. There are scads of resources on the internet to help you write better. A great beginning book about learning to be a better writer is Stephen King's *On Writing: A Memoir of the Craft,* available also in ebook and audiobook formats.

Remember to:

✓ Start strong and positive.

✓ Be brief. Less is more.

✓ Be concise. Get to the point.

✓ Be clear. Use bullet points to summarize your thoughts.

✓ Use simple language. "Fancy" words won't impress anyone.

✓ Pay attention to your spelling (Spell Check) and grammar (grammarly.com). Otherwise, it will make you look dum.

Chapter 46

Set Yourself Apart—Write a Book

> *"Writing a book is a business card on steroids, and so much more."*
>
> —Josh Steimle, *Entrepreneur* magazine

To set yourself apart from others, consider writing a book about an area in which you have some expertise. You don't need to be an expert—you'll become one researching the information for your book. Many non-fiction writers write books more for themselves than their readers. They want to know more about the subject of their book. Doing the research is a form of self-education. Tim Ferriss said he wrote *Tools of Titans* and *Tribe of Mentors* (big and excellent books) for himself first and his audience second.

According to Kelli Richards, CEO of The All Access Group, "writing a book is a great way to establish yourself as a credible industry expert. You can create a brand platform for yourself, increase your market value, differentiate yourself from competitors, and discover new ways to grow your authority in your field."

Tucker Max, a four-time *New York Times* bestselling author, says it's important to be realistic about your expectations. You won't likely make any money selling your book. But "for entrepreneurs, consultants, professionals, and other business people, the book itself creates credibility and authority that is the means to selling other, larger opportunities that can be very profitable."

A book automatically boosts your stock and can raise you to "expert level" in the eyes of many people. If there is a choice between two veterinarians to take Fido to for an exam and one has written a book (e.g. *How to Raise Healthy and Happy Pets*) and the other hasn't, nine times out of ten the person who wrote a book will be selected, all other things being equal. The same applies for job candidates. If you are interviewing for a job as a Marketing Director for a high-tech company and have written a book titled *High-Tech Marketing for Dummies,* you'll be the one who gets hired, all other things being somewhat equal.

Today, there are resources available that can enable you to do nearly everything a big name publisher would provide—editing, cover design, typesetting, printing (usually print on demand), audiobook conversion, ISBN number assignment, bookstore and library sales—and some things only the very top authors get such as marketing and promotion. All these things should cost less than $5,000.

HOW to write a book would take too long to include in this book. But you can find out much of what you need to know by reading Guy Kawasaki's book *APE: How to Publish a Book* (APE stands for Author, Publisher, Entrepreneur). If you do it correctly and devote the time and effort, there is no reason why you can't have your own book independently published within 90 days. Independent publishing is the faster way to get your book to market and has the added benefit of cutting out the agent and publisher (as well as their cut of your profits). Plus, you own the book instead of the publisher and you maintain control over the words, as well as the design.

Other key independent publishing and writing resources include:

Joanna Penn, CEO of The Creative Penn (thecreativepenn.com), has written several books on writing and publishing. She also provides many other tools (e.g. podcasts, blogs, courses) to help aspiring authors succeed. Her book, Author 2.0 Blueprint, is offered free as an ebook on her website. It's a great starting point to begin the process of writing your first book.

Penny Sansevieri is the CEO of Author Marketing Experts (amarketingexpert.com) and author of several popular books on writing, self-publishing, and book marketing.

John Kremer has been helping people write and market books for nearly two decades. His book, *1001 Ways to Market Your Books, Real World Edition,* is an enormous compendium of helpful tips and ideas to bring your book to market successfully. Check out his considerable resources at (bookmarket.com).

Joel Friedlander and his team at The Book Designer (thebookdesigner. com) offer a wide range of resources, including templates you can use to layout the cover and the interior design of your book. His book, *The Self Publisher's Ultimate Resource Guide,* is well worth the price to access its information.

A helpful site to improve your grammar is (grammarly.com). If it's been awhile since you were in an English Composition class (or didn't pay attention), this site will help you get it right. Another resource is (hemingwayapp.com), an online editor that helps with sentence and paragraph structure. It analyzes your writing, grades it for readability, and provides helpful suggestions to improve it. You can even publish directly to Wordpress or Medium or import what you've written to Microsoft Word .docx files, then export to text, PDF, or Word.

Writing a book will also improve your writing in other areas, like business communications. Your ability to communicate in writing is a key ingredient in professional success.

Here are a few tips to become a great writer from author Stephen King from his book *On Writing:*

1. **Stop watching TV and wasting time online.** Instead, read as much as possible. TV and social media are poisonous to creativity. If you want to be a writer, you must do two things above all others: read a lot and write a lot.

2. **Write primarily for yourself.** Author Kurt Vonnegut said, "Find a subject you care about and which you in your heart feel others should care about." In business, write about what you know. And don't worry if you don't know everything about a subject. As Benjamin Disraeli said, "The best way to really learn about a subject is to write a book about it." You'll find that one of the side benefits will be that your expertise in a subject with which you are familiar will increase dramatically.

3. **When writing, disconnect from the rest of the world.** Find a quiet place where you won't be disturbed and carve out an hour or two a day to write without distraction.

4. **Don't be pretentious.** Write the same way you speak. Don't use jargon or fancy language. As legendary adman David Ogilvy said, "They are the hallmarks of a pretentious ass."

5. **Avoid adverbs and long paragraphs.** Instead, use visual cues and be succinct in your writing.

6. **Don't get overly caught up in grammar.** Write as you speak. Check out Grammar Girl, Mignon Fogarty, for tips. Use Spell Check, and load Grammarly on your computer (grammarly.com) to stay within the bounds of accepted grammar.

7. **Write every day**—even if it's just a few paragraphs.

If you write just 500 words a day, you will have a respectable length book in three months (about 150–175 pages).

Writing a book will affect your life in many ways and can change the trajectory of your career. When the late Anthony Bourdain wrote his first book, *Kitchen Confidential,* his career was going nowhere fast. He had bounced around for years on the fringes of the restaurant business, experimented with drugs, and drank too much. The publication of the book led to his first cable TV show, more books, more TV shows, travel all over the planet—and more money than he ever dreamed of having.

Martha Stewart, a former model, began catering and home decorating in her late thirties, but didn't become successful until she published her first book—which led to television appearances and her own media company. She's now worth millions. And most importantly, she is doing what she loves.

You may not experience this level of success from your book. But we guarantee it will be one of the most valuable things you do to advance your career.

WRITING AS A KEY INGREDIENT IN CAREER SUCCESS

If you consider your career as a business (and it's not a bad way of looking at it), it's important to shape your public perception to your advantage.

You want to sell yourself to those who may hire you. To do this you must write about subjects that show you have knowledge and expertise in the areas employers (companies or clients) deem important. In this way, your name becomes firmly associated with your career expertise. Posting your writing content online, as well as media coverage of what you write, will position you favorably when someone searches online for information about you.

Many people have built successful careers from a base of writing books, articles, and blog posts. At the least, you can get on the "radar screen" when hiring authorities search for someone with the skills you have to offer.

There are several free platforms to publish your work online. If what you have to say is interesting or valuable enough, your online writing can often get picked up for use in traditional media. For example, a LinkedIn Publishing post might go viral and get picked up for use in, say, Forbes or Entrepreneur magazine. You might even make a little money from your writing.

You can start writing immediately here:

- ✓ Medium
- ✓ LinkedIn Publishing
- ✓ Your own blog
- ✓ Your own website (Wordpress, Wix, Squarespace)
- ✓ Quora

Another increasingly popular form of "writing" is posting your thoughts and images on Instagram. It's the favorite medium right now for Gen Z. Some "influencers" on Instagram earn millions of dollars by promoting the brands they support.

Mindful Career Rules: Learn to write well. Consider writing a book to advance your career. Create content that enhances your personal "brand."

Chapter 47

Be Tech Proficient

"There will be two types of people in the future: people who are told what to do by computers and people who tell computers what to do."

—Marc Andreessen, Co-founder of Netscape, Partner in Andreessen Horowitz investment firm

The integration of computer and internet-based technologies in all aspects of the workplace makes it imperative for nearly every professional to be proficient in their use. To be "computer illiterate" in the 21st century is committing career suicide. For many people over 50, it is their biggest career liability. If you don't understand how to use technology and the internet, you'll be at a disadvantage when competing with most younger workers who have been using technology almost from the time they were in the cradle.

✓ It may seem overwhelming at first but begin by learning how to use the basic tech tools like the Office 365 suite—Word, Excel, and PowerPoint. Be sure to get or upgrade to a Gmail account. Nothing makes you look "old school" than, say, an AOL email. Set up a LinkedIn account and become proficient using it. It's very easy. Study up on social media. Open Facebook, Twitter,

Instagram, YouTube, and Pinterest accounts. Again, these are all very simple to use and having them demonstrates that you have some competency in the new world of tech and the internet.

✓ Create a Zoom, Skype, or WeChat account to facilitate teleconference interviews with recruiters and potential employers.

✓ Get Dropbox, Google Drive or iCloud. Then store your resumé in one of these so that you can access it anytime and anywhere.

✓ Use a smartphone (we prefer the iPhone) and learn to use its many functions. Download useful apps like Slack, Pocket, Evernote, 1Password, LastPass, DocuSign, Arrangr, First Agenda, Grammarly, LinkedInJobs, Google Maps, and any of the tens of thousands that can make your life more productive, save time and money, and help you manage your career.

In the rapidly evolving 21st century it is difficult to keep up with all the change, but you must do your best to have any hope of success. Virtually every industry—from construction to retail—is being transformed by technology and the internet.

The world now is unsympathetic to those who don't stay current and relevant. You won't find much support among your fellow workers—especially the younger ones, who now have a valuable skill their older colleagues don't often have.

Mindful Career Rules: Be tech smart if you want to succeed in the 21st century.

Chapter 48

You May Be Your Own Worst Enemy

> *"Life is hard, but it's harder if you're stupid."*
>
> —From the 1973 film *The Friends of Eddie Coyle*

After owning several businesses with more than a hundred employees over the years, as well as working with thousands of job candidates through our talent recruiting firm, it's our strong opinion that people are frequently their own worst enemy when it comes to career success.

Plain stupidity—saying the wrong things at the wrong time, inappropriate behavior, bringing their own personal issues to the workplace, greed, lying, a poor work ethic, narcissism, being unreliable, stealing, and unethical behavior toward the company or co-workers— can sabotage even the most talented people.

> *"Once you replace negative thoughts with positive ones, you'll start having positive results."*
>
> —Willie Nelson, singer

A sizable number of people have, well, unpleasant negative personalities. They have anger issues. Or they are moody and dour. Frequently, they are lazy and undependable. An entire book could be written (and probably has) about the most important ingredient of all to career success: YOU.

Often, when people don't "fit the culture" and get "voted off the island" it's because someone who interviewed you picked up on some odd personality quirk or discovered it during reference and background checks. These are the "red flags" that signal potential problems with a job candidate.

Everyone knows someone (usually several people) with negative or peculiar personalities. If you're one of these people, your career and life will always be a struggle unless you work to correct the defects. Cognitive therapy can help, but you will need to do most of the internal work if you want fundamental change.

BE HONEST

> *"The foundation stones for a balanced success are honesty, character, integrity, faith, love, and loyalty."*
> —Zig Ziglar, author of *Create a Life You Can't Wait to Live*

We're fully aware that a sizeable percentage of resumés include "enhancements" if not downright lies. Protective work laws prevent us from doing too much investigation into our candidates. We do our best with the information we can find by searching online and conducting basic background checks.

We've been fooled (as have our clients) on more than one occasion by people who interview well, look good on their resumé, test well, and have managed to provide excellent references. Then, on the job they fail to live up to expectations. This ultimately is a waste of time, money, and energy for everyone involved. Bluntly put—if you can't do the job you are being hired to do then don't apply for it in the first place.

> *"The first thing is to be honest with yourself. You can never have an impact on society if you have not changed yourself."*
> —Nelson Mandela, human rights activist, former President of South Africa

As we've said elsewhere in this book, you must be willing to do the hard, introspective work to truly know and understand yourself, your strengths and limitations, and the goals you want to achieve. Fooling yourself, as well as us, is not a mindful existence. And doing something dumb during the job search process or while on the job is a serious career-limiting move. Think first about the repercussions of your actions.

THE KEY TO YOUR SUCCESS IS YOU

> *"Act as if what you intend to manifest is already a reality. Eliminate thoughts of conditions, limitations, or the possibility of something not manifesting."*
> —Dr. Wayne Dyer, author of *Manifest Your Destiny*

Living a mindful (and successful) life requires engaging in continual self-improvement, both spiritually and practically. *In A Plan for Life: The 21st Century Guide to Success in Wealth, Health, Career, Education, Love, Place . . . and You!* Eric describes how important it is to address the six key areas of your life that will lead to success and fulfillment. If you are relatively successful in each of these areas, your entire life will likely be a success—including your life's work.

Here are several tips to help you achieve a better YOU:

1. Take care of your health.

    ✓ Exercise every day.

    ✓ Rise early.

    ✓ Hydrate.

    ✓ Get adequate sleep.

    ✓ Only eat real, organic food.

    ✓ Get regular checkups.

    ✓ Learn to manage stress.

    ✓ Live in a healthy environment.

    ✓ Find work that you love and has meaning.

- ✓ Spend time with friends and family.
- ✓ Avoid wasting time on electronic devices or social media.
- ✓ Get a dog.

2. Take care of your mind.

- ✓ Meditate.
- ✓ Engage in lifelong learning.
- ✓ Read books.
- ✓ Travel.
- ✓ Do new things.
- ✓ Do different things.
- ✓ Keep a journal.

3. Take care of your career.

- ✓ Find what you want to do in life that makes you happy, earns enough money, and makes a difference.
- ✓ Develop a Career Plan.
- ✓ Learn how to speak in public.
- ✓ Learn how to work well with others.
- ✓ Constantly engage in training and education.
- ✓ Become an expert at something valuable.
- ✓ Develop a large professional network.
- ✓ Continually improve your technical skills.

4. Find the right places.

- ✓ Choose a state and city that aligns with your professional goals.
- ✓ Live where your "soul" belongs.
- ✓ Live in the best neighborhood you can afford.
- ✓ Keep your home neat and uncluttered.

5. Take care of your wealth.

   ✓ Continually study personal finance.

   ✓ Start a saving plan as soon as you begin working.

   ✓ Invest in a low-fee market index fund.

   ✓ Buy mostly what you need, not what you want.

   ✓ Avoid debt.

6. Be mindful about your relationships.

   ✓ Choose the people you include in your life wisely.

   ✓ Don't "settle" for a mate.

   ✓ Don't get married too young.

   ✓ Opposites may attract, but shared values and interests endure.

   ✓ Be kind and respectful to your spouse, children, relatives, and friends.

   ✓ Learn how to be a good friend.

   ✓ Always give more than you expect to receive in your relationships.

> *"When we get too caught up in the busyness of the world, we lose connection with one another—and ourselves"*
> —Jack Kornfield, author of *For a Future to be Possible: Buddhist Ethics for Everyday Life*

Don't become so distracted and consumed by the hectic business of everyday living that you don't pay attention to what is truly important. Take time to be with friends and family. Take care of your body. Learn new things. Make space in your life to relax. Laugh more. Connect with nature. Be open to love—and give love. Face difficulties with courage. Be introspective and correct the negative aspects of your personality. Meditate. Love what you do.

Be mindful in all things.

Mindful Career Rules: YOU are the most important ingredient to career success and happiness. Work on smoothing out the "rough" spots in your personality. Be honest. Be dependable. Be someone people trust.

Success and happiness in your career are multidimensional and require mindfully balancing and coordinating all the key areas of your life: Health, Wealth, Career, Education, Love, Place, and YOU.

IN CONCLUSION

"No person is free who is not master of himself."
—Epictetus, Greek stoic philosopher

Being truly mindful in your career requires an enormous amount of thought and effort on your part. But the payoff can be a life of fulfillment, love, contribution, reward, and happiness. World Champion boxer Muhammed Ali said he hated every minute of his intense training. But he said it was all worth it to know he would live the rest of his life as a champion—"The Greatest!"

Your career is one of the best investments you will make in your future. A mindful career requires a mindful life. Everything you do or think or say contributes or detracts from the goal of a mindful existence. Striving to live mindfully every moment of every day will lead you to your greatest potential in life. You only have one precious life to live, so live it mindfully.

Namaste.

About the Authors

Carol Ann Wentworth is the CEO and Founder of Wentworth Executive Recruiting in San Francisco. Her mindful approach to the recruiting process has helped position her firm among the top talent recruiters in the Bay Area. She has also served in the past as the President/CEO of the Woodland Hills and Sausalito Chambers of Commerce in California. She began her business career as the Founder/CEO of Carol Ann International Modeling & Talent, a modeling and talent agency affiliated with Eileen Ford in New York.

Eric Wentworth is a marketing veteran and serial entrepreneur who has owned an advertising and PR agency, an international travel firm, two restaurants, and is a co-founder of several internet startup companies. Eric is the Operations and Marketing Director for Wentworth Executive Recruiting. He is also the author of *A Plan for Life, the 21st Century Guide to Success in Wealth, Health, Career, Education, Love, Place . . . and You!*

Carol Ann and Eric live in the San Francisco Bay Area.

WENTWORTH
EXECUTIVE RECRUITING

Mindful Executive Search
Carol Ann Wentworth, CEO

> *"There is nothing more important than hiring the right team."*
>
> Sir Richard Branson, Founder, Virgin Group

Our mindful philosophy to finding the top talent for our clients is based on creating win/win matches in skills, personalities, and culture. We believe the extra time and effort devoted to achieving this goal is worth it to create long-term mutually rewarding relationships. It's why the retention rate for the career candidates we place is an extraordinarily high 97% for the first year of employment.

It is a matter of great pride when we see a client flourish because of the talent we bring to their company. Likewise, we take very seriously the responsibility to the job candidate. We have seen how the right match with an employer can change the entire trajectory of a person's life for the better.

We support our mindful approach to talent recruiting by investing in the most sophisticated search software available. We also utilize a variety of marketing methods to find the best people, including all major social media, advertising, and advanced SEO. And we are the only executive search firm in the world that produces a custom video for every search we conduct.

Combined with our own proprietary list of potential candidates, we are able to meet our clients' expectations in a timely manner, despite a challenging job market.

We invite you to read our book, visit our website, and check us out on LinkedIn. We think you will quickly see what makes Wentworth Executive Recruiting stand out from other search firms.

WentworthExecutiveRecruiting.co

CarolAnn@WentworthExecutiveRecruiting.co

LinkedIn: Linkedin.com/in/carolannwentworth

415-516-9343

amindfulcareer.com

Carol Ann is available for personal or group career coaching and as a speaker at your next event.

Testimonials for Carol Ann Wentworth, Wentworth Executive Recruiting

CRAIG ROSSI
President, Rossi Builders, San Francisco

"Wentworth's results are like a 275-yard drive right down the middle of the fairway. Since 2015, Wentworth has teamed up with Rossi Builders with terrific results. We look forward to playing the next holes."

STEVE ALLEN
CEO, Steve Allen Media and Public Relations
Los Angeles | San Francisco | New York

I've known Carol Ann for almost 13 years . . . worked with her close to four years . . . I am honored to write a recommendation . . . if she were a restaurant and you went to Yelp to view her reviews . . . there would be triple digits of reviews and they would be all five stars . . . the only complaint would be that she needs a day off and the restaurant is closed on Mondays . . . she's honest, smart, funny, loyal, great phone skills, people are attracted to her energy . . . and she makes the BEST chocolate chip cookies I've ever had . . .

COACH RON NASH
Founder, Get Hired Now!, Career Coach, LinkedIn expert

"I have had the pleasure of knowing Carol Ann Wentworth for several years now and she continues to be the amazing person I first met. The fact is that she recruited me to be part of an event she and her husband produced, called 'Career Reboot.' Carol Ann reached out to me, then followed up with a phone call. It only took a minute to know that she was a true relationship building expert! Carol Ann uses 'Old School' relationship building techniques along with 'technology' to effectively go anywhere she pleases, in any industry. She's a rarity, a Rock Star recruiter, and human being. I would highly recommend Carol Ann Wentworth as a business partner to assist with your career or as a professional to assist you with growing your business. Once you've interacted with Carol Ann, you will have a friend for life who really cares."

TOM THUMAN
Project Manager, Rossi Builders

"Carol Ann is easily approachable and a pleasure to talk with! When we first met we talked for hours about life, goals, family, and she always steered the conversation back to me and the potential employer's relationship. She provided sound advice and never stopped trying to get me further along in the process. Truly a pleasure to work with and always enjoy catching up with her."

TIFFANY DOUGLASS
Director of Global Marketing, Tigo Energy

"Carol Ann was very helpful, conscientious, organized, prompt, and encouraging during the recruitment process. I appreciated how transparent she was with me from the beginning."

FREDDY RAVEL
Grammy-nominated jazz musician,
creator of Life in Tune training system,
former member of the Santana and Earth, Wind, and Fire bands

"Carol Ann is very simply a great person. Total integrity, brilliant business acumen, and a staunch advocate for supporting, connecting, and recruiting the best of the best."

SHERIF F. ELDASH
Construction Engineer, Estimator, Rossi Builders

"My experience with Carol Ann was fantastic. What I liked the most about her recruiting strategy was her interest in looking out for both the candidate and potential employer. Not to mention her communication and transparency throughout the recruitment and hiring process. It is such a privilege to have worked with her."

KENN PHILLIPS

President and CEO The Valley Economic Alliance, Los Angeles, CA

In my over thirty-plus years as a Manager of Advanced Programs and Public Affairs Director for the Boeing Company and now as the President and CEO of The Valley Economic Alliance. I make it a point to surround myself with knowledgeable and successful people. Carol Ann is one of those people. Her capable "can-do" attitude provides leadership to businesses, mentoring to colleagues and support to community organizations, including Higher Education Intuition.

Carol Ann is also an influencer with strong communication, negotiations, and persuasion skills. She gets along with a wide range of people and works effectively with them. She brings a balanced sense of humor to her work. Carol Ann has worked with leaders in business across all industries, from Presidents and CEO's to the newest emerging leaders, assisting executives as they stretch to their next level.

KARESSA VANDER ZANDEN

Inside Sales, Tigo Energy

"Rarely do you come across people as genuine as Carol Ann! It was a breath of fresh air working with her and almost seemed too good to be true when she reached out to me. What really took me aback was the fact that she was not just looking to fill the position, as many recruiters or hiring managers do these days. Her goal was purely to make sure I would be a good fit for the company and the position, which consisted of having a lively conversation about where I was at in life and how the company may align with my current values and goals. It truly felt like I was chatting with a friend and there was no feeling of pressure to impress. Her attitude towards ensuring the 'perfect fit' shows leadership and is inspiring."

JUAN MARTINEZ
Product Manager, Enterprise Products @ Facebook

Carol Ann was a pleasure to work with in my pursuit of a new career. She helped me every step of the way, from our first discussion, through my interviews and eventual offer. She aided me in salary negotiations and helped me land with a company that was eager to hire me. I strongly recommend Carol Ann, as her network and experience would be an asset to any professional seeking employment.

TREVOR SMITH
EHSAS Specialist II, BioMarin Pharmaceuticals

"Carol Ann is undoubtedly the most personable, attentive, and genuine recruiter I've ever worked with. She and I had the opportunity to partner together and collaborate a successful working relationship that afforded me a refreshed perspective on my career. Through Carol Ann, I was able to finally realize exactly where I wanted (and needed) to be career-wise . . . and it was her diligence and experienced coaching that directly allowed me to look at my career through a new lens. I would happily recommend Carol Ann to anyone who needs wise counsel on their business and career endeavors."

TOM McCAMY
Branch Manager, Securitas Services USA, Inc

"Carol Ann assisted a long-time co-worker of mine who lost her job due to a company-wide reorganization. Carol Ann gave her time and specialized attention to help my friend prepare and refine her resumé to the point that it opened doors on its own. The end result was my friend not only found a job but a new career that suited her skill set, challenged her abilities, and made her excited to go to work. Carol Ann is both professional and personal, a rare combination in this day and age. I highly recommend Carol Ann Wentworth if you need help at any point in your career. You couldn't be in better hands."

A PLAN
— for —
LIFE

The 21st Century Guide to Success
in Wealth, Health, Career, Education,
Love, Place...and You!

ERIC C. WENTWORTH

A Plan for Life is a roadmap for everyone—recent college grads to Baby Boomers—who want the tools to create a more successful, happier, and fulfilling life in the fast-changing 21st century. Using the most most critical thinking of great minds past and present, cutting-edge scientific research findings, and more than 500 resources, both online and off, *A Plan for Life* can help anyone create their best life.

"A profound resource on how to live a good life. Everybody needs to read this book!"

–Patti Wilson, CEO, The Career Company

Index

Z